KIT CARSON

BY NOEL B. GERSON

Non-Fiction:

KIT CARSON: *Folk Hero and Man*
BELGIUM, *Future, Present, Past*
THE SEXUAL LIFE OF THE MAN PAST FORTY
(*with Louis P. Saxe, M.D.*)
FOOD
VALLEY FORGE
THE LEGEND OF POCAHONTAS
NATHAN HALE

Fiction:

OLD HICKORY
THE GOLDEN LYRE
THE TROJAN
THE LAND IS BRIGHT
THE HITTITE
THE YANKEE FROM TENNESSEE
THE EMPEROR'S LADIES
DAUGHTER OF EVE
THE SILVER LION
THE CONQUEROR'S WIFE
THAT EGYPTIAN WOMAN
THE HIGHWAYMAN
THE FOREST LORD
THE IMPOSTOR
THE GOLDEN EAGLE
THE CUMBERLAND RIFLES
THE MOHAWK LADDER
SAVAGE GENTLEMAN

KIT CARSON

Folk Hero and Man

BY NOEL B. GERSON

1964
Doubleday & Company, Inc.
Garden City, New York

Library of Congress Catalog Card Number 64–19276
Copyright © 1964 by Noel B. Gerson
All Rights Reserved
Printed in the United States of America

For
MERRILL S. DREYFUS

The man of short stature who hopes to triumph in battle arms himself with courage, and has no need of a long sword.

—Miguel de Cervantes

1. THE SUN SHINES BRIGHT

The rich soil of Kentucky has produced a bumper crop of American folk heroes, and legends about these supermen have grown as tall as the state's luxurious blue grass.

The first of the breed was Daniel Boone of Pennsylvania, who formed the pattern his successors followed. Boone was the "father of Kentucky," and although others had blazed trails through her wilderness of forests and hills before him, he was largely responsible for opening the region to settlers. In 1769, on the eve of the War of Independence, Boone was hired by a group of land speculators to prepare the way for colonists who wanted to settle in the rich valleys of the West, and performed his task with such ingenuity, imaginative daring and zeal that the first legends about him sprang up like weeds in that same year.

A fearless hunter, expert marksman and natural-born fighter, a man who never bragged about his exploits and let his deeds speak for themselves, Boone was the perfect choice for an exceptionally difficult job. Completely at home in the wilderness, he explored virtually all of what is now Kentucky. He fought hostile Indians, made it his business to become friendly with others and was a principal in the protracted negotiations that resulted in the purchase of large amounts of real estate from the Cherokees. Thereafter he acted as a guide and escorted immigrants from the East down the Wilderness Road to the new colony, Transylvania.

Thanks to his lack of business foresight, he himself failed to benefit from the financial windfall enjoyed by his partners, and spent his later years duplicating his feats of resourcefulness and courage elsewhere on the frontier. He traveled into Spanish territory west of the Mississippi River, halting for a time in what is now Missouri. He roamed across the prairies of Kansas, and probably penetrated deep into the Rocky Mountains, supporting himself as a trapper, hunter and guide. The monument erected in Frankfort, Kentucky, in 1845, a quarter of a century after his death, became a shrine for pilgrims.

But Boone, who became a legendary figure in his own lifetime, needed no memorials of marble or granite. He lived and worked in an era when a new nation was emerging, when men were consciously—and unconsciously—seeking an ideal totally divorced from their European past. Other, greater men bore the stigma of cosmopolitanism. Benjamin Franklin, as much at home in Paris and London as he was in Philadelphia, was too much the intellectual. George Washington was the austere patrician, and although he was almost universally admired, men could not identify themselves with him. John Adams, who put duty above popularity, deliberately shunned the public, and Thomas Jefferson was not only a radical but, like Franklin, was an author. A new nation of semi-literates could follow a man who expressed his thoughts succinctly on paper, but could not feel in complete harmony with him.

Daniel Boone fitted the needs of citizens of the new United States of America to perfection. Residents of the growing cities, Boston and Philadelphia, New York and Charleston, were removed from the frontier, but those who failed to earn satisfactory livings on the eastern seaboard knew they could go into country where land was cheap and and could start new careers. Immigrants from Europe who found opportunities limited in the established towns went west into Kentucky, Tennessee and the Ohio Valley, then pushed on even farther, encouraged by the Louisiana Purchase. And Yankee peddlers from New England went with them, selling them iron frying pans, bolts of cloth—and the American Dream.

Boone, the fearless pragmatist who fought the elements, Indians and corruption, who could adapt himself to nature and use the forest and plain, river and mountain to enhance his own comfort, was the epitome of that dream.

James Fenimore Cooper was aware of Boone's popularity, and used him as the prototype for Natty Bumppo, the hero of his *Leatherstocking Tales*. The image hardened into a solid, enduring mold.

Davy Crockett, who happened to be born across the border from Kentucky in neighboring Tennessee, came into the world at a time when Boone's reputation was at its height. He too was a backwoodsman, and he too was an expert marksman, a hunter and trapper and guide of great reputation. He entered politics, won election to the Tennessee state legislature and then to the national House of Representatives in Washington. Congressman Crockett was an eccentric who enjoyed telling tall tales about himself, but nevertheless was a genuine hero. Bewildered by politics, he migrated to Texas, and won immortality when he lost his life in the gallant defense of the Alamo.

A book allegedly written by him, and which he may have dictated to a professional newspaperman, was an autobiographical sketch that followed the Boone tradition. Crockett liked to tell wildly exaggerated stories with a straight face; this frontier brand of humor continued in the mainstream of American letters, and the technique was utilized by scores of authors from Washington Irving to Mark Twain. A second book supposedly written by Crockett and published shortly after his death in 1836, which purported to relate his adventures in Texas, was a thriller that went far beyond his own literary efforts to achieve its dramatic effects.

The scene was now set for another son of Kentucky, Kit Carson, who took the spotlight with the taciturn self-confidence that marked his breed. The "King of the Mountain Men," "Nestor of the Rockies" and "First Citizen of the West" was a monarch worthy of the buckskin mantle he inherited.

Many of the facts of his life are either unknown or have been disputed, but there seems to be no doubt that he was a son of Lindsay and Rebecca Robinson Carson. According to some accounts, he was their fifth child and fifth son. Others state that he was the eighth of their ten children, while a few say he was the youngest. Whatever rung he held on the family tree, he was the only member of the clan to become famous.

Boone was still living, and many of his exploits remained to be performed over a period of more than a decade when Christopher Carson was born late in the evening of December 24, 1809, in Madison County, Kentucky. Crockett had not yet achieved renown, but the tradition of the resilient, brave frontiersman was already well established.

It has often been claimed, though never proved, that Carson's father was a friend of the mighty Boone and often hunted with him. Whether they were actually acquainted is irrelevant. Of far greater importance is the fact that Carson, Senior, followed in the footsteps of the Great Hunter, traveling to the Kentucky wilderness late in the eighteenth century from the eastern seaboard, a long rifle in his hand, his bride close behind him in a mule cart.

The Carsons settled in the center of the state, south and slightly east of Lexington and Winchester, near the site of present-day Richmond. There the bridegroom chopped trees to make his first log cabin, cleared his land and kept hostile savages at a distance with his rifle. Wild game from the plentiful forests provided his family with food in the first, lean years, and he lived precisely as had Boone a decade or two earlier.

Like thousands of other settlers, he had no real choice in his way of life, but took pleasure in the knowledge that

Boone had set an example for him. "My father," Kit Carson once said, "believed that Daniel Boone was the greatest of Americans."

The family's first son was born before the wilderness had been pushed back, and was named Moses by his devout mother. He learned to handle firearms before he was taught to read, and no sooner could he walk than he was placed on the unsaddled back of a horse. Younger brothers were given the same treatment, and as there were no schools in the district, the children were taught their letters and numbers by their mother, a woman who believed passionately in another American Dream, that every child deserves the best education his parents can give him.

The wilderness had been tamed by the time Kit was born. Forests had vanished, and the land had been transformed into crop-producing farms. Domesticated cattle grazed placidly where deer had roamed, and early settlers even claimed that there were fewer fish in the rivers. Salt and nails and cloth could be bought at village stores or, if one preferred, from the peddlers who spoke with the nasal twang of Massachusetts, Rhode Island and Connecticut. Trails had been made into roads, and there was talk of building a county courthouse, a jail and, perhaps, a school.

Mrs. Carson wanted a daughter as a Christmas present, but quickly became resigned to the presence of another son in the house. After all, she was accustomed to handling boys, and Moses was old enough to help look after his baby brother.

Kit, who acquired his nickname in infancy, enjoyed many of civilization's benefits in his first years. The family drank water from a well that Carson, Senior, had dug, and several hearths kept the clapboard house warm. Mrs. Carson baked her own bread, of course, but made it from finely ground wheat flour purchased from peddlers. She was determined to give him an even better education than had been afforded his brothers, and—although some of his biographers claim he was illiterate—she may have taught him the alphabet when he was only three or four. The child was precocious, and by the time he was five supposedly could read verses from the King James Bible.

In one significant respect, Kit Carson departed from the pattern of America's folk-supermen. He enjoyed reading, and as a mature man owned a library of between one hundred and two hundred books. He wrote with clarity, if not precision, but disliked writing; he felt more comfortable with a rifle in his hand than with a quill pen. It was not accidental that he reached the rank of a brigadier general of volunteers in the Union Army during the Civil War. He certainly was no scholar, but had acquired a sufficient education to feel at home with stars on the shoulder-boards of his uniform.

As a child he enjoyed the best of two worlds, for the frontier tradition lingered in Kentucky, even though the wilderness had vanished. Like his older brothers, he learned to shoot as soon as he was old enough to hold a pistol, then a rifle in his hands. Moses taught him to ride at an early age, and although he was an unusually small boy, he rode Moses' large gelding.

The tranquillity of civilization often irked men who had known the dangers and joys of wilderness living. Carson, Senior, became infected with the virus of restlessness, and felt compelled to move on into country where his rifle would provide meat for his table. Once again the family was directly influenced by Daniel Boone, for word had filtered east that Boone had discovered another fertile paradise in far-off Missouri. Carson sold his farm, and moved west with his family in 1813, when Kit was in his fifth year.

They settled in Howard County, deep in the wilderness, and the boy was subjected to the direct influences of the frontier as he grew to adolescence. He stalked deer, shot buffalo and patiently hid in marshes, waiting for a chance to bring down a wild duck. Indians of the Missouri and

Osage tribes were resisting the invasion of the settlers, and necessity taught the boy to shoot first and talk afterward. He was exceptionally bright, and no one was surprised when, seemingly without effort, he picked up two of the area's savage dialects.

Howard County, located in the center of Missouri on a dip in the Missouri River, was deep in country that Boone had explored. Directly to the east was Boone County, just across the river to the south was the newly-settled town of Boonville, and most of the families moving into the territory came from Kentucky. The Carsons felt at home, and happily moved into a log fort, where the men and older boys took turns keeping a lookout for hostile Indians from watchtowers. Sentries stood duty twenty-four hours per day, and when men went out to clear fields and plant crops, they always worked in groups, with pairs on guard at each corner of the plot.

The children were forced to obey strict rules: under no circumstances were they permitted to leave the fort alone, and could go out into the wilderness only when accompanied by adult males.

Kit Carson found the restrictions annoying by the time he reached the ripe old age of eight years. One morning, when his father and two eldest brothers were out working on a field-clearing project, the lure of the unknown proved too strong for him to resist, so he armed himself with two of Moses' best pistols and wandered out into the forest in search of adventure.

The incident has produced many legends in the past one and one-half centuries. According to one, he felled a doe with a single shot between the eyes. Another states that he routed a small party of Missouri Indian warriors, shooting the pistols in the air and bringing the settlers to the scene. A tale that is still more romantic claims that a band of Sioux braves, who were making their way through the forest, saw the boy and captured him. They took him with them, but he showed no fear and, addressing them in their own tongue, assured them he wanted to become one of them. Therefore they did not tie his wrists and ankles that night, and after they fell asleep he crept out of their camp and returned to the fort.

The stories are exciting but untrue. Carson vaguely recalled the adventure when asked about it soon after the Civil War, and replied that, as nearly as he could recall, he wandered around for a few hours, observed several small animals in the underbrush and returned to the fort unharmed and undetected.

The danger of Indian attacks subsided sharply in 1816, due to events beyond the control of both settlers and savages. The natives, always susceptible to the diseases of the foreigners, were the victims of a smallpox epidemic that decimated their ranks, and the survivors, anxious to leave the scenes of death and suffering, moved farther west. Howard County became a civilized region almost overnight.

Another story about Kit, also completely without foundation, concerns this period. Once again he supposedly was captured by the Sioux, who intended to offer him as a living sacrifice to appease the gods who were destroying whole families. But Kit understood the principle of vaccination and, knowing enough of the Sioux language to make himself understood, persuaded his captors to let him vaccinate himself. He performed the operation with a hunting knife, which he dipped in a pool of the germs. The warriors were astonished when he lived, and willingly submitted to similar operations. They too remained healthy, and in gratitude granted him his freedom.

There is no evidence to suggest that Kit knew anything about vaccination, nor has any satisfactory explanation ever been offered for the claim that the Sioux captured him. He himself made no mention of any such adventure, and his "official" biographer, Dr. Dewitt C. Peters, presents an unidentified "young gentleman" as the hero of the tale.

What is known is that Kit received the first horse he ever owned as a gift from his father and brothers on his twelfth birthday. Thereafter he spent most of his time in the saddle, and when he completed his daily lessons in reading, arithmetic and writing, which his mother still taught him, he was inclined to roam through the now peaceful countryside. This tendency angered his father, as the boy was expected to put in his share of work on the farm to which the Carsons had moved, and the future folk hero's backside was warmed. This positive, corrective action had the desired effect, and Kit dutifully ploughed, weeded, sowed and reaped.

A boy of twelve was expected to do a man's work, and Kit did more than his share. He was smaller than average and unusually slender, so he compensated for his size by volunteering for the hardest tasks. When a boulder had to be hauled from a field, it was he who moved it; when a tree stump needed to be dug out by the roots, he labored with a shovel. His short stature made him the butt of other boys' rough frontier jokes at the jamborees and fandangos that enlivened frontier living, too, but he soon earned the respect of the entire community.

A jamboree was a gathering of people from the surrounding countryside at which sides of beef, venison and buffalo were roasted, gossip-starved women who spent weeks in isolation on their husband's farms could talk to their hearts' content and men who needed help arranged labor exchanges with their neighbors. A fandango was a similar affair, but usually included dancing as well. At both kinds of celebrations, young men and boys competed with each other in tests of skill and trials of strength. These competitions provided a healthy outlet for emotions and helped to curb the frontier tendency to fight duels, a forbidden practice. Families simply could not afford to lose manpower needed to till the soil.

Free-for-all fights, a frontier-invented form of mayhem,

were always highlights of a jamboree or fandango, and gave those carrying grudges the opportunity to settle scores with one or more enemies. Literally no holds were barred in such contests, and although participants were not allowed to carry guns, knives or other weapons into the arena, boxing, wrestling, gouging, kicking, biting and clawing were considered legitimate. As many as ten or twelve young gladiators usually climbed into the pit at the same time, and a youth fought until he either lost consciousness or, in a struggle that was truly a test in which the fittest—and luckiest—survived, emerged the victor.

Kit took part in his first free-for-all early in the summer of his thirteenth year, and was taunted by the other boys as the fight began. It soon became obvious to the spectators that he had planned his tactics with care, for he remained at one side of the arena, his shoulders almost touching the fence that had been erected to keep the participants inside and the spectators out. Assured that no one could attack him from behind, he concentrated on one opponent at a time, waiting until he was attacked and felling his foes, one by one, with his fists.

Accounts differ as to the number of boys he knocked out, but figures are unimportant. Suffice it that he was doing splendidly until the four or five who remained in the ring recognized their danger and converged on him simultaneously. He fought them furiously, but eventually was overwhelmed. A short time later, when he regained consciousness, he had to be restrained from returning to the arena.

That jamboree marked a turning point in his life. He earned respect for his prowess, and others were careful not to tease him. He, however, was not satisfied, and having tasted combat, sought a return engagement. His chance came at the fandango held early in the autumn of that same year, the last social event of the season, prior to the advent of winter. There he established a reputation that made even the most hard-bitten adult frontiersmen take notice of him.

He won the boys' rifle- and pistol-shooting contests by such wide margins that he recklessly challenged the men, and soon was pitted against his own brother, Moses, the best shot in the county. The pair destroyed target after target, each displaying such good marksmanship that the judges were ready to proclaim the contest a tie. Moses insisted that they continue, and finally beat the twelve-year-old Kit by a narrow margin.

The boy, taking his defeat with good grace, calmly announced that he could have won had he owned his own weapons instead of being forced to use guns belonging to his older brothers. His father promised him a rifle of his own, and the prospect gave him greater energy when the time came to enter the arena for the free-for-all.

He had learned from his previous experience, and immediately waded into battle, disposing of several opponents in the first few minutes. Then, with the strongest still to be faced, he repeated his previous tactics, facing them one by one. This time he refused to be drawn into a general melee, and displayed such skill that he was still on his feet when every one of the others was sprawling in the mud.

Kit climbed out of the pit groggily, the cheers of the spectators hailing the new champion. The applause was sweet, but meant far less to him than the self-knowledge he had acquired. In spite of the handicaps imposed on him by his size, his will had triumphed, and from that time forward he exercised a rigid self-discipline.

"I have found," he said late in his life, "that a man can accomplish whatever he wants, provided he sets his mind on his goal and refuses to accept adversity."

The new rifle provided Kit with a welcome relief from his chores, and he spent long hours shooting at targets he set up on a range in a wooded area at one end of the family farm. He amused himself by shooting from horseback, dis-

mounted and in a variety of cramped positions, explaining
to his amused brothers that in real combat a man often
had no opportunity to assume the proper stance. Their
laughter faded when they discovered he could put a home-
made bullet through a leaf regardless of whether he was
lying on his stomach, shooting backwards over his shoulder or crouching close to the ground.

When he reached the age of fifteen his parents became
concerned about his future. Most of his brothers had followed Carson, Senior, into farming, but Kit, like Moses,
was showing signs of restlessness, and the boy listened eagerly when the oldest of his brothers talked about moving
to the farthest of frontiers, the Californias. It might be mentioned in passing that Moses did make the long trek in
1824, establishing his home near Sacramento, where he and
his wife built their house. And there, in the great gold
rush of 1849, he became wealthy selling food and other supplies to the hordes who swarmed into the area searching
for gold.

It was obvious to everyone in Howard County that Kit
did not possess the placid temperament a farmer needed.
His father understood how he felt, having conquered two
wildernesses before settling down, but Mrs. Carson didn't
want her youngest needlessly exposed to danger. A number
of family conferences were held, friends were consulted and
it was finally decided that Kit should learn a trade. Consequently he was apprenticed to David Workman, the county's saddler, and spent two years in Workman's shop.

Many years later, when it was said that those years had
been wasted, Kit denied the charge. The training had been
valuable, he believed, for he had been taught patience, a
quality in which he had been lacking. And in the practical sphere, he had acquired a knowledge of how to work
with leather. He learned how to cure and cut hides, how
to preserve their elasticity, how to judge their strength, tex-
ture and resilience. This information was to prove impor-

tant to him in the years when his clothes and shoes, his saddle and traveling pouch, and at certain periods, even his blanket were to be made of leather he fashioned himself.

All he knew at the time, however, was that his work was dull. He had no desire to spend the rest of his days in Howard County making harnesses and saddles, and whenever he was allowed to leave the shop he sought the company of men who were traveling to alien New Mexico on trading ventures. The few who had been in the Rocky Mountains of the Far West spoke in glowing terms of the grandeur of the area, of the primitive life they enjoyed and of their battles with heat and cold, thirst and hunger and untamed savages who roamed through the region in large numbers.

Kit made up his mind to become one of that band, and was intrigued by the prospect of exploring the vast, virtually unknown prairies that stood between the Missouri River and the towering peaks of the Rockies. The Indians who lived in that area were said to be the fiercest of the fierce, the bravest of the brave; there were mountain lions and countless other wild beasts that menaced the human intruder, and there were other dangers too numerous to list.

Kit found the challenge irresistible, and on Sundays, when he went to his parents' home for dinner, he talked of nothing but the West. His father made no attempt to dissuade him, and his mother must have known that he was not destined to become a saddler.

In the spring of 1826 a small party bound for the Mexican town of Santa Fe paused in Howard County to buy flour and bacon, the reserve food supplies that wilderness travelers carried with them, and Kit knew his chance had come to live the life he wanted. He obtained Workman's permission to terminate his apprenticeship, then went to his parents, who reluctantly gave him their blessing.

Then, but only then, he approached the leader of the

party, whose name has been lost in the mists of time. The seventeen-year-old youth applied for a place in the company, and proved his worth by demonstrating his skill with a rifle and a pistol. He was accepted on the spot, and signed an agreement promising to provide his own horse, flour, bacon, weapons, ammunition and gunpowder.

Sometime in April he said goodbye to his proud father and tearful mother, shook the hands of his brothers and set off on the long journey that was to make him a folk hero greater than Davy Crockett, a superman of the frontier who was to become Daniel Boone's only rival in the affections and imaginations of the American people, and of millions in England and continental Europe as well.

2. THE TENDERFOOT

Only the leader of the expedition, Kit later recalled, had ever ventured into the lands beyond the Missouri River. All the others were tenderfeet, and he, the youngest of the party, was also the greenest. On the first day of the journey the men saw a large herd of buffalo, subsequently to become the most common of sights, and Kit excitedly killed a bull, using two rifles to bring down the beast.

The carcass was stripped, the men knew they had enough meat to last them for several days and happily resumed their journey. But, in their inexperience, they did not pause long enough to smoke the buffalo sides, and consequently attracted the scourges of the prairies, jackals and wolves, who trailed them and approached their camp every evening when they completed their day's journey.

It was relatively easy to rid themselves of the jackals, a few well-placed shots scattering the scavengers. But the wolves were far more menacing. Large, gray creatures that became increasingly bold, the pack ventured closer to the campfires each night. The party replied to the challenge by building larger fires, but were reluctant to make too large a blaze for fear of attracting the attention of Indians.

Rifle shots scattered the pack momentarily, but the animals quickly returned, and the horses became increasingly nervous. Twice the animals pulling the carts filled with trading goods bolted, scattering the contents of the wagons, and the travelers realized something drastic had to be done. A man named Broader tried to solve the problem by snatching a rifle from a wagon in which he was riding, hoping

to put a quick shot into the beasts following the little caravan.

Broader was in such a hurry that he handled his weapon
carelessly, with the result that it fired prematurely, putting a bullet through his arm. The accident was painful,
but seemed of little consequence, and the men finally rid
themselves of the wolves by firing several volleys at the
beasts. But Broader did not recover. A few days later gan-
grene had set in and was spreading, and the victim could
no longer walk.

The leader called everyone to a meeting, at which it was
solemnly decided that the arm had to be amputated in order to save the man's life. Broader agreed to submit to an
operation, and three members of the party were selected
to perform it. One of them was Kit, who knew nothing about
surgery. He learned rapidly.

A kingbolt was removed from one of the wagons, and was
plunged into the flames of a fire until it became red-hot.
The operation was performed with a razor and a small saw,
and the heated bolt was then applied to the wound to
prevent further bleeding. Out of consideration for Broader,
the journey was not resumed until the following morning.
Miraculously, Broader recovered, and eventually became a
merchant of substance in New Mexico.

The men traveled through what subsequently became
Kansas and Colorado, turned south and at last reached
Santa Fe. The party remained together until the leader
disposed of his merchandise and paid his hands their wages,
an event which took place in November.

The ancient city, capital of a vast Mexican province, was
the terminal point of the Santa Fe Trail from Missouri and
there were perhaps fifty to one hundred United States citizens there at the time Kit arrived. But he saw few friendly
faces and heard few words spoken in a tongue he understood. More than two hundred years had passed since the
Spaniards had taken possession of the ancient Pueblo

Indian community, and Spanish customs still predominated. The Mexican governor lived in a magnificent palace, where elegantly uniformed Mexican sentries stood guard duty, and a full regiment of Mexican troops kept the peace.

There were many hundreds of Pueblo Indians in the town, and perhaps two thousand half-breeds. The inns and taverns served Spanish and Mexican foods unfamiliar to a Kentucky- and Missouri-educated palate, and virtually everyone spoke the Pueblo dialect, Spanish or both. Dozens of prostitutes strolled up the broad streets, waiting patiently to take the money earned by men in the fur trade and, most astonishing of all, warriors from at least a dozen savage tribes of Indians roamed through the town, They too were eager to obtain Mexican and American gold they could use to buy guns and whiskey, ammunition and wine.

Even the climate was unfamiliar. The sun that burned down on the parched ground was hot, but the air was remarkably clear and dry, and Kit was surprised to discover that, no matter how great his exertions, he rarely perspired.

American traders were made to feel less than welcome in Sante Fe, and it was common knowledge that the governor, trying to preserve trade for the Mexicans, frequently threw Yankees into prison without cause and held them, without trial, for long periods in dungeons. The army officers were arrogant, and soldiers deliberately insulted the Americans, who were warned by veterans that they must not become involved in brawls. Only the ladies of joy treated the men from the northeast with kindness. It is not known whether Kit availed himself of their services during the period of his initiation into the mysteries of a hostile, bristling world.

In spite of the discouraging atmosphere, the youth kept his eyes wide open, and soon realized that it was possible to earn a good living in the fur trade. But it was necessary, first, to learn Spanish and some of the more prominent Indian tongues. Kit's curiosity and desire for knowledge attracted the attention of an elderly mountaineer, an American who made his home in the little Mexican town of Fernandez de Taos, slightly more than eighty miles to the northeast of Santa Fe. This man, sometimes called Kincaid and sometimes Kin Cade, came to the city every year with just enough furs to enable him to purchase necessary supplies.

He invited Kit to spend the winter with him, the youth accepted and they rode together to Kincaid's house. In the next four months Kit obtained a working knowledge of Spanish and of several Indian dialects, his elderly host serving as his tutor. In the spring Kit knew he had to find employment, and bidding Kincaid farewell, returned to Santa Fe. The year that followed was the most miserable he ever knew.

No one wanted to hire a hunter or trapper totally lacking in experience, and when Kit's wages from the previous year's journey had been spent, he was forced to ask permission to join a company that, its business concluded, was setting out for Missouri. A failure at the age of eighteen, he started out for home.

The group traveled more than four hundred and fifty miles and, immediately after fording the Arkansas River, met a party of traders moving in the opposite direction. Kit promptly asked the leader of this band for employment, and was hired as a guard. The next morning he was bound for Santa Fe again. But the worst was yet to come, for the traders earned less than they had anticipated, and Kit was paid off with a smile and an expression of regret.

There was enough food in his saddlebag to last for a week or two, and fodder for his horse was easy to obtain, but the shirt of heavy wool he had worn when he had left Howard County was now threadbare. He desperately needed a new one, but didn't have a copper to his name. Willing to accept any position that would pay him enough to buy a new shirt, he accepted a job as a teamster with a Mexican commercial expedition that was intending to travel to the city of El Paso, approximately three hundred miles to the south. The journey was uneventful, but he had ample opportunity to practice his Spanish, for he was the only English-speaking member of the party. He worked as a teamster on the return journey, too, and bought a new shirt as soon as he received his wages.

There seemed to be few opportunities for work in Santa Fe, and Kit had learned that it was far too easy to spend every penny he owned there, so he went to Taos, where there were more Americans. Through Kincaid he had met one Ewing Young, a wealthy trader who dealt with scores of trappers, and Young, struck by his plight, offered him his room and board if he would work as a cook.

For six months, from the autumn of 1827 to the spring of 1828, Kit was employed as the master cook in Young's kitchen, where he prepared enormous meals for his host and the many trappers who were his guests. There is no record that anyone ever complained about the chef's talents. And Kit was working too hard over a hot stove to feel sorry for himself. He was up at dawn, peeling potatoes and scrubbing vegetables, and he learned to hang all of his own beef, venison and buffalo meat. He became expert at baking bread, knowledge which he would find useful in later years, when he was destined to roam alone through the mountains, and Young is the authority for the statement that he made delicious pies.

It was Kit's hope to find work with one of the trappers who came to Young's house, but his lack of experience was still a great handicap, and in the spring of 1828, at the age of nineteen, he succumbed to Young's persuasion and joined a Missouri-bound caravan. But he remained stubborn, and when the group met a party coming in the opposite direction, he duplicated his feat of the previous year and persuaded the leader to hire him. A few weeks later he was back in Santa Fe, and his luck improved, or so it seemed at the time.

Colonel John Tramell of Illinois, a prominent but tight-fisted trader, was seeking a Spanish interpreter to accompany him on a trading venture into the Mexican province of Chihuahua, south of El Paso, and Kit was hired. He went with Tramell to the city of Chihuahua, where he fulfilled his obligations. By now he had become less innocent about money, and demanded his wages to date. Tramell argued with him, but finally paid him and, stranded in a Spanish-speaking land, tried to persuade the young man to remain with him.

Kit realized, however, that it would be almost impossible to force Tramell to pay him the rest of his wages after they returned to Santa Fe, so he looked for other employment. There were only a handful of Americans in the city, and he had no difficulty persuading one Robert McKnight to hire him as a teamster. McKnight had obtained the permission of the Mexican government to transport copper from the mines found near the Rio Gila River, and Kit spent the latter part of 1828 and the first months of 1829 sitting on the hard seat of a wagon, trying to persuade recalcitrant mules to haul copper ore.

It was his goal in life to become a successful trapper and professional hunter, but that career seemed unattainable as he spent day after weary day swallowing the dust kicked up by the wagon ahead of his in the unending procession. His determination and self-discipline prevented him from admitting total defeat and returning to Missouri. At least he was being paid regularly, and for the first time in his life had enough money in his pocket to give him some feeling of independence.

Life as a teamster at the copper mines was even more frustrating than existence as a cook, and in the early spring of 1829, at the age of twenty, he made up his mind to seek Ewing Young once more in the hopes that the trader would put him in touch with fur trappers. He had enough money in his pouch now to withstand a siege of unemployment for as long as four or five months, and leaving McKnight, went back to Taos.

There, at last, opportunity beckoned wildly.

Four or five experienced trappers hired by Young had been attacked by hostile Indians south of the Colorado River and, after fighting a futile, day-long battle, had been compelled to retreat into New Mexico. The situation was dangerous for everyone who earned his living in the fur trade, for word of the savages' victory would spread, and if they went unpunished, no American trapper would be safe in the wilderness.

Young was raising an expedition to accompany him, and loudly announced his intention of finding the Indians. He would force them to do battle, he declared, and kill every member of the war party. Any volunteer who could handle firearms, Mexicans excepted, was being accepted, and Kit leaped at his chance. While preparations were being made, he returned to Young's kitchen as a cook.

Not until Young took the men into his confidence did Kit realize that his true ambition would soon be fulfilled. The purpose of the expedition was twofold. Young intended to teach the savages a lesson, as he had advertised, but he was also planning to trap game on a large scale.

Neither Kit nor anyone else familiar with Mexican territory needed an explanation for Young's stealth. Mexican laws, which were strictly enforced, required every trapping expedition to obtain a license for the purpose. These licenses were issued by provincial governors, and orders issued in Mexico City prohibited the granting of permits to citizens of the United States, who were taking vast quantities of furs to New Orleans and eastern ports, thus robbing the Mexicans of revenue that was their due. Prices of furs having soared recently on the international market, the Americans, filtering into Mexican territory in ever increasing numbers, were determined to evade the law.

No one ever went to greater efforts to fool the authorities

than Ewing Young. He hired a company of forty marksmen, the vast majority of them Americans, with a scattering of Frenchmen and Canadians filling the ranks. He dis-
tinctly let it be understood that the Indians he intended
to pursue were far to the north, in territory owned by the
United States, and he openly bought provisions, gunpowder and lead for a long stay in the wilderness.

The Mexicans, naturally, were suspicious, and two platoons of troops were assigned the task of keeping watch on
Young's company. The wily Young offered the soldiers his
hospitality and, on the evening prior to his band's departure, ordered sides of beef and venison barbecued in their
honor. Kit Carson was an exceptionally busy young man
that evening, laboring in the kitchen and at the barbecue
pit.

The next morning, at dawn, he doffed his chef's hat for
all time.

Young's company marched due north at a rapid pace,
the Mexicans accompanying them, and in a day and a half
covered a distance of fifty miles. The commander of the
troops was satisfied that Young planned to live up to his
announced intentions, and turned back. The company took
no chances, and made camp shortly after midday. The men
remained idle until the following morning, when several experienced scouts went out on reconnaissance and reported
that the Mexican platoons were not lurking in the vicinity.

Young immediately changed his course, and his men
rode off toward the southwest, passing through territory
occupied by the Navajo nation. They skirted the Pueblo
Indian town of Zila, then traveled to the headwaters of
the Salt River, one of the tributaries of the Rio Gila. They
had come now into the area where the fight had taken
place, and again Young dispatched scouts, who fanned out
ahead of the company.

One of them returned within a few hours, reporting that
he had discovered traces of a band of savages numbering

at least three hundred warriors. The other scouts were ordered to probe in the same direction, and as nearly as they could judge, at least four hundred Indians were making their camp only a mile or two from the spot where the trappers had been defeated.

Young advanced cautiously, dividing his men into two groups. The first, only ten strong, made no attempt to maintain secrecy. The men called to each other in loud voices, and made a pretense of hunting for the savages. This group, presumably, was made up of the original party of trappers, reinforced by several friends.

To the rear and keeping within cover on the wooded hills was the second, larger group, which made every effort to conceal its presence from the savages. Kit was a member of this band, which Young himself led. The Indians discovered the advance unit nearby early in the afternoon of a cloudless day, and warriors by the hundreds rode out to kill the intruders who had dared, for a second time, to invade their domain.

The advance party of trappers halted near the crest of a hill, and the larger unit, still remaining carefully hidden, worked its way to the top of another hill on the right flank. A narrow, smooth valley stood between the two groups, and this level ground provided the savages with the best approach to their intended victims. The Indians rode into the little valley, the braves increasing their pace when they assumed that their foes' inactivity was caused by fear and confusion. By striking swiftly, they could wipe out the band of trappers with a minimum of losses, and in their eagerness to win a decisive victory they poured into the valley in large numbers.

Suddenly, as their leaders wheeled and started toward the crest of the hill, both of Young's units came to life, and the warriors were caught in a murderous crossfire. The marksmanship of the trappers was superb, the element of surprise contributed to the terror of the savages, and the fight ended almost before it began, the braves scattering in all directions. Before they could reach safety, however, fifteen of their number were killed and at least three times as many were wounded.

Kit, in his baptism of battle, was responsible for the death of at least one of the warriors, and was believed to have wounded two others. His comrades later commented that they had never seen anyone reload a rifle so rapidly. The long years of practice on the farm in Howard County were paying dividends at last, and the neophyte was accepted by his elders as an equal. The brief battle, in which not one trapper sustained even a minor injury, was the turning point in Kit Carson's career.

The Indians having dispersed, Young and his men were able to devote their energies to more lucrative pursuits, and trapped their way down the Salt River to the San Francisco River, then worked their way up to its headwaters. They had not seen the last of the Indians, however, and although the warriors did not dare to meet their enemies in another open battle, they made nuisances of themselves. Each night, after Young's men made camp, ate their supper and went to sleep, braves managed to creep past the sentries, sometimes stealing traps, sometimes killing a horse or a mule.

There was no way to counter these raids, and Young doggedly continued to push north. Eventually, as the group moved into country the hostile savages did not know, the warriors turned back, but by then the damage was done. At least one third of Young's beaver traps had vanished. In spite of this handicap, however, the party prospered. Beaver were so plentiful that the pack mules were soon carrying huge bales of pelts, the progress of the trappers was reduced to a slow crawl and Young had to make new arrangements.

He sent twenty-two of the men to dispose of the skins, and several of those who wanted to leave in order to reap their share of the profits immediately agreed to return with new traps to replace those that had been stolen. Eighteen members of the company, Kit among them, elected to follow Young into the valley of the Sacramento River in the Californias, which Americans had never visited. This wild region was said to abound in beaver and game, and the explorers were anxious to see the district.

Severe obstacles stood between them and their goal, however, for they were planning to travel through unknown territory and had no idea what terrain or weather they would find. A small band of Indians whom they encountered shortly after parting with the men who were leaving the expedition warned them that the land directly ahead was barren and that they would find no water anywhere.

They made their preparations accordingly, and Young ordered them to kill as many deer as they could find so they could use the skins as water bags. Luck was against them, and they found only one stag and two does. But the savages had also confirmed the stories that the region they intended to visit was rich with beaver, so Young decided to push ahead. The long march began, and for four days and nights the party traveled across desert and bleak rocks, with no water to be seen anywhere. Young himself doled out rations of water each night for men and animals, and everyone suffered from thirst.

The pack mules eventually led them to a water hole, and they spent two days at this little oasis, regaining their strength before resuming their journey. They were reduced to eating some of their emergency supplies of bacon and flour now, and were anxious to reach territory where they could find fresh game. One of the legends about Kit that sprang up in later years had it that he killed several rattlesnakes with his pistol, and that the men were forced to eat the meat of the snakes for want of other food, but Kit himself made no mention of the snakes in his reminiscences, nor did Young when discussing the venture in later years.

For four more days the party struggled across waterless soil, and on the afternoon of the fourth day met a small party of Mojave Indians, from whom an old mare was purchased. The animal was slaughtered and roasted, and although only an hour or two of daylight remained, Young ordered the march resumed, for the Indians had told him that plentiful supplies of water lay directly ahead.

At dusk the men came to the great Colorado River Canyon, later destined to become a tourist magnet, but the beauty of the place was of far less significance than the water. For three days the party rested, regaining its strength, and several mountain lions were shot. Their meat was so tough that it had to be stewed rather than roasted, but good fortune favored the group, for another party of Mojave warriors arrived at the site and sold them a supply of beans and corn.

Equally important was the information obtained from the braves, and when the journey was resumed the men traveled toward the southwest for three days, following a natural line of least resistance. There they found a small river that ran toward the northeast, and followed it, but the bed soon became dry. The dry bed was clearly marked in the sand underfoot, and they doggedly remained on the same course until, unexpectedly, they came to water again. They surmised that the river had run underground for many miles, a theory that was subsequently confirmed by others who came after them.

Turning due west, as the Indians had directed them, they made their way across another desert, and after four more days of battling heat, thirst and hunger, came to the Spanish town of San Gabriel, where the Roman Catholic church maintained a mission. A priest was in charge, a platoon of Mexican soldiers kept the peace and approximately one thousand domesticated Indians lived near the mission.

Their occupation was raising cattle and oxen, and Young later estimated that they owned eighty thousand head. There were grape vineyards growing on latticed frames, too, and vegetables of all kinds tended by the squaws. The hungry trappers thought they had reached heaven-on-earth, and Young had to restrain them from stealing and killing cattle.

The priest was friendly, but the soldiers were not, and the best barter deal Young could make was to trade four butcher knives for one ox, which was slaughtered at once. At the priest's instigation the Indians gave the party ample quantities of vegetables and all the water the men wanted. The trappers would have lingered at San Gabriel, but the commandant of the troops asked too many embarrassing questions about beaver trapping, so Young ordered the march resumed after a halt of only one day and night.

After another ride of a single day they reached the mission of San Fernando, a miniature version of that at San Gabriel, then went on again after an overnight halt. Their destination was the Sacramento River, and they traveled northeast through country where grass grew high, water was plentiful and game abounded. Young called a halt near the bank of a swift-flowing stream, and the party stayed there for more than a week. Hunting parties were sent out, and returned heavily laden with deer and elk, ducks and other wild fowl. There were fish in the stream, too, and hunger, like thirst, became a mere memory.

The priest in charge of the mission at San Fernando had given Young specific information, and he headed now for the San Joaquin River and its tributaries, where there were more beaver than even the most experienced of the veterans had ever seen. Another party of trappers appeared to be in the area, much to the men's astonishment, and when they heard rifle shots in the forests, they replied with shots of their own.

The two groups met, and the strangers proved to be Canadians employed by the Hudson's Bay Company. Their commander, Peter Ogden, agreed to join forces with Young, there being more than enough beaver for all, and the two parties worked together. The forest was teeming with elk, deer, antelope and a variety of smaller game, so both groups appointed hunting parties to take care of their present and future food needs.

Here Kit Carson really came into his own. His marksmanship was magnificent, he displayed a remarkable instinct for stalking his prey and no American or Canadian bagged more game than he did. Soon he and two of the Canadians were doing all of the hunting for both parties.

When the combined groups reached the Sacramento River they parted, the Canadians traveling north toward the Columbia River. Young elected to remain at the campsite on the Sacramento for the rest of the summer. The weather was delightful, there was more than enough to eat and, although the trapping season had now ended, neither he nor his men were in any hurry to start the long trek back to New Mexico. The memory of thirst and hunger made it imperative that careful preparations be made for the journey, too, so skins were treated and laid aside for use as water bags. And meat was converted into pemmican, after the manner used by the Canadian Indian tribes to the north.

Meat, preferably venison—in the absence of buffalo—was cut into small pieces and laid out to dry in the hot sun. When dried it was pounded into a fine powder and mixed with venison grease, then shaped into packages small enough to be carried in saddlebags or, if necessary, slung over a man's shoulder. Meat prepared in this way could be kept for long periods without spoiling, and it had been found that a man could subsist for weeks on a diet made up exclusively of pemmican.

The stay on the Sacramento was enlived by a call for help from the priest in charge of the little mission of San

Rafael. Several Indians who lived and worked at the mission had murdered one of their colleagues, then fled to a native village in the interior. The priest had sent out an armed party of soldiers and loyal warriors to demand the surrender of the fugitives, but the group had been repulsed after a short, brisk fight.

Kit and eleven others volunteered to help the priest, and joining forces with the soldiers and warriors, renewed the attack. A large number of the defenders were killed, the fugitives were given up and the trappers returned to their easy life on the Sacramento.

A short time later the priest returned the favor. The captain of a trading ship had arrived at the mission, and was interested in buying at least a portion of the party's furs. Young went to San Rafael immediately and sold the entire stock, receiving a fair price for his bales. He purchased a large number of horses from the mission's Indians, which he subsequently gave to his men, each also receiving a purse containing more than fifty dollars, a sum large enough to support an unemployed trapper for at least six months.

At this juncture another of the unproven and unprovable incidents concerning Kit's prowess took place. A band of hostile Indians, tribe unspecified, allegedly stole sixty of the company's horses and fled toward the east with them. Young sent Kit and a dozen other men in pursuit; the party rode one hundred miles in the direction of the Sierra Nevada Mountains, and came upon the savages feasting on the meat of six horses they had butchered.

Kit and his men crept close to the banquet scene, then launched a wild charge that was completely successful: the warriors fled, leaving the fifty-four remaining horses. Eight braves were killed in the attack, the trappers recovered the mounts and returned to their camp with the horses and three Indian children they had taken as prisoners. Until this point there is no mention in the tale of squaws accompanying the warriors, so the presence of Indian children in the party is an unexplained detail.

Kit neither affirmed nor denied the validity of the story when asked about it after the Civil War. By that time he had fought in so many battles and raids against so many Indians that one attack more or less was a trifling matter. Dr. Peters included the account in his biography of Kit, so the hero tacitly acknowledged that the raid had indeed taken place.

Whether the chase and fight are real or imagined is unimportant, however. What does matter is that, for the first time, Kit is seen as a leader of men. He had already gained experience as a trapper and hunter; now he was commanding others. Young purportedly had sufficient faith in him to make him a deputy, and Kit responded by accomplishing the mission assigned to him.

True or false, the story indicates that the twenty-year-old Kit had found his place under the sun. Veterans had accepted him as their equal, and now he was about to become their superior.

3. HIGH ADVENTURE

In September 1829, Ewing Young decided the time had come to return to New Mexico, as nothing could be gained by spending the winter in the Californias. The men started south, their considerable pack train carrying their pemmican, jerked meat and dried vegetables. They halted briefly at San Fernando, then made the mistake of visiting a small Indian town, Los Angeles, that was reputedly the shabbiest of the savages' communities.

Los Angeles lived up to its reputation and, even worse, the trappers were confronted by a strict Mexican official, a deputy governor of the Californias, who demanded to see their trapping permit. Young stalled, having no license, but was reluctant to let his men become embroiled in a fight with the seventy-five Mexican soldiers who made up the local garrison. The deputy governor wanted no fight, either, having learned that Yankee frontiersmen were unpleasant enemies.

The deputy governor quickly proved that he understood American trappers, and proceeded on the theory that honey catches more flies than vinegar. Blithely ignoring Young's refusal to show him the party's license, he sent the trappers several gallon jugs of potent brandy, distilled from local grapes, as a gift. The men had not tasted liquor in many months and, ignoring Young's pleas to throw the brandy away, sat down to dispose of it in a manner they considered more satisfactory.

It was plain to Young that the deputy governor had devised cunning tactics. When the men were too drunk to defend themselves, they would be arrested by the Mexican soldiers and thrown into the prison, the largest and most imposing building in Los Angeles. Desperate counter-tactics had to be devised at once, and Young turned for help to Kit, one of four men who had heeded his plea and was refusing to drink the brandy.

Kit and the other three were instructed to take the large number of spare horses, all of the mules and the camping equipment onto the trail that led to the southeast. They were told to travel at a pace slow enough so that Young and the roisterers could catch up in a day or two. If they were not overtaken, they were instructed to report, when they reached New Mexico, that the rest of the party had been massacred. Neither Young nor Kit stopped to consider that the penalty for disobeying the Mexican licensing law was death, and that under the law the execution of every one of the trappers would be just. The killing of United States citizens, no matter what the reason, was always considered a massacre.

Kit and the other sober men went ahead, and the following morning the drinkers, still imbibing, followed them, accompanied by the deputy governor and his troops. Reinforcements were waiting at San Gabriel, whose Indians were also considered more reliable by the Mexicans than those at Los Angeles, and there seemed little doubt that the trappers would be placed under arrest as soon as they arrived.

Young was frantic, but fate intervened on his behalf. Two of the trappers, one James Higgins and one James Lawrence, became involved in a drunken dispute as they rode side by side down the trail. One word led to another, and they began to shout; they called each other names, and Higgins ended the discussion by drawing a pistol and shooting at his friend. Either he was so drunk that he missed completely or, at worst, inflicted a minor flesh wound; accounts differ.

The result, however, was significant and spontaneous. The Mexican troops, who had grown indolent and soft after spending years leading an uneventful garrison existence, prudently went ahead to San Gabriel. Young saw his chance to escape, and coaxed, stormed and wheedled; in one way and another he persuaded his intoxicated companions to increase their pace and give San Gabriel a wide detour.

The party caught up with Kit and the faithful, sober trio late that afternoon. The reunited group pushed on to a river, where the drunken men presumably soaked their fevered brows in the water. That night Young, Kit and the trio stood guard while the others slept off the effects of their drinking. The following morning the sober, dehydrated men drank water greedily, and the march was resumed at a rapid clip. The trappers realized they had almost lost their lives, and needed no urging now. After a forced march of nine days, they reached the Colorado River.

There they rested, and the majority went out to set traps along the banks of the river. Kit remained at the camp, standing guard with a few others and, inevitably, another apocryphal incident demonstrating his courage and wisdom took place. A party of several hundred Indians, tribe unspecified, came upon the campsite and promptly professed friendship. According to the story, the savages were cunningly concealing weapons beneath their clothes.

The tale does not explain why the Indians would bother to hide weapons when hundreds faced a small handful of trappers, or where, for that matter, half-naked warriors would conceal rifles, bows and arrows, knives and hatchets. In any event, Kit felt certain the braves intended to kill him and his companions, and the other trappers looked to him for leadership.

None of the Indians spoke English, but one, fortuitously, knew a little Spanish. On Kit's orders the trappers pointed loaded weapons at the leaders of the band, Kit himself placing the muzzle of his rifle against the chest of the interpreter. This inhospitable gesture was accompanied by an order to leave the camp instantly. Kit, it seems, had acquired a master's psychological understanding of the warriors, and knew that the band would not attack if it stood to lose its chiefs. He was proved correct, for the braves withdrew, and were not seen again.

Young and his party proceeded at a leisurely pace, trapping down the Colorado River, then changing their camp to the banks of the Gila and working up that river to the mouth of the San Pedro. There they found a large number of horses and mules, and a closer study indicated that the animals were in the possession of the very warriors whom the trappers had set out to chastise earlier in the year. The Indians were taking their ease in huts they had built in the hills behind the river bank, so the trappers immediately charged them, Young and Kit leading the attack.

The savages fled, but soon rallied, and the fight continued for an hour or more. Eventually the warriors were dispersed, and Young's men gained possession of the whole herd.

That same night they acquired an even larger number of horses. The men were awakened from their sleep by the rumbling of many hoofbeats, and an investigation proved that a small number of Indians were driving at least two hundred horses toward the now abandoned village. Young immediately concluded that the horses had been stolen from Mexican ranchers living in the vicinity of the nearby Mexican town of Sonora, and without further ado the trappers attacked. The savages rode away, and Young now had more horses than he and his men could handle.

Apparently no one thought in terms of returning the animals to their Mexican owners, for the party was laden once again with beaver pelts, and Mexicans sufficiently wealthy to own herds of horses might have asked questions about licenses. So, when morning came, the best of the horses were kept, two were killed and butchered and the others were turned loose.

Driving their large herd before them, the men continued their trapping until they reached a point not far from the Gila copper mines. It was not easy to dispose of skins in New Mexico, and Young proved his resourcefulness by leading his men to the neighborhood of the mines, where Robert McKnight, Kit's former employer, had established a trading post. The bales of skins were hidden in mines no longer used, and McKnight agreed to keep watch over them.

Young and his men went on to Santa Fe, where they applied for licenses that would enable them to trade with the Indians. The governor of New Mexico made it a policy to grant such permits to anyone, even citizens of the United States. Young and the trappers then returned to the mines, collected their skins and went back to Santa Fe, where they announced they had acquired the furs in trade with natives.

Skins were currently selling at the high price of twelve dollars per pound, the men placed two thousand pounds on the market and received twenty-four thousand dollars in return. Young, as leader of the party, took half of the sum, and the seventeen others divided the rest. Their share, combined with their portion of the proceeds from the sale of the excess horses, amounted to slightly more than one thousand dollars per man, a staggering sum.

Each was paid when the party reached Taos, in April 1830, approximately one year after the expedition had set out. The party disbanded, and the men, somewhat dazed by their good fortune, went their separate ways. Several returned to Santa Fe, Kit among them, and by the autumn all were penniless again.

There is no direct evidence to indicate that Kit squandered his money on wine, women and song, but his pockets were as empty as those of his friends. Dr. Peters writes firmly that he "learned no bad habits," yet offers no explanation for the fact that he squandered at least one thousand and fifty dollars. According to tradition, folk heroes do not play cards for money, and they certainly avoid fancy ladies. Kit himself wisely remained silent and disclosed nothing about the activities that drained off his money in less than a half-year.

If he gambled, drank or found consolation for his loneliness in the company of painted women, he learned his lesson well at the age of twenty-one. Never again, at any time in his life, did he engage in activities of a questionable nature. He remained abstemious, scorned harlots and was bored by games of chance.

Whatever the reasons he lost his money, he needed work again, and by the autumn of 1830 had acquired a sufficient name for himself as a hunter that he had no trouble finding a place. Thomas Fitzpatrick, subsequently the most famous of the Mountain Men after Kit and Jim Bridger, was openly recruiting for men to accompany him on a party that, he said, would go into the unorganized American lands west of the Minnesota Territory, Iowa and Missouri, and east of the Mexican-owned Utah Territory and the Oregon Territory, which both United States and England claimed.

Anyone who knew Fitzpatrick took his disclaimers with a large scoop of salt from the nearest deer lick. Fitzpatrick was the first to trap for beaver in what later became the state of Wyoming, and in all probability it was he who discovered the South Pass through the Rockies. He was fearless, independent and hated all authority.

Therefore it could have been no secret to his friends that he undoubtedly planned to trap on the principal rivers of the Rocky Mountains, regardless of who might own the land. The expedition promised to be both lucrative and exciting, for Fitzpatrick was one of the most efficient of the Mountain Men—and one of the most ruthless.

Kit applied for a place in the company, and was accepted without question. He had earned his reputation, and Fitzpatrick was pleased to enroll him.

The men traveled north rapidly, and in October began trapping on the Platte River and its tributaries. But the weather turned too cold for them to work in comfort, so they made camp on a bluff overlooking the Salmon River, built themselves log huts and settled down for the winter. They ventured out infrequently, and went hunting for deer or buffalo only when their supplies of food began to run low.

On one occasion Kit shot a bear, but in no other way distinguished himself that winter. The only event of consequence was the killing of four men who went out on a hunting expedition. Their murderers were attributed to members of the fierce Blackfoot nation, a tribe with whom Kit was destined to clash frequently.

Winters spent in the mountain wilderness of Colorado, Idaho, Utah, Montana, Wyoming and Nevada were surprisingly carefree. The men made themselves snug in their log huts, and there was ample firewood in the forests. Sufficient quantities could be acquired by a work party in a single morning to last for the better part of a week. Fish could be obtained by dropping lines through holes made in the ice that caked on the surface of rivers, but the Mountain Men ate fish only when no red meat was available.

Meat was the staple of their diet, and veterans knew it was wise to make camp in or near small valleys, where animals would search for fodder. A party that camped too high on plateaus or in the mountains would run the risk of losing its food supply after a blizzard or during a cold spell. Buffalo were in the lowlands, deer were everywhere, and there were elk, moose and bear to be found, too. Mountain lions were palatable in emergencies, and self-respecting trappers ate wolf meat only when very hungry. Beaver tails were considered delicacies, but beaver was unobtainable in the cold weather.

There was literally nothing to do when a man was not

occupied on a wood-cutting detail or off hunting. Nevertheless trappers awoke at dawn, and after eating a breakfast
of bear bacon and a steak, settled down for a long day
of idle conversation. Storytelling became a fine art, and
in the main the Mountain Men spoke of their own experiences in years past. They talked of narrow brushes with
death, fights with Indians and escapes from wild animals.

The best storytellers usually acquired considerable reputations, but Kit Carson rarely boasted of his exploits. As
a rule he was a listener, remaining silent and letting others do the talking. Unlike lesser heroes whose names have
faded from history, he preferred not to dwell on his
achievements. It was inevitable that, through the years,
others began to tell tales about him, and certainly those
stories became inflated as snowbound trappers let their imaginations run riot. Many of the Carson legends came into
being before the fires built in winter huts, but Kit contributed little or nothing to them.

His position was similar to that of Jim Bridger, a pioneer hunter and trapper who spent all of his time in the
Rocky Mountains. Bridger was also close-mouthed, and the
less he talked, the more others said about him. Some of
the tales told about him and about Kit are interchangeable,
the hero of one appearing as the protagonist in another. It
is interesting—but fruitless—to speculate on the conversa-
tions these two held with each other. There is no record of
their conferences.

It was imperative that Mountain Men learn to get along
with each other, for explosions of temperament would
have decimated the tribe if trappers cooped up together in
tiny, smoke-filled cabins had failed to abide by the rule to
live and let live. In spite of good intentions, there were
disputes, of course, and disputes led to violence. Men who
chose to live in the wilderness battling the elements, savages and wild beasts were neither pacific nor placid by nature, and a slugging match often relieved the monotony

of sitting before the fire or going out into the snow for fresh air.

An unwritten code prevented the use of firearms, knives or other lethal weapons to settle arguments, however. The basic instinct of self-preservation forced the Mountain Men to use their common sense, and when tempers flared, men went out into the cold to settle their affairs with their fists. Noses might be broken and teeth smashed, but few lives were lost. The duel was reserved for serious differences in which the honor of the participants was at stake. Granted that the touchy pioneers were ultra-sensitive and often claimed that their honor had been slighted, yet everyone knew that a serious bullet wound inflicted at a remote mountain camp hundreds of miles from the nearest physician would, in most instances, result in death. So pistol duels were fought only when other forms of combat had been exhausted.

Kit Carson's first winter in the Rockies was spent peacefully, and he became involved in no unpleasant incidents. As he said many years later, he was living the life he had always sought for himself, and was content. As his marksmanship was superior to that of most of his colleagues, he went out more frequently than the others on hunting trips, but otherwise failed to distinguish himself. He was satisfied with acceptance as a professional trapper and hunter and, having adopted the philosophy of his breed that the future would take care of itself, did not look beyond the forthcoming beaver-trapping season.

Snow and ice began to melt early in April 1831, and late in April, Fitzpatrick ordered his party to resume their trapping. The men worked their way slowly toward the Snake River, then down to the Bear River, which empties into Great Salt Lake. Beaver were plentiful, but Kit and several others became restless, as Fitzpatrick was painstakingly thorough, and the pace he set was too slow for the taste of hot-blooded young men. So, when they encountered another party of trappers from New Mexico and learned that one Captain Gaunt was in the vicinity on a trapping expedition, Kit and four of his comrades terminated their relationship with Fitzpatrick and set out in search of the more dynamic leader.

After ten days of travel they found him in one of the many so-called parks of the Rocky Mountains. These areas were natural game preserves, often occupying many thousands of square miles, and their rivers were known to be teeming with beaver. Gaunt was pleased to receive the recruits, and they spent the spring and summer with him, working the streams in what is now Wyoming. Then, when autumn approached, they journeyed to the Arkansas River and made camp there while Gaunt went on to Taos to sell the considerable quantity of furs they had accumulated and to buy provisions, gunpowder and other supplies for the company, including the always needed woolen shirts.

Gaunt returned late in the autumn, and as the season was too far advanced to travel any great distance, the men went into winter quarters. Life remained tranquil until January 1832, when a band of approximately fifty Crow Indians invaded the camp one night and stole nine horses. The loss was discovered early the following morning, the men also finding definite signs that the savages had been responsible for the theft.

Kit made himself the head of a party of volunteers determined to recover the animals, and set out in pursuit at once with a dozen men. This incident, which Kit verified in later years, proved to be a formidable undertaking from the start. The trappers crossed a plain which had been trampled by buffalo after the Indians had ridden across it, and the beasts' hoofprints on the snow made it difficult to distinguish the savages' tracks and determine the direction they had gone. Nevertheless the task was performed, although several hours passed, and the party set out again. Late in the day, after traveling nearly forty miles, the fatigue of their horses forced them to halt, and as there was a stand of trees a short distance ahead, they decided to make camp for the night.

Soon after they reached the site they saw smoke not far distant, and two men who went out to investigate reported that they had found the band of Crows. Sheer accident had caused the trappers to halt only a short distance from the savages they were pursuing.

At Kit's instigation nothing more was done until night fell. Then, after eating a small quantity of cold jerked beef, the trappers crawled slowly toward their objective on their hands and knees across the frozen ground, taking care to maintain complete silence. It had been decided that, as the Crows were traveling northeast, it would be wise to approach them from that direction, as the braves would not be expecting an attack from the far side of their camp. Therefore it was necessary to make a wide detour, and the trappers were tired when they reached their goal.

The worst of the ordeal was yet to come. Observing the Crows through dead underbrush, the men saw that the Indians were sitting around a fire built between two hastily erected log huts, the presence of these structures indicating that the savages intended to remain there for an appreciable length of time. The nine stolen horses were tethered nearby, as were the Indians' own mounts, but it was impossible to approach the animals without being detected, as the warriors were sitting around the fire, eating. According to some versions of the story, they were celebrating their successful theft by staging a victory dance, but this embellishment appears to be a frill added in subsequent years to give the tale more spice, which it doesn't need.

The trappers crouched behind the bushes and waited in the numbing cold for the warriors to finish their meal and retire before trying to regain possession of the horses. The decision was Kit's, and it is of interest to note that in this, the first operation against savages of any consequence in which he was the undisputed commander, he elected to pursue a cautious course. He could have ordered an immediate surprise attack, but knew his men were tired after their unexpectedly long ride, and his primary concern was the stolen mounts.

The Crows, enjoying the warmth of their fire and food, were in no hurry, and time dragged for the shivering trappers, who were forced to remain virtually motionless. Eventually the savages banked the fire and went into the two huts, and Kit was ready to act. He divided his party into two groups and, accompanied by five of the men, crawled across the snow and ice to the horses. Halters were cut with knives, and the men then threw snowballs at the animals, driving them toward the members of the second group. All of the horses were recovered in this manner without the knowledge of the warriors.

The trappers then retired some distance from the huts to decide their next move. It would not have crossed Kit's mind to give orders at this point without first obtaining the views of his comrades; when Mountain Men risked their lives in a fight, they expected and received the right to vote in a council of war. The majority were in favor of withdrawing at once. They had recovered their horses, which had been the primary aim of the expedition, and saw nothing to be gained by attacking the braves.

Kit disagreed, and argued that the Crows would cause further mischief in the future if allowed to go their way unpunished. Two of the men supported his contention, and the others, after discussing the matter at some length, agreed that an assault on the huts was necessary. So three of the men were sent off to the bivouac with the mounts, and the others returned to the site of the Indian camp.

There are two versions of what happened next. According to the more likely, the trappers moved as close as possible to the huts, took up positions behind the trunks of trees and opened fire. The second, which is more dramatic, has it that a dog belonging to the warriors barked furiously, giving an alarm, and that the savages raced out into the open to meet their foes. There had been ample opportunity for the Indians' dogs to bark earlier, when the trappers had been hiding in the underbrush, so this detail should be taken with a liberal dose of salt.

In any event, the trappers opened fire, and the savages came out into the open. Kit and his men, badly outnumbered, had to make every shot count, and their furious volley drove the warriors toward the second hut, which they used as a fort. The two parties exchanged shots for some time, with neither gaining an advantage, and Kit would have been wise to withdraw at this stage of the battle, for several of the braves had been wounded in their first counter-charge, and he had accomplished his aim of punishing them.

But neither he nor his men thought in terms of giving up the battle. They sought a clear-cut victory, and waited for the Crows to emerge into the open again. The coming of dawn revealed to the savages that they were facing a small handful of men, and charged. The trappers were compelled to retreat, firing repeatedly as they ran from tree to tree.

Kit and his colleagues must have known they could not stand fast, yet it did not occur to any of them that the more intelligent decision would have been to call it a day. Mountain Men hated to acknowledge defeat, and would have thought it dishonorable to give up without a fierce struggle. They were accustomed to living and working under conditions of great hardship, and thought it only natural that the odds should be against them. Their admirers, whose ranks continue to multiply, applaud them for their stubborn refusal to admit defeat. The Mountain Men would have been astonished by such admiration, for it simply did not occur to them to run from the field, much less surrender. When they entered combat, they continued to fight until they won or were killed.

The three men who had gone to the rear with the horses heard the continuing sounds of gunfire and, realizing that their comrades were encountering difficulties, rejoined them. Bolstered by these "reserves," Kit halted for a last-ditch stand, and his men redoubled their fire, loading their rifles with the skill and speed born of long practice. Five of the Crows were killed, and uncounted others were injured; several of the trappers were also wounded, but none lost their lives. The savages lost their taste for battle, which often happened under such circumstances, and broke off contact.

Kit and his men were left in possession of the field, and of their recovered horses. They returned to the camp on the Arkansas River, and Kit's reputation soared. He had won a victory against heavy odds, and from that time forward was always recognized as a leader of men.

He was not invincible, however, as another incident soon demonstrated. Captain Gaunt led the company to the Laramie River as soon as the weather became warmer, and trapping was begun again. The men worked their way to the Platte, and while moving up the south fork discovered one morning that two members of the band had vanished. It was believed, at first, that they had been abducted by savages, but when a head count of horses was made, it was found that three of the company's best animals had also disappeared. Gaunt and Kit immediately concluded that the fugitives had gone to the previous campsite on the Arkansas, where beaver skins had been buried, for it was the custom of trappers to hide their bales of skins, so they could travel unencumbered, then recover them at a later date.

Kit and two other men were sent out to apprehend the pair, but found no sign of them anywhere. Proceeding to the Arkansas camp, they found that the entire supply of beaver that had been concealed there was gone. Three hundred pounds of skins had been taken, and Kit, who was becoming expert at reading trail marks in the wilderness, could find nothing to indicate the direction the thieves had taken. Neither was ever seen again, and although a rumor later arose to the effect that they had been murdered by Indians, there is no substantiation for this claim.

There was no opportunity for Kit and his two companions to dwell on thoughts of vengeance, for their own position was perilous. Bands of Crow warriors were prowling through the area, and Kit, displaying a healthy regard for his own life and those of his friends, decided to remain at the camp. Gaunt's partner, a man named Blackwell, was expected sometime in the spring with a party of reinforcements, so the trio waited for them.

The next month was grueling. The three took turns standing sentry duty, and all three worked hard to build a small fort where they could hold out, at least for a time, in case of attack. Indians came close to the camp, but had no idea it was defended by such a small party, and did not attack. Their proximity made it impossible to hunt for meat, however, and even though there was game in the forests, the trio had to live on the emergency rations they carried. One or another fished in the river, too, and after two weeks of meager fare Kit finally killed a deer that ventured close to the camp.

After one month of mounting tension, the siege was lifted when Blackwell arrived with fifteen men and a mule train containing supplies of all kinds for the entire company. A day or two later, four of Gaunt's men arrived at the camp, and were overjoyed when they found that Kit and his companions were safe, as they had been given up for dead.

The entire party set out to join Gaunt at some salt springs located at the headwaters of the south fork of the Platte. Trapping was exceptionally good there, so the men marched as rapidly as they could, not pausing en route to do any trapping of their own. One day, after traveling fifty miles, they paused for the night near the banks of a small stream, a tributary of the Arkansas, and that night a band of Indians invaded the area and made an attempt to stampede the horses.

The savages were driven off, and for the next day or two extra guards were maintained, but the Indians did not repeat their tactics, and the trappers eventually relaxed their vigilance. The lure of beaver proved too strong to resist, and when the four men who had come from Gaunt's camp said that beaver were supposedly plentiful on a stream some distance from the route of march, Kit took two of them to investigate.

During their absence the Indians again raided the main party late at night, and managed to make off with a number of spare horses. Four of the trappers chased after them and, in the fight that took place when they caught up with the savages, one man on each side was wounded.

The following morning, Kit and his two companions started back toward the main body. Their mission had been a complete failure, for they had found no signs of beaver on the banks of the river that was allegedly teeming with them. All three were irritated, having made a long journey in vain, and were riding hard in order to make up for lost time. They emerged from a patch of woods and rode out onto open grassland at the same time that four Indian warriors came into the clear at the far side of the plains.

Under such circumstances the trappers reacted identically. It was unnecessary for Kit to give any orders, and he and his companions immediately spurred forward. The Indians fled, the trappers gained on them and were drawing within rifle range when a large band of Indians, perhaps sixty or seventy in all, came out of the forest. The four had been an advance guard, and too late Kit and his friends realized they were facing odds too great for them.

The four warriors who had been fleeing promptly turned

back, the savages started to close in from both sides and the three Mountain Men were trapped. Their one hope of survival was to reach the forest quickly, and they bent low in their saddles, urging their mounts forward. They were caught in a crossfire and had to run a gauntlet, but there was no choice, and they made no attempt to return the fire as they rode toward the trees.

Their refusal to fire at the warriors was eminently sensible. Three rifles would have been ineffective against sixty or seventy, and even if the trappers had scored, every second was precious. Time meant more to them than the futile gesture of killing or wounding a foe. There was a principle at stake, too, a basic precept that was one of the unwritten laws of Mountain Men. A rider never fired his rifle if he had no opportunity to reload, preferring to save his single shot for a moment of dire emergency. If his horse were killed or some other circumstance forced him to dismount, the last rifle shot might mean the difference between life and death, freedom and captivity. Contrary to a later, popular myth, the Mountain Man was not quick on the draw, but used his rifle only as the final means of self-defense.

Kit and his friends were relying on the notoriously poor aim of the Indians to help them escape. Again, contrary to legend, the savages were not expert marksmen. Firearms were a novelty to them, they obtained meat by shooting almost blindly into the seething mass of a herd of buffalo, and as it was not easy for them to obtain bullets and powder, they had few chances to improve their skill. Their gunnery, like their war whoop, was more sound than fury.

The gamble succeeded, and the trio reached the cover of the forest safely. Not pausing, they continued to ride at a break-neck pace and managed to outdistance their pursuers. The Indians soon gave up the chase, and it was not difficult for Kit and his companions to guess the reason: the warriors had stolen horses from Blackwell's men and, having no desire to encounter the main body of trappers, quietly made off with their spoils.

Kit was satisfied with the results of the encounter, too. Recalling the incident in later years, he said, "The redskins made a good attempt, but failed, thank God."

He and his companions reached the main body without further trouble, but found that two of Blackwell's men had suffered severe wounds. Neither was well enough to travel, and as it was feared that the savages might attack again in strength, a strong guard was established, with Kit in charge. The night passed calmly, but the following morning one of the sick men was much worse, and it was decided to carry him by litter. A buffalo robe was stretched between two stout poles, which were then lashed to the backs of mules, and the patient was laid on the robe.

He was fortunate that there were enough pack animals for him to ride in relative comfort. Another, more primitive type of litter often was made by attaching the front handles to a single mule and allowing the rear handles to drag on the ground. Saplings were usually used for this purpose, as there was a natural resilience in green wood that caused the poles to spring as they dragged on the ground. But this method, at best, guaranteed a patient a rough ride as his litter bounced, jolted and swayed on rough ground, and it was not uncommon for a man to be thrown from his litter.

Blackwell's subordinate suffered no ill effects from the journey by litter, but it was necessary to travel slowly, and some days passed before the group finally joined Gaunt's company. Then further time was lost, as both of the injured men mended slowly and could not be moved again until they were healed. No one thought of abandoning them in hostile Indian territory, so the men dawdled for several weeks, willingly sacrificing the better part of the trapping season.

When the wounded recovered, the entire party set out again and, anxious to make up for its idleness, went to one of the natural "parks" stocked with game and beaver. They found deer, buffalo and elk in abundance, so there was plenty to eat, but the beaver had vanished. Perhaps other trappers had already worked the rivers, or it may have been that the beaver had decided to move to more remote areas. Whatever the cause, the trappers had no success, and the men became disgruntled.

Kit was as restless as the others, but did not waste his time grumbling. Instead he devoted his energies to thinking of ways the remainder of the summer season could be utilized to advantage. It seemed to him that, if he struck out on his own, he could make a profit by confining his trapping operations to the streams high in the mountains. He had observed that the Indians spent most of their time in the lowland prairies, rarely venturing into high mountain areas, so he reasoned that he would be fairly safe from attack if he remained on high ground. The reason that trappers usually traveled in large companies was for mutual protection, but he would need no help if he avoided the areas in which the Indians roamed.

He discussed his plan with Gaunt, who willingly released him from the company. Two veterans found Kit's scheme so attractive they offered to go with him, and he accepted them provided they too could obtain a release without incurring hard feelings. Gaunt and Blackwell were amenable, as they were intending to give up their operations for the year, and Kit set out immediately with his two friends.

He was, for the first time, the leader of his own trapping expedition. He and his companions enjoyed considerable success, and by the early part of August 1832 had acquired as many bales of furs as their pack mules could carry. They still had to carry out the most dangerous part of their plan, that of crossing the prairies in order to reach New Mexico, and they made careful preparations accordingly. They shot two deer and a buffalo, made large quantities of pemmican and then set out for Taos, traveling at a rapid speed.

The men made themselves as inconspicuous as they could, never firing their rifles nor drawing attention to themselves in other ways. The weather was sufficiently warm that they needed no fires at night, they lived exclusively on pemmican and each morning, on breaking camp, they took care to obliterate all signs of their presence in the area. As a result of their caution or good luck—or a combination of the two—they reached Taos without encountering a single party of savages.

Gaunt and Blackwell were not the only trappers who had encountered problems, and the demand for beaver was so much greater than the supply that prices were exceptionally high. Kit found an outlet for his skins in Ewing Young, who paid him three thousand dollars for his bales. As the leader of his group, he kept half of the sum, and having learned his lesson, saved the money.

At the age of twenty-two he was a success in his chosen work, he had acquired a considerable reputation and his character had matured. He was a slow-spoken young man who thought carefully before voicing an opinion, but when he made up his mind he rarely changed it without good cause. His courage and his ability to react quickly and decisively in moments of crisis had made him a leader. His marksmanship was superb, other trappers regarded him as their superior, for he had the talent of "smelling out" beaver and he had proved that he could keep his head in clashes with hostile Indians.

He had traveled extensively, too, and was familiar with vast areas unknown to many of his colleagues. In short, he had established himself as one of the foremost citizens in the world of Mountain Men, and his future was assured. Never again would he have difficulty in finding work, nor would he be embarrassed by the need to buy a new shirt.

Ewing Young, describing the changes in his nature, later

said that his self-assurance had increased, which was natural. He no longer displayed great eagerness when approached by traders and the leaders of trapping expeditions who offered him employment, but calmly discussed financial terms with those who wanted his services. His sense of humor remained sharp, but he laughed less often and less boisterously. The time he had spent alone in the mountains had weathered him, and he had become a man.

The image of the Kit Carson known to later generations had been formed.

4. THE RIFLEMAN

No company of traders was better known in the fur business than that of Charles Bent and Cerin St. Vrain, who bought skins, sold supplies to trappers and provided guides for those who went into the mountains for the first time. Captain Albert Lee, a former officer in the United States Army and now a partner in the house of Bent and St. Vrain, was in Taos at the time of Kit's arrival there, preparing for an expedition into the wilderness. It was his purpose to supply the trappers with supplies and obtain furs in return, and he was acquiring everything from bacon and flour to new rifles and gunpowder, blankets and skinning knives and hatchets.

Kit and Lee met at Ewing Young's house, and almost immediately struck up a friendship. Lee offered Kit a place in his party, and his terms were flattering: he promised the young man the basic wage of one hundred dollars per month, plus a percentage of all profits made by Bent and St. Vrain on the expedition. Kit accepted, and in October, 1832, the group of about ten men set out on the so-called Old Spanish Trail, a mule path that led in the direction of the Californias.

Then they turned north into the mountains, where they met a larger party of some twenty men, led by one Robidoux, who was trapping mountain streams. An unexpectedly early heavy snowfall made both groups realize it would be wise to go into winter quarters, and they established a joint camp in the country of the Utah Indians, with whom they were on good terms. The traders and trappers set up skin tents, in which they made themselves comfortable, and as the natives in the area had often demonstrated their desire for peace, it was logical to assume that the winter would be quiet.

But the peace was disturbed within a short period of time by a California Indian employed by Robidoux as a guide. The man was an excellent horseman, a first-rate marksman and had frequently demonstrated great physical strength and endurance. Several of the trappers were uneasy in his presence, but he went out of his way to be accommodating, and eventually they forgot their fear of him. Then, when they least expected him to create trouble, he suddenly disappeared with six of Robidoux's best horses, which were worth approximately two hundred dollars each.

Robidoux asked Kit to follow the Indian and regain possession of the animals. Captain Lee granted his permission, and Kit departed at once, first going to the nearest village of Utah Indians to obtain the help of a warrior as a guide, for he himself was not sufficiently familiar with the territory to travel alone through the wilderness.

A warrior accepted the offer of a rifle in return for his services, and the two men set out. They had some difficulty in finding the fugitive's trail, which led toward the west, but once they ran across it, their troubles were at an end, for the six horses left tracks that were easy to see. Kit and the Utah rode rapidly, covering one hundred miles in two days, and it appeared that they were gaining on the criminal, who seemed to be headed in the direction of the Californias.

The Utah's horse was taken sick on the third morning of the journey, and the warrior refused to continue the chase on foot, which would not have been practical in any event. Kit therefore decided to proceed alone, even though unfamiliar with the surrounding countryside, and to meet the warrior on his return.

He covered another thirty miles in less than a day, a remarkable feat considering that he was following a trail through territory he did not know. Late in the afternoon he saw that the tracks were fresh, and unslung his rifle. The events of the next quarter of an hour provided the raw material from which legends are made.

Kit, riding now at a canter, caught sight of the fugitive in the distance, and spurred his horse to a gallop. The Indian, seeing his pursuer a few moments later, headed for the cover of a large boulder. If he reached it, he would have time to fire and reload at will, while Kit, completely exposed, had to depend on a single shot.

Still riding at full speed, Kit took careful aim, waited until the fugitive reached the boulder and then fired before the man could duck out of sight. His one shot felled the thief, and he recovered the six stolen horses.

An embellished version of the story states that the fugitive fired at the same instant Kit squeezed the trigger, but that the Indian's shot went wild. The facts of the case speak for themselves, and a coat of varnish adds little to the tale. It seems obvious that the Indian, riding hastily for cover, could not have turned in time to take aim and fire when his adversary had already drawn a bead on him.

Whether the Indian actually fired or not is an irrelevant detail. What does matter is that Kit killed the thief, and added to his soaring reputation. It was later said that if a man had a serious quarrel with Kit, he should not permit Carson to get the first sight over his rifle, for if he succeeded, his enemy was as good as dead. The fugitive, certainly, was dead.

Kit returned to camp with the horses, pausing en route to take the Utah warrior back to his village. There, even though the brave had not been able to accompany him on the last, climactic stage of his mission, he ceremoniously presented the man with a new rifle. In the process, of course, he made a lasting friendship and won the respect of the entire tribe, for other, lesser traders might have been inclined to withdraw the offer of the weapon on the grounds that the warrior had not fulfilled his part of the bargain.

The rest of the winter passed quietly, and early in the spring, when the men were preparing to break camp, several trappers, riding south, came into the bivouac to rest and to report that Fitzpatrick and Jim Bridger were encamped on the Snake River, about fifteen days' march distant. They had enjoyed good luck the previous season, the men said, and had acquired large quantities of beaver.

Lee and his party started north the following day, and after a hard journey that lasted more than twenty days, finally reached the camp of Fitzpatrick and Bridger, where Kit was reunited with many of his old friends. All of Captain Lee's supplies were purchased by the group, Fitzpatrick and Lee paying for the goods in beaver. The profits promised to be large, and Lee planned to return at once to Taos.

Kit preferred to remain in the mountains, the new trapping season having begun, so Lee arranged to pay his share to Ewing Young, and Kit joined Fitzpatrick's company. Bridger went off on his own, and Kit soon concluded that the veteran had been wise, for the company was so large and the beaver so few that the profits reaped by any one man would be slim. After spending only four weeks with Fitzpatrick, Kit decided to follow the same plan he had used the previous year, and announced his intention of leaving for the higher mountains.

A large number of volunteers wanted to go with him, but he accepted only three. With them he went up into the mountains to the headwaters of the Laramie River, and they enjoyed a busy and profitable summer, repeating Kit's success of the previous year. He had developed his own trapping system, and it is surprising that others did not employ the same technique. It can only be deduced that the majority of trappers were sufficiently gregarious that they preferred larger companies to the greater profits they would have reaped had they emulated Kit.

When the autumn approached, Kit began to think in terms of going into winter quarters, and was reluctant to try to duplicate his feat of making a dash for Taos with his skins. He didn't want to push his luck, and rather than run the risk of being attacked by Indians on the prairies, he buried his pelts in a safe place until the following spring and led his men to Jim Bridger's winter quarters. A number of independent trappers made it their practice to congregate at Bridger's camp, where everyone was welcome, and it was natural that Kit, who admired the veteran, should want to join him.

Soon after arriving at the spot, the exact location of which has not been handed down to posterity, there occurred an alleged incident that had become one of the most noted of the Kit Carson stories. It is impossible to determine whether there is even a germ of truth to substantiate the tale. Kit himself neither confirmed nor denied it, and there were no witnesses who could verify the story. It was widely believed, regardless of its authenticity, and Dr. Peters, who accepted every legend about Kit at face value, tells it with gusto.

It seems that, immediately after reaching Bridger's camp, Kit discovered that the trappers gathered there were short of food, a drought having made meat difficult to obtain. So he appointed himself hunter for the company, and after turning his horse over to one of the other men to lead into camp, immediately went off into the forest, rifle in hand, to search for game. In spite of the supposed absence of game, he found elk tracks only one mile from the campsite, and following the trail, discovered several of the animals grazing on a hillside. Only a short distance from the elk was a stand of low, bristling pine trees, and he started toward them, noting with satisfaction that a breeze was blowing toward him, which would make it difficult for the elk to scent him.

Just before he reached the pines, however, the beasts started to move away rapidly, and he could only assume that he had stepped on a twig or had given away his presence in some other careless manner. There was no time to dwell on the matter, for the elk would be gone in another moment, so he raised his rifle and, allowing for the inevitable leap of the stag at bay, brought down the largest of the elk with a single shot.

He took no more than a single step toward his prey when he heard a ferocious roar from the woods behind him. Turning his head, he saw two large grizzly bears bounding toward him. There was no time to reload his rifle, which was useless, and he raced toward the pines, the bears closing in behind him. He reached up for a branch, and as he hauled himself up into the tree, one of the bears brushed against his legs. He pulled himself higher into the tree and discovered, to his dismay, that in his haste he had dropped his rifle.

He knew, of course, that bears also climb trees, and realized he would be helpless unless he took energetic measures to defend himself. Drawing his hunting knife, he quickly severed a stout branch. This feat is itself worthy of comment. Anyone who has ever tried to saw or cut a limb of a living tree knows it is extremely difficult to slice through green wood. Pines, which are gummy, are particularly resilient, so it must be presumed that Kit, who slashed off the branch with a single stroke, was using an exceptionally sharp knife.

Using the branch as a lance, he deftly poked each of the bears with it, rapping them smartly on their snouts, which are very sensitive. They had just started to climb the tree after him when he struck them, and they dropped back to the ground again, howling. He climbed into the highest branches that would support his weight, and when the bears came after him again, he repeated the tactics. For several hours the duel continued, the bears trying to reach their intended victim, Kit holding them off.

The bears roared angrily, but Kit's maneuver succeeded, and when their snouts were bleeding and sore, they finally withdrew. The man was afraid they were lurking in the nearby forest, however, and remained in the tree for some time before taking the risk of leaping to the ground, snatching his rifle and hastily reloading it. The bears were no longer in the vicinity, however, and did not bother him again.

Perhaps the strangest aspect of the tale is that the carcass of the slaughtered elk had not been molested. The bears, it seems, were so intent on destroying their living prey that they completely ignored the elk, whose meat would have more than satisfied their hunger.

Kit cut as much of the elk meat as he could carry, then returned to the camp, and other members of the company hurried out into the forest for the rest of the carcass, which they managed to save from hyenas, jackals and wolves. Thanks to Kit's heroic efforts, the trappers had food again.

Few accounts of Kit's life and career omit the story of the two bears, which strains credulity to the breaking point. Such a tale is essential to the legend of Kit Carson, however, for the grizzly was considered the king of the wilderness, and every hunter worthy of note killed at least one of the monsters at some time during his career. Kit shot his share of bears, but only he was considered capable of facing two of them, without firearms, and surviving. One wonders, in passing, what had happened to render his pistols ineffective. Perhaps he wasn't carrying them in his belt that day.

Soon after the narrow escape, Kit and Bridger led their men to Rendezvous, the first time this gathering of the clan appears in the life story of Kit Carson. Trappers, hunters and guides usually gathered for what was tantamount to a convention of Mountain Men at the end of the summer season.

As a rule they met on a plateau below the great peaks of the Rocky Mountains, and Rendezvous combined some of the aspects of a sales meeting with those of a carnival. A generous pinch of religion was added to the brew, too.

The purposes of Rendezvous were many. The trappers could sell their furs to traders, and in return could buy supplies for outrageously high sums. Men who saw few other humans through the better part of the year had an opportunity to mix with their fellows. Gossip was exchanged, there were discussions on the current state of the fur market, and men learned which streams were supplying beaver in quantity.

Peddlers provided the participants with whiskey, rum and strong wines, which sold at high prices, and professional card players were usually on hand hoping to separate the trappers from the money they had just been paid. Missionaries were drawn to a Rendezvous, too, and frequently made converts, for the Mountain Men needed faith to sustain them in their unceasing battles against privation, the forces of nature or Indians who resented their presence in the territory.

Colorado was a favorite meeting ground, and the annual Rendezvous was often held near the site of present-day Estes Park, with Twin Sisters and Meadow Mountain looming nearby, and mammoth Long's Peak casting its shadow on the tents of animal skin that the men erected. No one kept count of the number who attended these business-social meetings, but it has been estimated that at least two hundred usually gathered together, and the figure, at times, may have been double that number.

Mountain Men, cut off from civilization at their own instigation, were in no position to haggle over prices, and they paid exorbitant fees for their purchases. They were charged two dollars per pint of sugar or coffee, which cost only a few cents in the cities of the eastern seaboard, and frequently they paid as much as two to three dollars per pint of gunpowder, for which they would have spent no more than twenty-five cents in Illinois or Indiana. They were charged three dollars for a gallon of whiskey, which cost about seventy-five cents east of the Mississippi, and wines were even higher. By far the most expensive items were blankets of rough wool, which cost consumers about one dollar and fifty cents in Boston or Hartford. At the beginning of Rendezvous, traders charged the Mountain Men as much as twenty-five dollars for a blanket, and even the wary buyer who waited until the end of the convention and ran the risk of finding that the traders were completely sold out could not purchase one for less than fifteen dollars.

In the years prior to the Civil War, when Rendezvous was an economic and social necessity, no women were present at the conclaves. Only in postwar years, when the meetings had become so highly publicized that hardy tourists attended them out of curiosity, did ladies of pleasure from the growing frontier towns enliven the proceedings. In Kit Carson's day, no woman was rugged enough to make her way across the prairies and mountains to Rendezvous, nor brash enough to force her way into the company of the roughest, most independent-minded men in the civilized world.

Kit dug up the bales of fur he had buried and took them with him to his first Rendezvous, where he sold the skins for a good price. He kept most of his profits, buying only the supplies he needed, and although he remained at the meeting for a period of six to eight weeks, neither drank to excess nor gambled. He kept busy, however, for he had already acquired a name for himself, and men who were not acquainted with him made it their business to seek his company.

There were snow flurries in the air when the Rendezvous was adjourned, but the trappers, always optimistic, hoped to find at least a few beaver before winter came. Kit went into country he had never before visited, the headwaters of the Missouri River, and traveled with a company of about fifty men into portions of Montana that had never been thoroughly explored.

The trappers soon realized their hopes were unjustified. The weather was bitterly cold, beaver had disappeared from the streams and not a single skin was obtained. The company was in the country of the Blackfeet, and Kit soon realized that this tribe had earned its reputation for stubborn persistence. Running attacks were made on the trappers at irregular intervals, and the men never knew when the warriors might strike next. An attempt was made to establish a winter camp on the bank of the Missouri, but the site faced an open valley on two sides, and the Blackfeet made life miserable for the trappers.

Kit and the other leaders realized they would have to find better quarters if they hoped to avoid trouble through the winter, and the march was resumed. The Blackfeet continued to harass the company, and on two occasions men who fell behind the main body were killed and scalped. But the trappers were not in a position to retaliate, for they had not yet found a base from which to operate, and the cold was causing severe discomfort. The Blackfeet, of course, mistakenly assumed that their foes were cowards.

At last a site was found near the Big Snake River, and the trappers went into camp on a hill that was a natural fortress, or so they thought. They erected their tents and began to build a palisade, but on their second night at the bivouac the Blackfeet sneaked into the incompleted compound and drove off eighteen of the company's horses. The loss was discovered during the night, a council of war was held and at dawn a band of twelve men, with Kit acting as captain, set out in pursuit.

Snow had fallen shortly before the theft, so it was easy to follow the savages' tracks, and Kit set a hard pace, covering fifty miles by midafternoon. They made better progress than had the Blackfeet, who had been forced to break a trail through the snow, and the savages had already halted and made camp for the night when they were discovered.

The horses were grazing on the southern slope of a hill, where there was relatively little snow, and the trappers, in an attempt to recover their property immediately, opened fire. The Blackfeet party, about fifty strong, returned the fire, and neither side gained an advantage. But Kit was apprehensive when he saw that the natives were equipped with snowshoes, and when the Blackfeet sent forward a brave under a flag of truce, who asked for a talk, he consented.

The emissary told him, at some length, that the warriors had no desire to make war on trappers and had assumed they were stealing the horses from their ancient enemies of the Snake nation. Kit was skeptical, and demanded to know why the warriors had not laid down their arms at once when they had learned their error. The emissary replied, with unassailable logic, that men on the receiving end of rifle fire are inclined to shoot first and talk later.

Kit tried another approach. The warriors now knew they had taken property belonging to trappers, not Snake Indians, and the entire matter could be settled without further ado by returning the eighteen horses to their owners. The emissary went back to his brothers to carry the message, and the trappers, alert for trickery, held their rifles ready for use. The Blackfeet surprised them by sending the messenger forward a second time with a request that both groups sit down together to settle the problem amicably.

The wary trappers agreed, and all twelve dropped their arms, then advanced fifty paces to the spot where the council would be held. The Blackfeet did the same, approaching the place from the opposite direction, and a blazing fire was lighted. The men seated themselves on the snow, a pipe of peace was passed from hand to hand, and after every man present had taken a puff or two, the chief of the Blackfeet made a long, rambling speech. In it he made a number of vague promises of friendship, but did not refer to the horses.

Kit controlled his impatience, and when it was his turn to speak, he declared bluntly that there could be no peace until the trappers' mounts were returned. The savages, who outnumbered their foes by more than four to one, became overbearing, and after conferring briefly among themselves, sent off two of the younger braves, who returned a few moments later with five thin horses, none of them belonging to the trappers. These were the only horses, the chief said, that he could return.

Kit tried to argue with him, but the Blackfoot remained adamant. The peace parley dissolved instantly, and both parties ran for their weapons.

Kit and a trapper named Markhead were the first to recover their rifles, and consequently led the advance on the Indians, who were taking up positions behind trees that stood between their campsite and the open area. The most logical targets were two warriors who scurried into partial cover behind the two nearest trees, and Kit, seeing one of the braves aiming at Markhead, brought the man down with a single shot.

In protecting his friend he neglected his own safety, and realized too late that the other warrior had taken aim at him. He flung himself forward onto the snow, but the Indian's shot grazed the skin of his neck and passed through his left shoulder, shattering the head of the armbone and narrowly missing the main artery.

Kit made an attempt to reload his rifle, but his left arm could not be moved, and when he discovered that he was powerless, he crouched on the ground in order to make himself as small a target as possible. He was unable to take part in the rest of the battle, and watched helplessly as his companions launched two attacks, but were driven off in both. The trappers finally withdrew, taking Kit with them, and rode off for a distance of about one mile.

There they halted and made camp for the night, posting two of their band as outposts. Kit's wound was dressed, but he suffered agonies, for the trappers were afraid to light a fire for fear of drawing the Blackfeet to them. The wound bled freely, and it was so cold in the open that the blood froze to the bandage, which became as stiff as a sheet of ice. He made no complaint, however, and to the best of his limited ability took part in the council of war that followed the retreat.

The men sensibly concluded that they were no match for the Blackfeet, notwithstanding the fact that they had suffered only one casualty, Kit, while killing and wounding an undetermined number of warriors. There was the danger that the savages would attack again, and it was possible that the outnumbered Mountain Men would be wiped out. They therefore made up their minds to return to their base at once.

Kit was placed in his saddle, and when he lost consciousness several times on the long journey, his companions lashed him to his horse. The men rode hard all night, increased their pace at daybreak and arrived at the base camp at noon. A second party of about thirty men was organized and left at once under the command of Jim Bridger, but the savages had vanished, and neither they nor the stolen horses were ever seen again.

Kit spent the winter convalescing. Fortunately he was young, his health was good and his wound healed. The bone in his shoulder was not set, but managed to mend, and he exercised his arm for hours each day, showing great patience. By spring he was recovered, and took an active part in trapping operations through the season.

The men worked the Green and Snake rivers, and enjoyed the best trapping success Kit had ever known. His injury had made him more taciturn than ever, but he made no secret of his pleasure when the company traveled into Colorado for Rendezvous and his share of the profits amounted

to more than one thousand dollars. He was acquiring a
small fortune, and certainly was becoming one of the
wealthiest of the Mountain Men.

At Rendezvous Kit became embroiled in his first serious
quarrel, an event which he later regarded with little pride.
Perhaps his own injury the previous winter had made him
somewhat short-tempered, but it is certain that his adversary was an unpopular man. He was a Frenchman who
called himself "Captain," and whose name has been spelled
St. Nane, Suenan and Shunan. This last, obviously, was an
attempt on the part of the American westerner to grapple
with unfamiliar spelling and pronunciation, and he has generally been recorded as Shunan.

A thorn, no matter what its spelling, is prickly, and Captain Shunan was a known trouble maker. He had lived in
Montreal for a time, and sometimes spoke of having been
a *voyageur*, or canoeman in the vast Canadian fur trade.
There were rumors, unverified but generally believed, that
his presence in French-speaking Canada had become un-
welcome, as he had committed the error of killing an employee of the powerful North-West Company, which had
recently consolidated with the older and even more influ-
ential Hudson's Bay Company.

Shunan, for whatever his reasons, took care not to set
foot on Canadian territory. He confined his operations to
the American West, where he was considered a good trapper, an indifferent hunter—due to a lack of patience he
could not curb—and a first-rate marksman. No society of
teetotalers would have elected him to its board of direc-
tors, and whenever he was drunk, which was most of the
time, he was inclined to be quarrelsome.

Frontiersmen were not inclined to search for a fight, and
no one wanted to tangle with a brute who stood more than
six feet tall and had a chest as thick as a barrel of hard
cider. Ever mindful of his ability to drill a hole through a
walnut, allegedly at fifty paces, the trappers gathered at

Rendezvous thoughtfully avoided Shunan whenever possible. That task became increasingly difficult as the days passed, for the captain mistakenly assumed that anyone who failed to stand up to him was a coward.

One day he went too far. In the morning he deliberately provoked arguments with two smaller, weaker men and, challenging both to fist fights, knocked them out. Eyebrows were raised and a few mutters were heard, but at this point no one reached for a gun. Fisticuffs were common at Rendezvous, and anyone who lost was expected to bear his swollen jaw and black eye with good grace.

Shunan, never one to leave well enough alone, went through the camp boasting that he could fell any Frenchman with a single blow. As for Americans, he supposedly said, they weren't worth soiling his hands, and he would be delighted to cut a stick and switch any such vermin who annoyed him.

Whether Kit Carson heard these incendiary comments or whether they were reported to him by others is unimportant, although some accounts insist that the words were addressed to him and that he burned with righteous, patriotic zeal. It is sufficient to note that, in one way or another, he became aware of Shunan's gratuitous insults.

The more exalted versions of the events that followed state that some trappers, fed up with the captain's abuse, conceived the not unlikely idea of escorting him across the prairie to the nearest tree and hanging him from the highest branch. Kit, these romantics declare, was horrified by the proposal, feeling that a lynching would besmirch the reputation of frontier justice. Therefore he supposedly countered with the suggestion that he act as his comrades' spokesman and champion, and promised to put the bully in his place.

Other accounts indicate he was afraid that Shunan, if unchecked, would start using men's heads instead of walnuts as targets for rifle practice. Still others say that the company gathered at Rendezvous was mortally afraid of the captain, and that no one was willing to knock the chip from his shoulder. So Kit cast himself in the role of a pacifying avenger.

Sheer logic might induce one to suppose that Kit's motives for trying to halt Shunan's reprehensible conduct might have been somewhat less lofty than those later ascribed to him. It is possible that his own patience gave way. Even the monarch of the Mountain Men was mortal, and presumably had a temper.

Whether he lay in wait for the chance to call Shunan's bluff or whether the garrulous captain handed him an opportunity on a rough wooden platter cannot be determined. Let it suffice that Kit was a member of a large group engaged in desultory conversation, that Shunan approached the men and, shouldering several aside, laughed contemptuously.

All accounts are in unanimous agreement that Kit promptly challenged the Frenchman to a duel.

He may or may not have called Shunan names, may or may not have shouted at him. But it is unlikely in the extreme that he made the little speech attributed to him by Dr. Peters, and here repeated verbatim:

"Shunan, before you stands the humblest specimen of an American in this band of trappers, among whom there are, to my certain knowledge, men who could easily chastise you, but, being peacably disposed, they keep aloof from you. At any rate, I assume the responsibility of ordering you to cease your threats, or I will be under the necessity of killing you."

His true words, whatever they may have been, had an immediate effect, and both men walked off to their tents, which stood at opposite sides of the camp. Word that a duel would be fought spread with the speed of a brushfire at the end of a hot, dry summer. Peddlers quickly removed their wares from the central open area of the bivouac, and hundreds of men gathered to watch one or the other of the principals shed blood.

Sporting instincts were aroused, and everyone who knew Kit placed bets on him. Notwithstanding the confidence of his friends, the odds were against him. He was a crack shot, it was true, but so was his opponent, and Shunan's experience was greater. Not only had he spent a much longer time in the wilderness, but he had fought a number of duels through the years. Kit, on the other hand, had never fired a shot at anyone in anger. Others had been known to fail when facing that test.

In any event, a new legend was in the making.

Kit and Shunan soon reappeared, and both were mounted. The captain carried his rifle, and whether Kit was similarly armed is open to question. Some versions of the story say that he, too, carried his rifle, but others claim that he had been in such a hurry that he had snatched the first weapon he had seen, a single-barreled pistol. It may be stretching plausability to believe that the cards were stacked so heavily in favor of the villain.

The antagonists spurred to a canter when they saw each other, their weapons ready for instant use. When they came closer, they engaged in a brief exchange of dialogue that, at first glance, cannot be accepted at face value.

"Am I the person you're looking for?" Kit shouted.

According to some accounts, Shunan answered, "Yes." Those who paint him in the darkest colors declare he called, "No," for reasons that will be discussed shortly.

There was neither the time nor the need for more talk, as the horses were now only a few paces apart. Shunan raised his rifle, which he aimed at his adversary's chest, obviously intending to kill him. But a ball from Kit's weapon crashed into his arm and broke a bone. It also spoiled the captain's aim. His shot was too high, and Kit escaped serious injury. Shunan's bullet may or may not have creased his scalp, and he may or may not have been sufficiently

close to the Frenchman to have received a powder burn
from the rifle. Accuracy was rarely observed in the retelling
of Kit Carson's exploits.

One fact emerges: Kit was the winner of the duel. Shunan's blood had been spilled, and the wound he had sustained made it impossible for him to continue the fight. Kit
was hailed by his companions, and it is safe to guess that
those who cheered him the loudest were the friends who
had bet on him. A chastened Shunan was carried off to his
tent.

Legitimate questions may be raised regarding several aspects of the duel.

Why did the combatants walk to their tents for horses
and weapons, rather than run? There is no logical answer.

Assuming that Kit was content to walk, why didn't he
take a few seconds longer to find his rifle, instead of picking
up the relatively weak pistol? For that matter, would a man
whose livelihood depended on his rifle have mislaid the
valuable gun, particularly at Rendezvous, where burglary
was not unknown? Reasonable replies are self-evident.

Why the curious question asked by Kit? Here, at least,
the ground underfoot is firm. In all probability, Kit did indeed ask, in one way or another, whether he was the man
Shunan was seeking. The query may seem absurd to the
modern reader, but it fits into the pattern of the early
nineteenth-century American frontier.

The wilderness of mountains, plains and forests was the
refuge almost invariably sought by the fugitive. Hence a
strictly enforced unwritten code was observed. No one
probed into a stranger's past; a man was accepted on the
basis of present deeds, and was assumed to be friendly unless his conduct indicated otherwise.

Privacy was considered sacred, and no man ever asked
another's name. One who wished to identify himself did so.
But it would have been rude to the point of begging trouble
to pry. And if a man chose to keep his identity to himself,

that was his business. His reasons were assumed to be valid.

Kit's inquiry, seen against this background, proves to have been part of the fabric of the Mountain Man's chivalric banner. In effect, one said, "Let there be no mistake about this. Are you sure that I'm the fellow you want to fight?"

One's opponent in a duel was obliged to answer affirmatively.

It should be remembered that neither Kit nor his foe was aided by seconds. There was no referee or other neutral arbiter to tell the antagonists when to begin shooting. Kit and Shunan, then, were simply observing a custom of their era, common in the West. The formalities having been observed, they were free to blaze away at each other.

Shunan's bewildering response, "No!" which is reported by Dr. Peters, and is repeated by J. S. Abbott, Charles Burdett and other nineteenth-century biographers, is no more than a clumsy attempt to portray the Frenchman as being totally evil. Presumably, by responding negatively, Shunan was trying to catch Kit off guard, to shoot him down in cold blood the instant he lowered his own weapon.

This attempt to blacken the captain gives neither combatant credit for possessing any intelligence. Shunan could not have been stupid enough to attempt the perpetration of such an absurd hoax, nor could any sane man have been taken in by it. The mere suggestion that the ever alert Kit Carson could have been fooled into believing that someone other than the man he had challenged to a duel was thundering toward him is ludicrous.

Why then did Dr. Peters, Abbott and the others go to such extreme lengths to show Shunan as a villain? These authors considered themselves responsible biographers, not tellers of tall tales, and certainly they did not believe their readers dim-witted or naïve.

Here again, the puzzle is solved easily, if one remembers that principles changed over the period of a half-century.

At the time Kit Carson was earning his living as a trapper in the very wild West, duels were fought frequently. No law enforcement officers were patrolling the frontier. A man was his own peacemaker, and his firearms were his pacifiers. When two frontiersmen developed a feud, they settled their affairs with bullets. Those who lived by the gun died by it, and no one thought worse of the killer.

But the Civil War and its immediate aftermath created a distinct change in climate. Dueling, which had been a fashionable inheritance of southern gentlemen, imported from England along with fox hunting and other games, was no longer in vogue. Northern arms had triumphed, the Confederacy was crushed and the stern Puritans of New England, many of whom had moved to other regions of the country, superimposed their own codes on the nation.

Dueling, in brief, had become worse than illegal. It was wickedly immoral.

So the authors who wrote biographies of the peerless Kit Carson were confronted by a vexing problem. That the folk hero had fought a duel was an incontrovertible fact. It had to be justified in order to make it palatable. Following the line of least resistance, they portrayed Captain Shunan as Beelzebub incarnate in order to lather Kit with an unnecessary coat of whitewash.

The men who attended Rendezvous felt no moral qualms after the duel, and certainly attached no blame to Kit. David had defeated Goliath in fair combat, and Kit's popularity soared. Men who had not known him previously sought his friendship, and he was paid the compliment of being considered Jim Bridger's equal. He could have received no higher tribute, for the taciturn Bridger was universally believed to be the most experienced and reliable of all trappers, guides and hunters in the band of Mountain Men.

The time was not far distant when Bridger would be called second only to Kit Carson. The young man from

Kentucky was already becoming so renowned that he seemed to be ten feet tall.

It was during this period that Kit's name first appeared in print. The New York *Post*, one of the most conservative of eastern seaboard newspapers, was running a series of articles in its financial section on the fur trade, and the name of "Mr. Christopher Carson" was included in a list of trappers who would, the *Post* declared, insure a profit to those who wanted to invest in trapping expeditions.

If Kit was aware of this honor, he made no known attempt to capitalize on it. Ewing Young, who was also listed, promptly sent an agent to New York and Philadelphia on a fund-raising hunt, and acquired so much money that he rarely went into the field again. Instead he stayed at home, hired others to work for him and became one of the wealthiest Americans in the Mexican Southwest.

It is doubtful that Kit would have been happy with such an existence. Even in later years, when he could afford to sit on his own front porch and direct the operations of others, he continued to spend the better part of his time roaming through the rapidly diminishing wilderness. He was one of the breed whom the intellectuals of the eighteenth century called a "natural man," one who lived his life strictly in accordance with his own desires. Fame and financial rewards meant nothing to him, and to the end of his days he regarded their acquisition as incidental.

What mattered to him was that he was free to do what he wanted. He had earned that freedom, and it was his most precious asset. Certainly in the hectic years when he was in his twenties he was a hedonist in the highest sense, finding deep satisfaction in spending long, lonely hours trapping along the banks of wilderness rivers, eating fresh-killed meat roasted over a fire and sleeping in the open. He had chosen his vocation and had become one of its leading practitioners, and was now enjoying life to the hilt.

5. STILL HIGHER ADVENTURE

The problem of unemployment no longer existed for Kit Carson, who received a number of offers from the financial backers of trapping expeditions. In fact, his reputation was now so great that he neither kept a record of which one he accepted nor, in later years, could remember who his employers had been. All that is known is that, once again, he preferred to join a small company, willingly taking greater risks in the wilderness so he could reap a larger share of the profits.

The autumn and early winter months passed uneventfully, and trapping operations were disappointing. He and his companions wandered through the mountains from one river to another, from the Yellowstone to the Big Horn, from all three major forks of the Missouri to the Big Snake. The beaver had taken themselves elsewhere, and the party went into winter camp near the Big Snake with virtually nothing to show for its efforts.

Soon after they had made camp a large company of Canadians and Americans came to the bivouac. This group was commanded by Thomas McCoy, a trader who held the rank of senior clerk in the Hudson's Bay Company, and was therefore a man of considerable power and influence. He persuaded Kit and five others to join him, and Kit became an employee of the largest organization in the fur trade. His affiliation with "The Company," as Hudson's Bay had been known for the better part of one hundred and fifty years, did not change his luck, however, for beaver remained scarce.

The energetic McCoy had heard rumors that there were large numbers of beaver on the Humboldt River, at that period called Mary's River, and showing greater zeal than common sense, led his men there in the dead of winter. The beaver were hibernating, of course, and game was scarce, so the expedition was doomed, and when provisions shrank, McCoy realized his mistake. Leaving the majority of the company in the mountains, he went off with a few companions to buy provisions at Fort Walla Walla in what later became the state of Washington.

Kit and the other members of the party who stayed behind were soon going hungry. Hunting parties found no trace of deer or elk, and for a week or ten days the men subsisted on edible roots, occasionally augmenting their meager diet with fish caught by dropping lines through holes cut in the thick ice that covered the rivers. Eventually they were forced to bleed their pack mules and drink the animals' blood, but did not dare repeat this desperate measure, for fodder was scarce and they knew the mules would die if bled again.

Fort Hall, the closest trading post, was a three-day march from the snow-covered hills where the men were camping, so they set out for it, hoping they could buy flour, bacon and other provisions there. They traveled on empty stomachs, and there was considerable doubt that they could reach their destination. On the second day of their journey they encountered a band of Indians whose tribe was not recorded. These savages proved amicable, but had only enough food for their own needs and refused to sell the trappers any supplies.

Kit promptly dangled tempting bait before the Indians, offering them butcher knives in return for a large, fat gelding. The savages expressed interest, but wanted rifles. No Mountain Man in his right mind would sell firearms to Indians, so Kit refused, but offered to throw in a few skinning knives, and at last the horse trade was completed.

The gelding was slaughtered and roasted; the tougher parts were boiled, and the trappers gained enough strength to stagger on to Fort Hall, which they reached late the following evening. They were cordially received by the American traders who were in charge of the establishment, and although they had no furs to offer in exchange for provisions, were given all they wanted on the liberal credit terms of the frontier. They promised to repay the debt, in one way or another, as fast as they could.

Forty-eight hours after their arrival at the fort, opportunity knocked. A professional hunter employed by the traders returned from a journey to report that a large herd of buffalo was grazing in a valley off to the south. Kit and his companions set out at once, and although still in a weakened condition, reached the valley after a single hard day's ride. The hunter's story proved to be right: Kit, who went ahead of the others on reconnaissance, saw hundreds of the beasts in the little, protected valley, where grass was still green.

As the wind was blowing from the south and would not carry the scent of humans to the animals, camp was made for the night. The men made careful preparations for the following morning's hunt, and no one slept for more than a few hours. It was arranged that Kit and several others who were marksmen would do the actual hunting, with the rest of the company handling the meat as soon as the beasts were slaughtered. At dawn the men moved out of their bivouac, and the hunt began.

In less than two hours, approximately one hundred and fifty buffalo were killed, the rest of the herd stampeding and vanishing in panic. There was so much meat now that it was impossible to return at once to Fort Hall, so the company remained in the valley, butchering and curing. Poles were driven into the ground, and rawhide ropes were strung, much in the manner of wash lines. Long strips of buffalo meat were hung on the ropes, and were left to dry in the sun. When dried, meat prepared in this manner could be preserved for long periods.

There was nothing to do now but establish guards to prevent wolves from stealing the spoils, and for the next week or two the company feasted on the delicacies of the frontier, the livers and tongues of the animals, and the fat found along both sides of the backbone of the buffalo.

The winter sun beat down steadily in the dry highlands, and at last the meat was cured. The men would not go hungry again for a long time, even after paying their debt to the traders by giving them large quantities of meat. Heavily laden, the company started back toward Fort Hall, and traveled at such a slow pace that the men spent three days on the march.

Neither Kit nor his friends knew it, but they were being watched by a band of Blackfeet, who had discovered them at their camp and had kept them under discreet observation. The Indians followed them to the fort, but concealed themselves some distance from the stockade.

The trappers' horses were placed in a corral, together with those of the traders, a sentinel was stationed at the corral gate and the rest of the company spent a merry evening. The trappers were wealthy enough now to buy whiskey, and for the first time in many weeks they relaxed completely, drinking as heartily as they ate.

At daybreak the chilly sentinel saw two men approach the corral. Both were dressed in buckskins, so he assumed they were friends from the fort who intended to lead the animals to a nearby hollow, where they could graze. He called a cheerful greeting, and they shouted pleasantly in return; not until later did he realize that their words were indistinguishable. Anxious for a drink of warming whiskey and a sizzling buffalo steak, the sentinel opened the corral gate and hurried off to the blockhouse. His companions were sleeping, so he ate and drank alone, then went to bed.

The rest of the company awoke an hour or two later, and

soon someone discovered that the horses had vanished. The sentinel was awakened, and told his friends what had happened. Kit and several others dashed out to the corral, and a close study of the ground indicated that the sentinel's mistake had saved his life.

The two men who had walked toward him in the half-light had been Indians, and the bulk of the war party had remained in hiding, ready to act instantly if the advance guard met resistance.

All of the horses at the fort were gone, including those belonging to the traders. Kit and the other trappers were forced to swallow a brew of bitter gall when they realized that the Indians had made off with the animals in a raid that could not have been better executed. Not one of the Blackfeet had suffered a single scratch.

It was impossible to chase the savages on foot, so the men were compelled to remain at the fort, brooding in impotent rage. There they stayed for weeks. The majority, Kit among them, believed that the raid had been made by braves of the Crow tribe, which was a logical assumption, for the Crows lived in the mountains, while the Blackfeet were prairie dwellers. The two nations were at war with each other, so it was thought unlikely that the Blackfeet would have invaded enemy soil in winter.

Spring came to Fort Hall, and so did Thomas McCoy of Hudson's Bay. The trappers were pleased to see him, but were far happier to find that he had traveled with a large herd of spare horses, as he was planning to expand his operations. The men now had mounts again, but revenge had to take second place to trapping, and the spring and summer were spent gathering beaver and making up for the previous autumn's failure.

Everyone then adjourned to Rendezvous, and at its conclusion Kit left the Hudson's Bay Company and entered the employ of one Fontenelle. It might be noted that his frequent moves from one company to another were typical of the Mountain Man, who prized his independence above all else and consequently refused to remain in the pay of a single trader for more than a season or two.

Fontenelle's company was large, consisting of more than one hundred men. In all probability Kit changed his custom of going out with small parties because it was rumored that both the Crow and Blackfeet were unusually active. In any event, he was engaged in the dual capacity of hunter and trapper, and spent the entire autumn with the company, which felt strong enough to travel wherever it pleased, often penetrating deep into Indian-held territory.

Fontenelle's ranks grew, for there were rumors that the Blackfeet were angry and intended to attack in strength. One day, however, two Crow scouts appeared, carrying a peace proposal from their own chiefs and bringing news about their enemies. The Crow, a highly intelligent nation, had no desire to fight a large, heavily armed company equipped with rifles whose power all Indians of the wilderness knew. An agreement was reached, and Crow warriors began to arrive at the campsites on the Yellowstone River in ever increasing numbers. Some of the trappers were afraid the savages would create trouble as soon as they gained a substantial majority, but the fears proved groundless.

There was no reason to be afraid of the Blackfeet, either, for an epidemic of smallpox, long a curse of the aborigines of North America, had rendered the fierce tribe impotent.

Kit, whose memory was long, questioned various Crow braves individually, and finally satisfied himself that the Blackfeet had been the culprits in the previous winter's humiliating horse-stealing incident. Contrary to a widely held belief fostered by romantic novelists and since disseminated even more intensively by the entertainment industry, the Indian of the frontier was neither poker-faced nor an expert liar. A primitive barbarian incapable of hiding his true feelings, he lied when afraid, in the way a child lies.

So it was not difficult to discover the truth when dealing with him.

Kit accepted the explanations of the Crow, and when Fontenelle proposed that the trappers spend the winter with the tribe, he agreed. The two groups journeyed together to a long, narrow valley, and there the frontiersmen built their huts, the warriors erected lodges for themselves and their families, and hunters spent every daylight hour searching for game before the beasts of the wilderness disappeared.

The winter that followed was the coldest and most ferocious Kit had yet experienced. It was fortunate that provisions were ample, and that unlimited quantities of firewood were at hand on the hills that lined the valley. Fodder became so scarce, however, that the horses and mules were in grave danger of starving. The Crow resorted to ingenious emergency measures to feed their own animals, and the trappers were forced to follow their example. Cottonwood trees were cut down, chopped into two-foot lengths and then thawed before huge fires. The bark was peeled off and shredded, and the smaller branches were cut into tiny pieces. The hungry animals willingly ate these rations.

It had long been believed by the frontiersmen that large quantities of bark would kill, but the Crow insisted that the notion was mistaken. Kit listened carefully as the elders of the tribe explained that the inner bark of cedar and other trees was considered a great delicacy for humans by the tribes who lived on the Pacific coast. These Indians, the Crow had learned, preserved this rind by drying it and keeping it for long periods in a dehydrated state. When needed, they poured hot water over it and ate it with relish.

Certainly the horses belonging to the Crow were healthy, and Kit argued with his companions that they had nothing to lose by following the example of the Indians. They were reluctant, but agreed rather than watch their own animals starve.

In a sense, the bitter winter was uneventful. Guards were posted to prevent wolves from attacking the domesticated animals. Years later Kit allegedly said that even buffalo were so desperate for fodder that the sentries had to prevent these starving beasts from goring the horses and stealing their meager fare. It is difficult to imagine buffalo forcing their way into a corral and driving horses out of the lean-to shelters that had been erected to protect them from the snow. If Kit did make any such claims, he must have been talking with his tongue planted firmly in one cheek.

The winter proved valuable in that it enabled Kit Carson to take a post-graduate course of study in frontier living. Most of the other trappers had limited contacts with the Crow, confining their relations to going off on joint hunting parties. But the curious Kit spent the better part of his days in the lodges, where he talked by the hour with the warriors and elders. He absorbed precious information on the savages' philosophy and religion, and was fascinated by their concepts of good and evil. He learned how they lived, how they made war and became proficient in their language. He gained an understanding of their customs and taboos, and the knowledge he acquired was helpful to him for the rest of his life. It was not accidental that, in later years, he enjoyed extraordinary success when he was employed by the United States Government as an Indian agent.

With the coming of spring, the trappers and Crow went their separate ways, their friendship cemented after living side by side. It is not strange that the Mountain Men, themselves not the most civilized of humans, should have promised the Crow that they, like the savages, would make war to the death against the Blackfeet. According to the frontier code, one stood firmly at the side of one's friends. And those trappers who recalled the horse stealing at Fort Hall undoubtedly needed little urging to pledge the Crows their support.

Fontenelle and Kit, who was acting as his deputy, soon began to receive reports on the Blackfeet from smaller parties of trappers. Either the reports of the smallpox epidemic of the previous year had been exaggerated or else the Blackfeet had made an almost miraculous recovery, for they were very active again, stealing horses, harassing trappers and otherwise making nuisances of themselves.

Trapping was still the primary purpose of the expedition, of course, and not even the most bloodthirsty members of the company thought of taking to the warpath instead. Beaver were plentiful on the Yellowstone, and after acquiring many pelts there, Fontenelle led the men to the headwaters of the Missouri, in what later became the state of Montana. Trapping was excellent, so they followed the Missouri east into what subsequently became the state of North Dakota. Here they found themselves in the heart of country dominated by the Blackfeet, and the long-simmering feud made a clash inevitable.

Thanks to some source of information not identified for posterity, the trappers learned they were only a few days' journey from one of the principal villages of the Blackfeet, and the whole company, now consisting of ninety-eight men, clamored for battle. If Fontenelle would have preferred to continue trapping, he wisely held his own counsel, for the trappers surely would have left his employment had he opposed their desires.

Kit, accompanied by five men, went ahead on reconnaissance, and scouted the village. As nearly as they could estimate, there were approximately two hundred to three hundred braves in the settlement. Kit's nineteenth-century biographers say that they found the Indians preparing to leave on a journey for parts unknown and for reasons unmentioned. Whether the Blackfeet were actually so engaged seems irrelevant, and the detail may have been added to give the story a heightened sense of urgent drama. No such spice is needed, for the facts are dramatic enough.

The whole company gathered to hear the report of the scouts, and it was unanimously agreed that an attack should be made on the savages. Forty-three of the party, among them all of the best marksmen, made up the assault column. The rest were to travel more slowly with the spare horses, mules and the small fortune in beaver skins that had been accumulated. It is significant that this body, which would also act as a military reserve force, was the larger. Even those who yearned for revenge had no desire to lose the hard-earned bales of fur that would bring them their only income for the year.

Kit was in command of the attackers, his companions having elected him their captain without a dissenting vote. He had left the ranks, never to return to them.

He and his volunteers reached the village after a ride of less than a day, reaching their goal undetected. The horses were rested behind a rim of hills, and Kit decided that, rather than wait until morning and thus run the risk of being discovered by the enemy, he would commence the battle immediately.

Approximately three hours of daylight remained, and Kit hastily explained his basic scheme to the others. He hoped to drive the savages out of their village and push them toward the north, past a field of boulders into the open prairie. Under no circumstances did he want the Indians to head west, where they could take cover in a patch of woods behind some scrub pines and other small trees.

The trappers rode toward the village at a gallop, and the men fired at will as they burst into the clearing. The Blackfeet, taken completely by surprise, made perfect targets, and at least ten were killed by shots fired in the first volley. One of those felled was shot by Kit.

The warriors fled, and the trappers succeeded in driving them toward the north. But Kit found that the field of rocks provided the braves with perfect cover. The chiefs of the Blackfeet rallied their warriors, who quickly responded to discipline, and the headlong, panicky flight was transformed into an orderly retreat. The Blackfeet were renowned horsemen, and proved they were good as their reputation. They rode in a loose, open formation and made no attempt to return the heavy fire of their foes.

Kit and his men soon discovered that the rugged hill country of North Dakota was not terrain ideally suited for a wild cavalry charge. Even the best of marksmen found it extremely difficult, when riding at a full gallop, to reload and fire their long rifles with accuracy. Volley after volley was fired at the retreating Blackfeet, and shot after shot missed. The frustrated trappers increased the tempo of their fire, and recklessly wasted ammunition.

The Blackfeet, finding they were intact, deliberately led their pursuers on a chase through the hills. Eventually the firing slackened, for the trappers began to run short of bullets and powder. Whether Kit was a sufficiently experienced captain to have urged his men not to waste ammunition is not known.

But he certainly must have realized that his men had used the wrong tactics when, after the trappers' fire had become ragged, the Blackfeet suddenly turned. The warriors, who had only a few rifles, preferred close combat, and brandished knives, tomahawks and spears as they raced toward their tormentors. The counterassault was totally unexpected, but Kit's men held firm and, using their pistols for the first time, sent the Blackfeet reeling toward the north again.

But the warriors had just begun to fight. Forming their ranks anew, they counterattacked a second time, and their drive was so fierce that the trappers were compelled to fall back from the crest of a hill onto rocky ground. Kit tried to halt the retreat, but was unsuccessful.

One of the trappers, a man named Cotton, was not the

most polished of equestrians, and lost control of his mount. The horse fell, throwing its rider and pinning him to the ground. Five or six braves who were leading the Indians saw Cotton's plight. They veered toward him, for it was the custom of the Blackfeet to scalp living enemies, when possible, in preference to dead men.

Kit saw what was happening, and shouted to others for help. His own horse pranced skittishly when he halted, making it hard for him to aim his rifle accurately, so he jumped to the ground, and dispatched the first of the warriors with a single shot. A volley fired by several of his companions sent the other warriors into retreat, and Cotton, who finally succeeded in freeing himself, was saved.

He ran groggily toward the others, and at that moment Kit's riderless horse bolted. Kit, Cotton and five mounted men now faced the entire band of Indians, the main body of trappers having retreated to the slope of the next hill before halting.

Myths to the contrary, Kit Carson was a realist who refused to fight when facing impossible odds. He hoisted himself onto the back of another trapper's horse, Cotton followed his example, and the group hurriedly rejoined the others. The Indians halted to take possession of Cotton's horse, and having lost the momentum of their drive, were forced to stop and take stock of the situation, too.

One member of Kit's company went after the captain's mount, recaptured it and brought it back to him. The trappers were relieved to have been granted a breathing spell and, following the example of the savages on the slope facing them, took refuge wherever possible behind boulders and rocks.

At this point the reserve force under Fontenelle's command arrived on the scene, which was fortunate for the trappers and helped to preserve Kit's reputation as an invincible battlefield leader. The odds against the trappers were now reduced to two or three to one, a comfortable ratio in Indian fights. Relatively fresh recruits had joined forces with very tired men and, most important of all, Fontenelle's reserves carried saddlebags filled with ammunition. The trappers now breathed easier, and the Blackfeet dug in behind boulders and rocks to make a final stand.

They would have been wiser to retreat, for their courage could not match their foes' firepower. They elected to fight, however, and when the trappers moved forward to dislodge them, again resorted to tactics of hand-to-hand combat. Night fell before they were compelled to flee from the field, the trappers following and firing at them repeatedly as they scattered in all directions.

The battle had ended in a complete victory for Kit and his men. The trappers had suffered the loss of three men killed and eight or nine severely wounded, while the Blackfeet casualties had been high.

The Mountain Men preferred to take no unnecessary chances, however, and that night strong sentry outposts were established. But the Blackfeet had been beaten decisively, and did not reappear. The trappers remained in camp for several days, treating the injuries of their wounded and burying their dead in a funeral service which Fontenelle conducted.

The victory had achieved more than the immediate goal of obtaining revenge. The power of the Blackfeet had been destroyed, at least for the present. Trapping operations were resumed, and the company traveled wherever it pleased through Blackfeet country without molestation. Vast numbers of beaver were found, and at the end of the summer the men departed for Rendezvous with as many bundles of furs as their mules could carry. Kit had good reason to feel satisfied with his accomplishments. His share of the profits would earn him about fifteen hundred dollars, the better part of which he intended to invest for safekeeping in a bank. And his reputation as a frontiersman had reached a new high.

A young Englishman, Sir William Stuart, attended Rendezvous; he was one of the first British aristocrats to travel into the American West, a pastime that later became fashionable. He and Kit became friendly, and Stuart enthusiastically wrote a description of the young American which appeared in print, in his *Memoirs*, a few years after the Civil War.

"One of the most popular of the mountaineers' leaders is Christopher Carson of Santa Fe, called Kit by all," Sir William wrote. "A brief acquaintance with him sufficed to cause one to understand the loyalty shown him by his comrades. Kit is a man of rare intelligence, and displays neither the evil habits nor humours which afflict so many of the mountaineers and cause them to die whilst still in the prime of life.

"His stature is short, and I judge that he stands no more than five and one-half feet tall. I estimate his weight at ten stone (140 pounds), all of it marble-hard sinew and muscle. He shaves his face. His hair is shaggy and he wears the badly stained leather clothing of the mountaineer, but there is in his demeanor something that catches the attention of a new acquaintance. The boldness of his unwavering glance proclaims that he is endowed with a noble character. When he gives his friendship, that nobility is confirmed.

"He is one of a small band about whose heads swirl tales of conquest and daring, yet only he of that band has been granted the grace to abstain from the telling of such tales about himself. No man who has lived for less than thirty years in this world could have committed so many great deeds.

"When I came to know Kit, I asked him to tell me, in the strictest confidence imposed by the bonds of friendship, whether these tales be true. He smiled as he replied that those who dwell in the mountains encounter many perils and are often beset by adventures. More than that he would not say, even when pressed. It is my impression that he enjoys hearing tales told about others of the band, but that his innate modesty is so deeply ingrained in his character that he is embarrassed when his comrades spin webs of fact and fancy with him at their center as they sit nightly around their fires.

"I saw no mountaineer save Kit refuse a cup of spirits, and even when he dined alone with me he would not accept a glass of mild wine. It was his habit, he said, to drink nothing but water. That which ran in mountain streams he drank by taking it dripping from the running stream. But that which he finds in the prairies he first boils, and perforce must let it cool for some hours before it becomes potable. He attributes his robust health to his diet of drink and of food. At no time did I see him fail to live up to his word, and even on the occasions when I encountered him at breakfast saw him drinking water rather than tea or coffee.

"He displays a hearty and zestful appetite for vegetables and for cooked fruits, which are not commonly available in the mountains. He eats prodigious quantities of meat, as do his comrades, but they subsist exclusively upon a diet of red meat, whilst Kit seeks such vegetables as are obtainable. He retains in his head all of his teeth, and holds that his partiality to vegetables is responsible for this evidence of good health. The toothless gums so common in the heads of other mountaineers would seem to confirm his opinion.

"Mountaineers whom I have seen at their games display less skill with firearms than reputed. Being myself no stranger to the military life, I have seen soldiers whose aim in shooting at targets both still and moving is superior to that of these fellows. But Kit Carson is exceptional, and well deserves the laurels earned by his prowess. Rarely have I seen any man shoot at targets both still and moving with an accuracy and grace approaching that of this remarkable man. His ability to load his clumsy mountaineer's rifle a second, third and fourth time with a speed so blinding that it defies all description must be seen to be fully appreciated, for his speed and delicacy cannot be captured in mere words. Whilst performing these necessary tasks he holds his eye fast on his target, which his bullets strike to the innermost core. Many emulate him, but none possess his skill. He wastes no motion as he goes about his required work. This, I believe, is the secret of his proud success. He boasts not of his prowess, as is his nature, yet is too sensible to decry his skills. When speaking of them to me, he said that others could become as skilled if they applied themselves with diligence and zeal to the study of the rifle, but it is my belief that this remarkable man is endowed by Nature with a keenness of eye and a nimbleness of hand denied to ordinary mortals."

Kit was an admirer of Sir William, returning the compliment, but his only recorded statement on the subject of his friend was expressed with typical brevity and the stilted wording of one unaccustomed to reducing his thoughts to paper. "For the goodness of his heart and numerous rare qualities of mind," he said, "he [Sir William] will always be remembered by those of the mountaineers who had the honor of his acquaintance."

The months passed quickly after Rendezvous, and Kit's pattern remained unchanged. He and a small group went to a trading post called Brown's Hole, and from there traveled into what subsequently became the state of Arizona to trade with the people of one of the wealthiest and most cultured of all Indian nations, the Navajo. Under Mexican law, United States citizens were not allowed to engage in such trade, but Kit and his colleagues blithely ignored the inconvenient prohibition. The Navajo wove blankets that brought exceptionally high prices from traders everywhere, they owned huge herds of fine sheep, horses and mules, and Americans of the eastern seaboard cities were becoming aware of their talents for making beautiful pottery and unusual jewelry. So Mountain Men intent on earning a profit shrugged at the law and took their chances.

Kit's venture into the land of the Navajo was successful. He had made no plans to spend the winter high in the mountains, and therefore accepted an offer to act as a professional hunter for the traders at Brown's Hole. This is an indication, perhaps, that he was beginning to tire of his life as a trapper after spending the better part of a decade searching for beaver.

In the spring, however, he returned to his former vocation, and went with Jim Bridger on a trapping expedition into the Black Hills of what later became the states of Wyoming and South Dakota. Virtually nothing is known of the time spent together by these taciturn superheroes. They spent almost the entire spring and summer in each other's company, and apparently worked and lived together in harmony, for they agreed to spend the winter together at a camp on the Yellowstone.

In December the bivouac was attacked by Blackfeet, and several inconclusive skirmishes with the savages were fought, the trappers eventually building a small fort. The following summer Kit and Bridger went their separate ways, and Kit, trapping on the Missouri's upper reaches, engaged in several more brushes with the Blackfeet. None were noteworthy, although several tales extolling his exploits in these engagements were told in later years.

Perhaps the most important work accomplished by Kit that year, in the summer of 1838, was the trapping expedition he undertook into territory he had never before visited. He went to the Pacific Ocean with a large, well-armed party of trappers, crossing the Great Divide and trapping on the mighty Columbia River. His education was almost complete now, for he had visited literally every portion of the West that was to comprise the continental territory of the United States.

Kit returned to the Rockies for the winter, then trapped in the land of the Utah Indians. One of his companions during a portion of this, his last trapping season, was one of the most eccentric of Mountain Men, "Parson" William Williams, a one-time Methodist clergyman from Missouri. Williams, one of the oldest of the mountaineers, had gone into the Rockies as a missionary, and had such a quick eye and ear for languages that several of Kit's nineteenth-century biographers claim he could translate the better part of the Holy Bible into a number of savage dialects.

There was no one wilder in the West than Williams. He had become a hunter and trapper and, wandering through vast reaches of previously unexplored territory, had been the first civilized man to set eyes on many parts of what later became Utah, Wyoming and Montana. Whether Williams could be called civilized was questionable, however, for the rugged life he led had radically changed his nature.

His capacity for liquor was enormous, and when he drank he quarreled with almost everyone. He eventually became so irritable that few men could remain friendly with him even when he was sober. It was wise to avoid him, for he was a crack shot. He had also picked up a few of the less refined customs of the aborigines, and on more than one occasion scalped a living opponent during a fight.

For a time he lived in Mexican territory, and his temper was so violent that the authorities avoided him when possible, threw him in jail only when desperate and were contemplating expelling him from their soil when he himself suddenly vanished. He lived with one or another of the Indian tribes for periods ranging from a few months to a year or two, and by 1839 few men, meeting him for the first time, could believe he had once been a clergyman.

He constantly drank to excess, yet remained a first-rate hunter, and could shoot a deer or an elk even when drunk. He frequently daubed war paint on his face, and no one knew when he might change into Indian clothing. He had recently spent all of one winter in a cabin with three Indian squaws, and had sired children by all of them.

At this stage of his unpredictable career he had developed a penchant for cutting off the ears of anyone he disliked, and he was so easily offended that the leaders of most trapping expeditions firmly refused him a place in their ranks. Consequently he spent most of his time wandering alone through the wilderness, and none of the Indians molested him. He had established a rapport of sorts with the Blackfeet, and like another eccentric, a man named Mitchell, had also spent time in the villages of the fierce Comanche.

Mitchell had later explained his defection from the corps of the Mountain Men by saying that he had heard a rumor to the effect that the Comanche had discovered gold, and that he had only pretended to become one of their band, deserting them as soon as the story proved false. His comrades, who appreciated pure gold as much as other, lesser men, had forgiven him.

Williams, however, never apologized to anyone for anything he did. A sure way to provoke a fight with him was to ask him why he had chosen to cast his lot with tribes engaged in a relentless war to the death with the mountaineers. Kit Carson, in later years, once said he had seen Williams stab a man who dared to inquire, in all innocence, why he habitually rode his horse crouched low in his saddle.

Kit had no trouble with Williams when the Parson suddenly joined him and eight or nine companions while they were trapping on the Arkansas River, in what later became the state of Colorado, not far from a trading post known as Bent's Fort. The trappers were apprehensive, but Kit promised there would be no difficulty with the prickly Parson, and took Williams off for a private talk while the others stayed at the campfire.

There is no record of what was said by either man. In later years Kit refused to discuss the incident, stating, "Bill Williams was my friend. We knew each other well."

Whatever may have been said, Williams quarreled with no one during the three weeks he spent with the company, although he drank prodigiously most of the time. The talent for conciliation displayed by Kit in this affair ranks among his more notable achievements, even though it is not regarded by the creators of folk-hero stories as a great accomplishment.

As the summer of 1839 drew to a close, Kit, who had been thinking about his future, came to the conclusion that he did not want to spend the rest of his days as a trapper. Perhaps his advancing age was responsible, for he would be thirty years old in a few months. Perhaps the examples set by men like Williams and Mitchell caused him to ponder. It may be that, having acquired a vast knowledge of the whole West, he was anxious to put what he had learned to better and more profitable use.

Whatever his reasons, he went to Rendezvous early in the autumn of 1839 with word that startled everyone who knew him. He had no intention of living the uncertain life of a trapper any longer and was seeking employment more suitable to his taste.

An era had come to an end, but another, still more hectic and, if possible, action-filled period of his life was about to begin.

6. DOMESTICITY—AND DANGER

The one-time cook had no need to worry about his future, although he didn't know it, for his financial security had been destroyed by forces beyond his control. Kit was met at Rendezvous by an eastern banking representative who told him that the money he had saved—a sum estimated at somewhere between five thousand and ten thousand dollars—had vanished when the bank had been forced to close its doors. The United States was in the grip of the first severe economic depression in its history, and President Martin Van Buren had no idea how to stem the tide of business bankruptcies.

Hundreds of men from the eastern seaboard appeared at Rendezvous. These pale, nervous refugees with soft-palmed hands had been drawn to the frontier by the glamorous accounts of life in the West that they had read in newspapers, and were anxiously seeking any work they could find. A few of the more promising found places as clerks at trading posts, but the majority were brusquely rejected. Anyone who wanted work in the mountains had to carve his own niche.

The neophytes regarded Kit Carson with awe, for he had already become a symbol of the West, and wherever he went at Rendezvous, there were several men in neat suits of wool and white shirts staring at him. Perhaps their blatant hero worship put ideas into the heads of land speculators. The activities of these unscrupulous real estate project developers had been responsible, in part, for the depression. They bought large parcels of land, some of them comprising many thousands of acres, usually obtaining titles to the property by means that the law courts of the states and territories concerned found questionable.

The system used by the speculators was simple. They acquired property at twenty-five cents per acre, or some other absurdly low sum. They then offered land to the eastern city dwellers at one dollar per acre. Many who wanted to start new lives snatched at these "bargains," and only after traveling west to take up residence on their new homesteads discovered that the titles they had acquired were shaky or, in many instances, fraudulent.

Now, with the country in the depths of a depression, land was more plentiful than ever. Army veterans and others who were entitled to claim as much as one thousand acres in the territories often were pleased to sell their rights to purchase, and disposed of these rights for small sums. The speculators who bought them usually knew that no one but the veteran himself had a legitimate claim to the land, but questions of law or ethics did not deter the hardy entrepreneurs. There were tens of thousands of desperate people in the cities, all of them eager to pay a dollar or two for a piece of paper that, they believed, would entitle them to build new homes on land of their own in the West.

The speculators appeared in large numbers at Rendezvous, and Kit was deluged with offers of employment from them. His duties would be simple, he was told. He would travel to the larger cities, and would describe the vast virgin wilderness that he knew.

He replied that he was not a speaker.

The speculators countered with other offers. They told him he would be required to do nothing more than sit on a platform while others talked. At the most, he would be expected to say a few words. One particularly shrewd speculator suggested that he give demonstrations of his skill with rifle and pistol before audiences who would be admitted free of charge to these exhibitions. Once a crowd had gathered, of course, the speculator and his assistants would offer cheap land for sale.

Kit was appalled, then indignant. He was neither a freak nor a theatrical performer, he declared, and wanted no part of the speculators' ventures. One of these gentlemen, greedier and more foolhardy than his colleagues, persisted in his offers and succeeded in making a nuisance of himself.

Kit pulled his nose, and is alleged to have said, "Were you a man, I would call you out and have done with it. But you are a vulture who preys upon the good people of the United States, and I will have nothing to do with you and your vile schemes. Let me not see your face again, for I assure you, upon my word as a mountaineer, that I will treat you less gently should our paths cross again."

The frightened land speculator does not appear again in any of the chronicles that deal with the life and times of Kit Carson, so it is fair to assume he knew when he was well off and discreetly vanished.

Kit received many legitimate offers, all of which he weighed with care. If he had entertained hopes of buying property and building a home in the vicinity of Taos, as Ewing Young had done, he had to abandon the idea now. He loved the country there, and had often mentioned the thought to Young, but now was strapped for funds. What he needed was steady employment that would give him a guaranteed income, yet at the same time would leave him sufficiently free to work on money-making projects of his own. Above all, he sought work that he would enjoy.

One offer seemed tailored to his needs. The large and prosperous trading company of Bent and St. Vrain, for whom he had worked previously, asked him to take the position of permanent professional hunter for their trading post in the Colorado country, Bent's Fort. He would be held responsible for supplying the inhabitants of the post with meat during the winter months, but would be expected to perform no other duties.

Kit accepted at once. He knew that game abounded in the area, which was dotted with low-lying valleys as well as with the highest mountains he had seen anywhere. Of primary importance, for his purposes, was that he would be kept busy for only four and one-half to five months of each year. He would be expected to report around the middle of November, and would be free to leave around the end of March. Even if spring thaws were late in coming, he would not be detained beyond the middle of April. Bent and St. Vrain offered him the liberal salary of five hundred dollars in gold per year, a sum sufficiently large to pay all of his expenses.

And he would be free to engage in other enterprises from early April until mid-November. A handshake with the partners sealed the bargain, and for the first time since Kit had left his parents' farm in Missouri, he had a home.

Kit certainly knew his work would not be easy, and that he was not being paid a handsome wage because of the reputation he had earned. While it was true that deer, antelope and elk were usually plentiful in the Colorado country, the permanent staff of Bent's Fort consisted of twenty-five men, so large quantities of meat would be needed and he would have little chance to rest. Buffalo, which usually traveled in large herds and were the principal source of meat when it was needed in quantity, were prairie animals seldom found in the small valleys that nestled high in the mountains. If he should go hunting for buffalo, he would have to ride far to the east, taking with him a number of pack mules to carry the dressed carcasses of the beasts he slaughtered.

He realized, too, that he would encounter many foes in the Bent's Fort region, some human and some animal. A number of roving Indian tribes frequently traversed the area, among them two of the most warlike nations, the Cheyenne and the Comanche. He had noted in previous years that there were more mountain lions in the area than in other parts of the Rockies, and wolves were numerous, too, as were hyenas. All were beasts of prey anxious to snatch spoils from the hunter who failed to keep a sharp watch on his prizes.

Kit felt confident of his ability to fulfill his obligations, but preferred to take no risks that could be avoided. Therefore he went to Bent's Fort as soon as Rendezvous ended, even though he was not expected to report for eight weeks. He spent those two months painstakingly exploring the land on both sides of the Arkansas River, drawing maps and making notes for future reference.

During this period he had an encounter with a band of warriors belonging to the Cheyenne nation. He was prepared to defend himself, but found them unexpectedly friendly, for his reputation had preceded him into the region. On the invitation of two chiefs who were in charge of the party, he accompanied the group to a village located near the present-day resort town of Estes Park. There, according to stories which may or may not be true, but are as accurate as any, he first met the Cheyenne maiden called Rai-Du. The spelling of her name differs in various accounts, and it is possible that she was an Arapaho rather than a Cheyenne. Both have claimed her. Perhaps the confusion is due, at least in part, to the fact that the two tribes were related. In view of the close bond between Kit and the Cheyenne in later years, and in particular to references he supposedly made to those ties when his relationship with the nation became strained, it seems more likely that she was a member of that tribe.

Her name, freely translated into English, was Mountain Flower. Kit called her Alice.

His taste in women's names always leaned toward the prosaic. Their daughter was registered at Bent's Fort as Adaline when she was born, but Kit preferred to call her Mary. This created some confusion when he married for a second time: the lady's name was Maria Josefa Jaramillo.

It was too much for Kit to deal with a Mary and a Maria, so he solved that problem by lopping off the first name of the second Mrs. Carson and called her Josefa.

When Kit and Mountain Flower—or Alice—met is a matter of conjecture. The actual date is less important than the fact that they did meet and that Kit, for the first time in his life, fell in love.

Literally nothing is known of their romance. Mountain Men, reticent to discuss personal matters, concealed their strictly private lives, revealing details to no one. The date of the ceremony is not known. Many years later, at some time after Kit's death, his daughter—then a matron living in California—revealed that her parents had been married at Bent's Fort by a Protestant clergyman summoned there for the purpose.

Mrs. Carson moved to the fort after her marriage, and was cordially received by Bent and St. Vrain, neither of whom entertained personal prejudices against such a marriage. Their attitude was reflected by everyone else with whom the couple came in contact, and Mrs. Carson was universally accepted, although the Cheyenne, as a nation, remained the enemies of most Mountain Men.

The position taken by the partners was important, for they were two of the West's leading citizens. Charles Bent was destined to become the first civil governor of New Mexico appointed by the United States Government, in 1845, and two years later was assassinated in Taos when Indians and Mexicans loyal to the old regime revolted. Cerin St. Vrain, who had been born in France, became wealthy in the fur trade, and later settled in New Mexico, where he and Kit lived in close friendship to the end of their days.

Mrs. Carson lived with her husband at the trading post in a cabin that Kit built for his bride in the compound, and they spent the winter of 1839-40 there together. Kit, of course, went out to hunt every day, and during the worst of the winter weather was often absent for several days at a time. Certainly his marriage influenced all of the Indian tribes of the region, for no warriors attacked him on his travels and he felt free to visit the lodges of the Cheyenne, Comanche and Kiowa.

Late in 1840 Mrs. Carson gave birth to a daughter, Adaline—or Mary. A delicate young woman, the mother suffered from complications at childbirth and, there being no physicians nearby, died within a few days.

Kit was heartbroken, and frantically but unsuccessfully searched for someone to take care of the infant. The task fell to Mrs. St. Vrain, the only woman in permanent residence at Bent's Fort, and she discharged her duties ably. Kit was not happy with this temporary arrangement, however, and was aware of his own inability to give the baby a home. He realized, too, that the primitive conditions prevailing in the mountains made it impossible for a girl to grow up on the frontier.

The tragedy of his wife's death and the problem of what to do with his daughter matured Kit as had no other experience in all the years that had passed since he had left his parents' home. It is not strange that he should have thought once again of the family he had left behind in Missouri, and in the early spring of 1842, when his season's work as a hunter ended, he felt free to travel east.

Bent and St. Vrain were sending a wagon train laden with furs to St. Louis, and Kit went with the party, but assumed no responsibilities on the journey. He left his companions at the Missouri border and, riding hard, soon reached the region where he had spent the better part of his childhood and early youth.

There fresh shocks awaited him. Both of his parents were long dead, and when he stood at his mother's grave, he wept bitterly. Only once before in adult life, when his wife had died, had he shed tears. His family's house was in ruins, the farm was abandoned and the family had scattered. Most of the nearby residents were total strangers, only a few of whom knew his name. From one neighbor he learned that his brother Robert now lived in St. Louis, so he went there at once.

No city in the United States was growing more rapidly than the great metropolis located on the Mississippi River, a few miles below the junction of the Missouri. The population of St. Louis in 1842 was estimated at twenty-five thousand, and was increasing so rapidly that no one could keep an accurate count. Eight years later the inhabitants numbered approximately eighty thousand.

Miles of wharves lined the waterfront, and literally thousands of steamboats sailing up and down the Mississippi docked there. Warehouses larger than any buildings that Kit had ever seen stood side by side in rows that stretched far down the west bank of the river. Streets were cobbled, and hundreds of substantial houses made of red brick caused the frontiersman to halt and stare at them in open-mouthed wonder. He was bewildered by office buildings and schools, taverns and hostelries, and listened in dumb astonishment as men spoke of building railroads into the far reaches of the West.

Yet, in spite of all the bustle, Kit was not a total stranger, for the lifeblood of St. Louis was the fur trade. Every Mountain Man was familiar with the giant of the industry, Pratte, Choutou and Company, which eight years earlier, on the retirement of John Jacob Astor, had bought out the western branch of his American Fur Company. Kit halted long enough for a meal in a tavern, where he felt conspicuous in his buckskins, and then asked directions to the central offices of Pratte, Choutou.

There he was greeted with a respect tinged with awe when he gave his name. Samuel F. Dickinson, one of the principal executives of the concern, extended a warm welcome to the frontiersman, and insisted that Kit spend the night at his home while the company's employees searched for Robert Carson. Kit's dinner that evening was an occasion he long remembered, for he was served four different vegetables with his meat and drank a cup of coffee sweetened with sugar. He developed a strong liking for coffee on that occasion, and afterward drank it with his meals whenever it was available, continuing, however, to consume large quantities of water.

The next day Robert Carson was located. He was employed in a position of responsibility by one of the steamship companies, was married and had two daughters and a son. He was delighted to see his brother, about whom he had heard many stories, and Kit, equally happy, accompanied him to his home.

Robert's wife received her famous brother-in-law graciously, and the children, who were shy at first, soon cast aside their reserve and bombarded their uncle with questions about the wilderness. Kit spent a pleasant ten days with his relatives, and before leaving made arrangements to send his daughter to them. Robert and his wife agreed to give the little girl a home and provide her with the best education available. And Kit insisted on paying his brother the sum of forty dollars per month for her room, board and other expenses. The allowance was more than enough to meet the child's needs, but Kit wanted to make certain that his daughter would want for nothing. If he could not give her a home under his own roof, he was anxious to compensate in other ways to the best of his ability.

St. Louis continued to fascinate the Mountain Man, and he spent long hours wandering through the city alone. The pace of living bewildered him, and he confessed that he was far more tired at night than he had ever been when pushing through an uncharted forest or scaling a rugged peak. He thought the steamboat the most remarkable invention he had ever seen, and Robert Carson arranged for him to inspect several of the vessels tied up at the wharves. The West, he realized, would soon be conquered by ships and he was even willing to concede the possibility that some day railroad tracks might be built across the wilderness, although he believed it likely that many years would pass before tracks and ties could be laid.

His interest in steamboats led him to decide that he wanted to travel west on one, and when he learned that a ship was planning on making a voyage up the Missouri River, he asked Robert to arrange passage for him on it. He was dumfounded when he was assigned a comfortable private berth in a tiny cabin he would share with only one other person. He departed after spending ten days in St. Louis, and was not sorry to put the city behind him.

Several of the passengers knew him, and he soon became acquainted with a man who was to become his closest associate. Sheer chance threw them together on the boat, and the history of the West might have been different had they not met. In any event, they fell into conversation, and soon recognized each other as kindred spirits.

John C. Fremont, who was four years younger than Kit, was one of the most talented Americans of his generation. A native of Georgia who had grown to manhood in South Carolina, he was a mathematician of extraordinary ability who, after receiving a degree from the College of Charleston, taught mathematics to midshipmen on a United States Navy sloop that made an extended voyage of more than two years along the coasts of South America.

That journey whetted the young man's appetite for exploration and map making, and at the time he and Kit met, he had spent six years as a surveyor. His family connections were powerful, for he was the son-in-law of Thomas Hart Benton of Missouri, the Democratic floor leader in the United States Senate.

In a long career that would continue until 1890, Fremont was to prove himself an explorer and surveyor of the first rank. He would also be a courageous soldier who, unfortunately, would be pitted against such geniuses as Thomas "Stonewall" Jackson. He would take a brief dip into politics, where he would be nominated by the radical wing of the Republican party to oppose the re-election of President Abraham Lincoln. Eventually he would delve into railroad building and finance, fields in which he was totally incompetent, and finally would redeem himself as an administrator when appointed governor of the Arizona Territory.

When he and Kit encountered each other on board the steamboat, Fremont held the rank of lieutenant in the United States Army Corps of Engineers, and had been assigned the difficult task of charting a route to the mouth of the Columbia River on the Pacific. A methodical and practical man, he thought it unlikely that he could complete his survey in a single year's journey, and was planning to make two separate trips. If all went smoothly, as he hoped, he would finish the mammoth survey in two years. But he had already suffered a severe setback, for the man he had hoped to engage as a guide had not appeared in St. Louis, as promised.

Fremont gave no indication in his correspondence or other writings whether he had been familiar with Kit Carson's reputation. Nor is it known for certain whether Kit volunteered for the post of guide, as his nineteenth-century biographers claim, or whether the idea was Fremont's, as his early biographers state. Let it suffice that Kit was hired at a fee of one hundred dollars per month.

He and Fremont immediately started to work, and decided that their goal for 1842 would be the trail that cut through the towering Wind River Mountains of the Rockies in what later became the state of Wyoming. The program was ambitious, even though it was now only the first of June.

The party assembled in the northwestern plains of Kansas, and made final preparations for the scientific assault on the wilderness. In all, Fremont commanded a group of twenty-eight men, himself included. His second in command was Charles Preuss, a native of Germany, who was an experienced topographer. A Mountain Man named Maxwell had been engaged as the professional hunter. Two youths who were expected to contribute little or nothing were nineteen-year-old Henry Brant, son of the prominent Col. J. H. Brant of St. Louis, and Fremont's brother-in-law, twelve-year-old Randolph Benton. Kit was the other member of the working party. Brawn would be provided by twenty-two *voyageurs,* or canoemen, most of them Canadian veterans.

Before setting out on June 10, Fremont made certain that everyone understood the routine he expected to follow. At dawn, horses would be released from their pickets to graze, breakfast would be eaten and the party would start out as soon after six o'clock as possible. A halt of one hour would be made at noon, then the march would be resumed until sundown. Horses and pack mules would be picketed every night, carts and wagons would be formed in a circle around the tents to establish a defense perimeter against the possibility of Indian attack and sentries would stand guard duty.

The journey began on an exciting note, for the travelers saw a herd of buffalo only a few hours after starting out on their first day. Fremont described the occasion in a letter to his wife, repeating portions of it in his official *Report* and, late in his life, in his autobiography:

"A few miles brought us into the midst of the buffalo, swarming in immense numbers over the plains, where they had left scarcely a blade of grass standing. Mr. Preuss, who was sketching at a little distance in the rear, had at first noted them as large groves of timber. In the sight of such a mass of life, the traveler feels a strange emotion of grandeur.

"We had heard from a distance a dull and confused murmuring, and, when we came in view of their dark masses, there was not one among us who did not feel his heart beat quicker. It was the early part of the day, when the herds were feeding; and everywhere they were in motion. Here and there a huge old bull was rolling in the grass, and clouds of dust rose in the air from various parts of the bands, each the scene of some obstinate fight.

"Indians and buffalo make the poetry and life of the prairie, and our camp was full of their exhilaration. In place of the quiet monotony of the march, relieved only by the cracking of the whip, and an *'avance donc! enfant de grace!'* shouts and songs resounded from every part of the line . . .

"Three cows were killed today. Kit Carson had shot one, and was continuing the chase in the midst of another herd, when his horse fell headlong, but sprang up and joined the flying band. Though considerably hurt, he [Kit] had the good fortune to break no bones; and Maxwell, who was mounted on a fleet hunter, captured the runaway . . .

"The wind was favorable; the coolness of the morning invited to exercise; the ground was apparently good, and the distance across the prairie (two or three miles) gave us a fine opportunity to charge them before they could get among the river hills. Kit Carson, Maxwell and I started together.

"The buffalo were now somewhat less than half a mile distant, and we rode easily along until within about three hundred yards, when a sudden agitation, a wavering in the band, and a galloping to and fro of some which were scattered along the skirts, gave us the intimation that we were discovered. We started together at a hand gallop, riding steadily abreast of each other, and here the interest of the chase became so engrossingly intense that we were sensible to nothing else. We were now closing upon them rapidly, and the front of the mass was already in rapid motion for the hills, and in a few seconds the movement had communicated itself to the whole herd.

"A crowd of bulls . . . brought up the rear, and every now and then some of them faced about, and then dashed on after the band a short distance, and turned and looked again, as if more than half inclined to stand and fight. In a few moments, however, during which we had been quickening our pace, the rout was universal . . . When at about thirty yards, we . . . broke into the herd. We entered on the side, the mass giving way in every direction in their heedless course. Many of the bulls, less active and less fleet than the cows, paying no attention to the ground, and occupied solely with the hunter, were precipitated to the ground with great force, rolling over and over with the violence of the shock, and hardly distinguishable in the dust. We separated on entering, each singling out his game . . .

"In a few moments my horse brought me alongside of a cow I had selected, and, rising in the stirrups, I fired at the distance of a yard, the ball entering at the termination of the long hair, and passing near the heart. She fell headlong at the report of the gun, and checking my horse, I looked around for my companions.

"At a little distance, Kit was on the ground, engaged in tying his horse to the horns of a cow which he was preparing to cut up. Among the scattered bands, at some distance below, I caught a glimpse of Maxwell; and while I was looking, a light wreath of white smoke curled away from his gun, from which I was too far to hear the report. Nearer, and between me and the hills, toward which they were directing their course, was the body of the herd, and giving my horse the rein, we dashed after them.

"A thick cloud of dust hung upon their rear, which filled my mouth and eyes, and nearly smothered me. In the midst of this I could see nothing, and the buffalo were not distinguishable until within thirty feet. They crowded together more densely still as I came upon them, and rushed along in such a compact body, that I could not obtain an entrance—the horse almost leaping upon them.

"In a few moments the mass divided to the right and left, the horns clattering with a noise heard above everything else, and my horse darted into the opening. Five or six bulls charged on us as we dashed along the line, but were left far behind, and singling out a cow, I gave her my fire, but struck too high. She gave a tremendous leap, and scoured on swifter than before. I reined up my horse, and the band swept on like a torrent, and left the place quiet and clear. Our chase had led us into dangerous ground. A prairie-dog village, so thickly settled that there were three or four holes in every twenty yards square, occupied the whole bottom for nearly two miles in length. Looking around, I saw one of the hunters, nearly out of sight, and the long dark line of our caravan crawling along, three or four miles distant."

Fremont caught the flavor of a buffalo hunt, but some of his details appear confused. It is unlikely that Kit could have resumed the hunt after being thrown from his mount and waiting until Maxwell captured the horse. The accident must have taken place toward the end of the hunt, for it seems probable that the herd of buffalo would have left him behind before he could resume the chase.

Certainly a hunter of Kit Carson's experience would not have been foolhardy enough to dismount after shooting a buffalo cow, tie the carcass to his horse and prepare to butcher the meat while still surrounded by wild, stampeding beasts. He probably would have been trampled to death had he been reckless enough to stand in one place for any length of time. And he would have found it difficult—if not impossible—to prevent his horse from stampeding too.

If he followed the usual custom of the hunter, as he must have done, he would have ridden on after dispatching the cow and sought another. Later, after the herd had disappeared, he would have returned for the animals he had killed, and there would have been an opportunity at that time to butcher the game without risking his own life.

In any event, he appeared to have suffered no real injury

from his tumble, for he immediately resumed his duties, and Fremont makes no further mention of his disabilities.

The party followed the trail taken by the early pioneers who were going out to the Spanish Californias, and Kit, who was thoroughly familiar with the whole territory, guided the company unerringly. The journey was without incident until the men reached Fort Laramie, where they learned that the whole region was in a state of alarm. A band of Sioux warriors had been unexpectedly attacked by a joint party of Snake Indian braves and trappers, and the Sioux were now seeking revenge. The whole nation was on the warpath, and hundreds of savages were roaming through the country into which Fremont proposed to travel.

The traders at Fort Laramie agreed unanimously that the topographers and their aides would be massacred, and advised Fremont to postpone his departure.

Fremont consulted with Kit, who said that the risks undoubtedly would be great, but that he believed nothing would be gained by waiting. The Sioux might cause trouble all through the summer and into the next year, thus delaying the entire project. He felt the party was sufficiently large and well armed to give a good account of itself and, as a veteran Indian fighter, he declared that although he respected the power of the Sioux, he was not afraid of them.

The commander pondered alone, then announced that the journey would be resumed. He was under orders from the Army to perform his task with dispatch, and was obliged to do his duty, no matter what obstacles stood between him and his goal.

Kit was pleased, but took the precaution of making out his will. He no longer had only himself to consider; his daughter was probably in St. Louis by now, as he had written to Mrs. St. Vrain, asking her to take the baby to his family, and he left everything he owned to the child.

The Sioux, contrary to expectations, did not appear, and the party reached the South Pass, the gateway through the

Great Divide. There Fremont and Preuss went to work in earnest, making detailed scientific observations, recording everything of note and exploring the surrounding country-side under Kit's guidance.

When the immediate task was finished, Fremont con-ceived the idea of scaling the highest mountain peak in the area in order to make still more observations. The base camp was strengthened, and on August 12, with Kit leading the party, eleven men set out on the adventure. By August 15 the group reached a point about halfway up the slope, but a crisis had developed. Neither Kit nor Fremont had esti-mated that it would take so long to make the climb, and food supplies were running short. Rather than send some of the group back to the base camp for food, the commander decided to proceed with a smaller party.

Fremont decided that he and Preuss would continue, as they were the only men capable of taking the observations he wanted. He would take a few of the *voyageurs* with him, he said. Kit, the only man competent to lead the rest back to the camp, was directed to retrace his steps, and therefore lost the chance to reach the summit of the peak, more than 13,000 feet high and subsequently found to be the second tallest in the range, which subsequently bore Fremont's name.

The reunited company started back to Fort Laramie late in August, arriving there in the first days of September. Fremont knew how to find his way back to civilization, so Kit's work was done, and the two men parted company. No arrangements were made at this time for Kit to ac-company the next year's expedition, but the two men, who had become close friends, promised each other that their separation was temporary.

Kit had been in touch with his employers at Bent's Fort, and they had offered him employment for the winter more remunerative than that of a hunter. St. Vrain wanted Kit to represent the firm in Taos, promising him basic wages of one hundred and fifty dollars per month, plus a percentage of the profits earned on the merchandise that passed through his hands.

He accepted, and immediately went to Taos, where he made his home with Ewing Young. There were many Americans in New Mexico now, and the Mexican authorities were trying in vain to stem the flow of emigrants to the region. Nearby Texas, where thousands of United States citizens had settled, was still involved in a violent dispute with Mexico. Texas had declared her independence in 1836 after fighting a brief but bitter war with Mexico, and was now recognized as a republic by a number of powers. The demand for the annexation of Texas by the United States was growing stronger on both sides of the border, and it was being said openly and repeatedly that a war between the United States and Mexico was inevitable. So Mexican apprehension over the future of the province called New Mexico was understandable.

Kit showed little interest in politics at this time. In fact, he set a good-will pattern of his own by falling in love with an attractive and charming young lady of aristocratic Mexican birth, Maria Josefa Jaramillo. He paid court to her through the autumn and early winter, and when she accepted his proposal of marriage, he bought a house in Taos. They were married in February 1843, with leaders of both the American and Mexican communities attending the ceremony.

Kit and his bride moved into their house, and soon afterward the new Mrs. Carson sent a letter to her in-laws in St. Louis, asking that Kit's daughter be sent out to Taos in the spring, when weather would make long journeys possible. The little girl did join her father and stepmother during the summer, and made her home with them. The family lived in harmony, and later, when Mrs. Carson bore three children, Mary was a devoted older sister. The girl never forgot the period she spent in St. Louis with her aunt and uncle, however, and when she became older, returned there to complete her education.

Kit, with a wife and child to support, could not afford to be idle, and Bent and St. Vrain saw to it that he was kept busy. In the early spring he left Taos for Bent's Fort to escort a wagon train laden with furs to St. Louis. He had been assigned the post of hunter and chief guard for the party and hoped, upon reaching his destination, that he himself could bring his daughter to New Mexico.

While traveling north, Kit met a company of United States infantry commanded by a captain named Cook, who told him that somewhere behind him and moving in the same direction was a wagon train containing many thousands of dollars' worth of merchandise owned by one General Armijo, a prominent Mexican trader. The Texans hated Armijo for his alleged mistreatment of prisoners during Texas' war of independence, and it had been rumored since the previous autumn that a large band of Texans planned to capture the wagon train. Armijo, who had heard the reports, had hired one hundred guards to protect his wagon train.

A clash seemed likely. The maneuvers on both sides were known in Washington, and President John Tyler, who was anxious to prevent the United States from appearing in the wrong, had directed the War Department to prevent a clash from taking place on American soil. It was Captain Cook's duty to make certain that the Texans did not resort to violence on the American side of the border.

Kit remained with Cook for twenty-four hours, and before he departed, the wagon train reached the camp. The commander appreciated Cook's protection, but was afraid that the company of soldiers was not strong enough to prevent a raid, for he believed that the Texans had mustered one thousand men or more to make the raid.

Unwilling to rely exclusively on the American troops, he wanted reinforcements from Santa Fe. Therefore he offered

Kit the huge sum of three hundred dollars in gold to carry a message to Armijo, asking for reinforcements. A man in Kit's position could not refuse, so he turned south the same day and rode hard for Taos.

There he gave the message to the local governor for forwarding to Santa Fe. Conscious of Mexican sensitivities and of his own position as a resident of New Mexico, he preferred to go through official channels rather than raise an alarm in person. He waited at home for a reply, and in a few days received word that Armijo had already sent one hundred Mexican infantrymen north and was himself following with a full regiment of six hundred.

Kit immediately started north again, knowing he could travel far more rapidly than foot soldiers and hoping he could overtake the wagon train in time to give the commander the comforting news.

He heard, while en route, that the Texan marauders had fought a pitched battle with the advance guard of one hundred Mexican troops—on Mexican soil—and had won an overwhelming victory. He learned nothing more until he reached Bent's Fort. There Bent told him that Cook had intercepted the Texans, who had bowed to his authority and had allowed themselves to be disarmed. The wagon train was now safely on its way east, traveling across the American plains, and Armijo and his regiment had gone home.

Kit was three hundred dollars wealthier, but Bent and St. Vrain had not been able to delay the departure of their own wagon train, and had hired another hunter to take his place. But another venture, far more lucrative and infinitely more exciting, was beckoning. Only three days earlier John C. Fremont had stopped at the post, hoping to find Kit there and wanting him to act as the guide for the second stage of his journey to the Pacific.

Wasting no time, Kit wrote a hasty letter to his brother and sister-in-law in St. Louis, asking them to send his daughter to Taos with a reliable escort. He left the sum of one hundred and fifty dollars with Bent and St. Vrain to pay the wages and traveling expenses of the baby and her companion, and so informed his relatives. Then, hastily re-assembling his gear, he started out in pursuit of Fremont.

7. THE GREATER GLORY

Two problems of international importance dominated the thinking of United States citizens in the spring and summer of 1843. The nation was suffering growing pains, and newspapers devoted long, daily columns to the simmering dispute with Mexico over Texas and the southwest territories. Equally important was the feud with Great Britain over the undefined border in the Northwest. Both London and Washington claimed the better part of the Oregon Territory, the British insisting that the area south of what became British Columbia belonged to them, while the Americans, equally adamant, declared that the region north of what eventually became the states of Oregon and Washington was theirs.

Unusual public interest was, as a consequence, focused on John C. Fremont's second expedition. Many thousands, tired of living in the slums of the eastern cities, were waiting for his definitive maps before setting out for the Pacific Northwest, which was being described as an earthly paradise. Immigrants from Europe, who were arriving at New York City and other ports of entry in ever increasing droves, hoped to go to the Far West, too, and eagerly wanted Fremont to show them the way.

The federal government was no casual bystander, for Fremont's maps and charts would strengthen Washington's claims to the territory. Newspapers controlled by both the Whig and Democratic parties spoke darkly of a third American war with England, but calmer students of the international scene predicted that the dispute could be settled amicably and to the satisfaction of the United States, provided that Fremont returned with masses of accurate data that would bolster the position of the State Department.

With the whole country awaiting the report of the lieutenant of Engineers, the government did not stint in the support it gave him. He carried the best scientific equipment available, including a recently invented rubber boat, which he intended to float on the waters of Great Salt Lake. The War Department, hoping to protect him and his company, provided him with a convoy of forty experienced cavalrymen under the command of a major. And he was supplied with enough funds to purchase all of the provisions he might want, with enough in reserve to take care of every conceivable emergency.

Great publicity had attended the departure of the explorers, and a number of dinners had been given in Fremont's honor. Senator Benton was so pleased that he declared, in a speech on the floor of the Senate, that he was now known as Fremont's father-in-law.

The applause was far behind and the members of the expedition had settled down to business by the time that Kit, traveling rapidly, joined the party seventy miles from Bent's Fort. Fremont was delighted to see him, having been uncertain whether Kit would appear in time to be of use. The two men came to an immediate agreement on the previous year's terms, and Kit conducted an inspection of the men and their equipment.

He believed that Fremont was relying too heavily on horses for the carrying of supplies and equipment. Mules, he said, were better pack animals in the mountains, for their energy was almost inexhaustible and they were more sure-footed on mountain trails. Fremont accepted his word and sent him back to the trading post for mules, arranging to meet him on the South Platte River, not far from the site of the present-day city of Greeley, Colorado. Kit took two men with him, and traveled rapidly, rejoining Fremont at the appointed place. Major Fitzpatrick and his cavalry had arrived, too, and Fremont believed that the party was too large to permit him the freedom to explore in earnest wherever he pleased. Kit, who had encountered several groups of trappers, assured him that the Indians of the region were showing no signs of hostilities, so Fremont sent the cavalry ahead with the bulk of supplies and equipment.

Kit led the commander and fourteen others to the North Platte, then took them east toward Great Salt Lake. Fremont wished that Kit had been a member of his planning staff, for he found himself short of such essentials as ropes and iron skillets, and sent his guide to Fort Hall to purchase the necessary items. Again Kit performed the errand quickly, and cutting through a number of small mountain passes he knew, came upon Fremont again at the upper end of Great Salt Lake.

Fremont and Preuss were fascinated by this unique body of water, and asked Kit to take them around to its eastern side, which he did. Several islands were seen in the lake, and the rubber boat, the first of its kind ever used for purposes of exploration, was launched. Kit, Fremont and Preuss, accompanied by two others, rowed out to the island, which was completely barren, and climbed a high, bleak hill, from which they surveyed the surrounding area. They could find no signs that any other humans had ever set foot on the place, and before leaving carved their names and the date at the summit.

The air-filled boat proved somewhat less than reliable. A storm blew up as the party was rowing back toward the mainland, huge waves crashed over the vessel—and the boat suddenly developed a leak. One of the men hastily snatched the bellows, and tried to pump air into the craft as rapidly as it was escaping. The men considered themselves fortunate when they finally reached dry land, for the storm was so severe that the water level rose rapidly.

The march was resumed up the Bear River, and a junction was made with Major Fitzpatrick at Fort Hall. Then Fremont and his company of fifteen pushed on as a vanguard. Kit led them northwest to the Snake River, which in time would become the boundary between the states of Idaho and Oregon, then cut through the Blue Mountains to the Columbia River and followed it to the Pacific.

Fremont and Preuss, like countless thousands who came after them, found the salmon delicious. Kit continued to eat meat, and thought it strange that anyone would prefer fish when game was available.

After spending several days carefully charting and mapping the mouth of the Columbia, Fremont and a few companions went north to Vancouver Island, in British Columbia, to make some purchases at a Canadian-owned trading post. Kit was in charge of the camp during the commander's absence, and welcomed Fitzpatrick when the cavalry arrived.

Fremont returned a few days later, and his mission, in a sense, was completed. But he was not satisfied, and knowing that the American people wanted as much information as he could give them, he decided to extend his journey in order to explore territory that was completely unknown. Kit agreed, and was forced to rely upon his instincts as a guide, buttressed by information he obtained from local Indians whose dialect was not too difficult for him to understand.

The full company went south through the fertile, well-watered lands of western Oregon, then moved east, where Kit, encountering no trouble, took them to Klamath Lake. Careful observations were made there, and new pages were added to the bulging notebooks of the map makers.

Deer and elk were still found in abundance, the rivers were stocked with fish and there were wild berries, edible roots and onions everywhere in the wilderness. It had been unnecessary to touch any of the supplies the expedition carried other than coffee, tea and sugar, and Fremont, decided to continue still farther. The United States was showing great interest in the Californias, so he made up his mind to go there.

The nature of the country changed south of Klamath Lake, game became increasingly scarce and Kit edged toward the southeast, going wherever he could find antelope and deer. His official position was still that of guide, but in practice he had become the chief hunter for the party, too. After marching through the barren foothills of the Sierra Nevada Mountains, snow-covered peaks could be seen directly ahead, and Fremont faced a crisis that had been growing in recent days.

A command of sixty-five men consumed huge quantities of food, and it was obvious that the supplies he carried, and on which the company now relied, would give out if not augmented. But Kit said that it would be necessary to travel more than one hundred and fifty miles before reaching the game-filled region he remembered so vividly from his first visit to northern California.

Fremont realized he was taking a chance, but refused to turn back, and the expedition plunged into the mountains. Snow became deeper and the weather was bitterly cold. Kit, traveling in advance of the main party, tested the snow in the passes, and found that in some places it was at least six feet deep. A halt was called, and Kit showed the men how to make snowshoes of the sort fashioned by the Indians of the Rocky Mountains out of the branches of bushes and small evergreen trees.

The animals could not make their way through such deep drifts, however, so a vanguard had to shovel through the passes, tamping down the remaining snow with spades, shovels and mallets. The pace was reduced to a crawl, provisions started to run low and the hungry pack animals were faltering. After spending almost two weeks in the mountains, most of the company thought it likely that they would die of starvation and cold, but Kit, who had caught a glimpse of the Sacramento Valley and the coastal mountains from the heights, insisted that a land of plenty lay ahead.

His knowledge of the terrain and his indomitable optimism, Fremont subsequently wrote, were the most important factors in preventing the members of the expedition from giving in to despair. Men unaccustomed to the mountains suffered severely, but Kit felt at home, took the discomforts in his stride and lost none of his strength. His companions watched him in awe, and the tales they told, the stories and letters they later wrote added new substance to the image of a folk hero that was taking shape.

An excerpt from Fremont's diary, later incorporated into his *Report*, is a typical description of the hardships encountered and of the role played by Kit:

"This was our most difficult day. We were forced off the ridges by the quantity of snow among the timber, and obliged to take to the mountain-sides, where, occasionally, rocks and a southern exposure afforded us a chance to scramble along. But these were steep and slippery with snow and ice; and the tough evergreens of the mountains impeded our way, tore our skins and exhausted our patience. Some of us had the misfortune to wear moccasins with . . . soles so slippery that we could not keep our feet, and generally crawled across the snow beds. Axes and mauls were necessary today, to make a road through the snow. Going ahead with Carson to reconnoitre the road, we reached in the afternoon the river which made the outlet of a lake. Carson sprang over, clear across a place where the stream was compressed among the rocks, but the . . . sole of one of my moccasins glanced from the icy rock and precipitated me into the river.

"It was some seconds before I could recover myself in the current, and Carson, thinking me hurt, jumped in after me, and we both had an icy bath. We tried to search awhile for my gun, which had been lost in the fall, but the cold drove us out, and making a large fire on the bank, after we had partially dried ourselves, we went back to meet the camp. Carson afterwards found that the gun had been slung under the ice which lined the banks of the river."

The company spent fifteen and one-half days in the mountains, losing most of their pack animals. Everyone was exhausted when Kit led the men into the Sacramento Valley, and a halt was called to repair equipment, give the remaining horses and mules a chance to graze and give Kit the opportunity to kill fresh game.

In a single day of shooting he brought down enough deer and antelope to give the members of the expedition more than they could comfortably eat. Then he and six others went ahead to Sutter's Fort to purchase supplies and animals. They completed the mission quickly, taking food, horses and mules to Fremont and his advance party, then to Fitzpatrick, who brought up the rear.

A few days later the explorers staggered into Sutter's Fort. The march had been the longest in the history of such expeditions, for Fremont and those who had accompanied him from the first had left Kansas on May 29, 1843, and it was now March 6, 1844. The commander gave the men a one-month holiday in which to recuperate.

Kit took advantage of this respite to pay a visit to his brother Moses, who lived less than a day's journey from the fort. Moses Carson, now a prosperous farmer and the father of a large brood, had lost his own wanderlust, and spent several evenings trying to convince his youngest brother that he too should settle down. It was wrong for a family man to roam all over the face of the earth, he said. It was the duty of a husband and father to spend his days with his wife and children, who needed his physical presence as well as his financial support.

Kit, who had always respected Moses' opinions, listened carefully to these views and offered no rebuttals. Moses repeated his arguments on a number of occasions during the month when Kit again visited him, and the folk hero became preoccupied. The better part of a year had passed since he had seen his bride, and he had not set eyes on his little daughter in almost two years. He had enough food for thought to digest on the rest of the journey.

The departure from Sutter's Fort was delayed when one of the men, who had not heeded Kit's advice to eat sparingly as he recovered his strength, became temporarily deranged and vanished from the fort. Kit directed the searching parties, but the man was not found, and Fremont finally decided to leave without him. A few days later he reappeared and eventually returned to the United States, so Fremont was able to boast, as he did, that he had fulfilled his assignment without the loss of a single man.

Kit led the party through the San Joaquin Valley, crossing the Sierra Nevada and coastal ranges where they joined to form a low-lying pass. They traveled south across the Mojave Desert, then followed the Mojave River toward the east where, beyond the great Colorado River, lay the land later to become the state of Arizona that Kit knew intimately.

The topographers-explorers now had an opportunity to see Kit Carson in action as a frontier Indian fighter. On the trail they came across a forlorn, middle-aged Mexican named Andreas Fuentes and a boy in his early teens, Pablo Hernandez. They had been members of a Mexican trading party, which had included Fuentes' wife and Pablo's parents. Indians had attacked them unexpectedly, and had captured all but the two fugitives, also taking the party's horses, equipment and trading stock. Fuentes was afraid that the others, including the women, had been murdered.

Fremont, who related the story in his *Report*, offered the man and boy food, clothing and sympathy. Kit Carson offered Fuentes practical assistance, declaring he would find the Indians and, if those who had been captured were still alive, would obtain their release. Fremont disapproved of the venture, for Fuentes believed that there had been at least thirty warriors in the attacking band. But he readily granted Kit permission to make the attempt.

Richard Godey, a Mountain Man and professional hunter who had been a member of the expedition since it had been in Colorado the previous summer, volunteered to accompany his friend, and Kit immediately accepted the offer.

Fremont had halted at noon, and it was now about one hour later. Fuentes insisted on going with Kit and Godey, but his tired horse faltered after they had ridden only a few miles. He turned back to rejoin Fremont, and the two Mountain Men went forward alone. The trail of the savages was faint but distinct, and they had no difficulty in following it. Night came, and they rested until the moon appeared, then went on again. The trail was now much clearer, and they did not halt until midnight, when their own fatigue and that of their mounts made a respite necessary.

The animals were fed and watered, and the two men ate a cold meal, not daring to light a fire. They rolled up in their blankets for a few hours of sleep, but the weather was too severe. So they took a calculated risk and, descending into a narrow ravine, lighted a small fire and snatched two or three hours of sleep.

At daybreak they were on the trail again, and at sunrise approached the camp of the Indians. The warriors were roasting meat over a fire, and the unguarded herd of horses was grazing nearby. The first task that awaited the avengers, as Kit and Godey saw it, was to gain possession of the horses and thus make it impossible for the Indians to flee. There were more than thirty warriors in the band, but neither of the Mountain Men seemed unduly concerned. They were accustomed to fighting against heavy odds.

They dismounted, tethered their own horses in a stand of trees and, leaving their blankets, saddlebags and other possessions behind, advanced with loaded, primed rifles. Then they cautiously approached the herd, creeping on hands and knees whenever they thought the braves might see them.

As they drew near to the animals, one of the horses neighed and kicked its heels nervously. The others began to stamp, and the Indians, realizing something was happening, jumped to their feet. One of them saw the intruders, and gave the alarm.

Kit unhesitatingly aimed his rifle at the warrior whose body paint identified him as the chief, and put a bullet between his eyes. Godey missed his first shot.

While the pair feverishly but efficiently reloaded their weapons, the warriors shot several volleys of arrows at them, but missed. Then, when the pair raised their rifles again, the braves became panicky, and several began to run away. Kit brought down his second warrior, and this time Godey's aim was accurate, too.

The rest of the Indians fled, scattering in all directions. One of the warriors who had been shot was still alive, so Godey put him permanently out of his misery by hitting him with the rifle butt. Two men had triumphed over more than thirty, and were in sole possession of the battlefield.

Before proceeding to the next order of business, Kit and Godey calmly scalped the three dead braves. Not until years later did Kit explain their reason for this act. During the months they had spent with Fremont, members of the expedition had listened with skepticism bordering on outright disbelief when they had heard stories about the exploits of Mountain Men. Kit and Godey wanted to present them with concrete proof that they had fought and killed the Indians.

The horses were rounded up, and the pair instituted a search for the missing Mexicans. They soon found the men, who had been murdered and scalped, but they had to hunt for some time before discovering the remains of the women, who had been tortured and burned to death at stakes.

Nothing more could be done in the vicinity. In the meantime, Fremont and his men, accompanied by the two Mexicans, had been moving toward the east. Fremont, who related the story in full detail in his *Report*, concluded on a stirring note:

"Their object accomplished, our men gathered up all the surviving horses, fifteen in number, returned upon their trail, and rejoined us at our camp in the afternoon of the same day. They had rode about one hundred miles in the pursuit and return, and all in less than thirty hours. The time, place, object, and numbers considered, this expedition of Carson and Godey may be considered among the boldest and most disinterested which the annals of western adventure, so full of daring deeds, can present.

"Two men, in a savage desert, pursue day and night an unknown body of Indians into the defiles of an unknown mountain—attack them on sight, without counting numbers—and defeat them in an instant—and for what? To punish the robbers of the desert, and to avenge the wrongs of Mexicans whom they did not know. I repeat: it was Carson and Godey who did this—the former an American, born in Kentucky; the latter a Frenchman by descent, born in St. Louis; and both trained to western enterprise from early life."

The account of the stirring raid, coupled with Fremont's high praise, fired the imaginations of the American people when they read the explorer's *Report*. This affair, more than any other single incident, made Kit Carson's name familiar to millions of his fellow citizens, but at no time in his life could he understand why he won so much praise for his deeds on this occasion. At other times and in other places he had done far more. As far as he was concerned, the raid was just another day's work.

The expedition moved slowly through the Rocky Mountains toward the northeast, arriving at Bent's Fort at the end of June 1844. On July 2 a banquet was given for the entire company by Bent and St. Vrain, toasts were exchanged and Kit actually drank a glass or two of wine. The next morning Fremont and his men set out for the plains. Kit arranged with Bent and St. Vrain to represent them once more at Taos, and started off on the long ride to New Mexico.

John C. Fremont's official *Report of the Exploring Expedition to the Rocky Mountains, 1842, and to Oregon and North California, 1843–44* was released by the War Department in Washington early in 1845. The demand for copies was so great that the printers hired on a contract basis by the government were swamped, and more presses were rented in order to meet the insistent need. Newspapers were granted permission to quote the document at length, and the more flamboyant portions reappeared. Kit's exploits had caught the attention of astute editors, and he was featured in most of the accounts.

Overnight Kit became a nationally known figure, and even people who cared little about the West considered him a hero second only to Fremont himself, who was now being called "the Pathfinder." More than 250,000 copies of the *Report* were printed, making it the most widely disseminated document in the history of the United States to that time. Resolutions were introduced in both houses of Congress, thanking Fremont and his followers, and singling out Kit for special commendation.

Never again, as long as Kit Carson lived, could he dwell in obscurity. Newcomers to New Mexico from the United States thought it a privilege to shake his hand, and men came to him seeking advice on every subject under the sun. So many letters were addressed to him that Bent and St. Vrain, who held a contract from the Post Office Department to deliver mail addressed to Americans in the West, looked at the mound of overflowing sacks, shrugged helplessly and sent Kit a note asking him what he wanted done with the correspondence.

He was too bewildered by his sudden fame to know what

to reply. Most of the letters did not actually reach him until late in 1848, some months after the conclusion of the Mexican War, by which time there were many, many more filled sacks. Thereafter Mrs. Carson appointed herself as a one-woman secretariat to sort out the letters in her spare time, but found the task too great for her.

Kit refused to take his enhanced reputation seriously. His own character was the same, he believed he had done nothing out of the ordinary and, as taciturn as ever, wanted only to escape back into obscurity. Events beyond his control made it impossible for his wish to be granted.

8. CALL TO DUTY

Many Americans opposed the annexation of Texas by the United States, some because they wanted no new slaveholding states, others because they believed the act would push the country into a war with Mexico. But the most powerful men in the nation were demanding annexation. Andrew Jackson, the most universally beloved of Americans, wrote from his deathbed, urging annexation. President John Tyler demanded it, and President-elect James K. Polk had been elected on the promise that both Texas and the Oregon Territory would enter the Union.

Late on the night of February 28, 1845, Congress finally voted in favor of annexation, and on the morning of March 1, President Tyler, in the last important act of his administration, signed the bill. Less than a month later the Mexican Government, certain that the lusty and growing neighbor to the north wanted more of her domain, broke diplomatic relations with the United States.

President Polk began to prepare for war, but kept his intentions quiet. John C. Fremont, now a captain in the Corps of Engineers, was directed to begin preparations for a third journey of exploration, but was given to understand he would have other duties as well. In the event of war, he was told, he was to take energetic steps to help bring California into the American camp.

In sleepy Fernandez de Taos, located in the vast Mexican province of New Mexico, Kit Carson neither knew nor cared about the great events that were taking shape. He had never developed an interest in politics, and discussions of international affairs bored him. His friends—and he himself—confessed as much to his nineteenth-century biographers. Nevertheless the thunderclaps emanating from Washington and Mexico City sounded over Taos, and were heard by other men. But Kit remained deaf, and his conduct in the spring of 1845 reveals a remarkable degree of naïveté.

After pondering for many months on the advice of his brother Moses, Kit had decided to give up his vagabond life and become a farmer. Mrs. Carson and Mary needed him, and a new baby was on the way, so he made up his mind to spend the rest of his life behind a plow.

He and a fellow Mountain Man, Richard Owens, who also wanted to settle down, spent their spare time during the winter of 1844–45 traveling around the Taos district, and finally found the spot they were seeking. Approximately forty-five miles east of the town was a wild, uncultivated tract of land on a small stream, the Cimarron River, that seemed ideal for their purposes.

Early in the spring of 1845 they bought the land, split it between them and, hiring a number of Mexican laborers, went to work. First they built temporary huts to house themselves and their employees, then they purchased quantities of sound timber. Construction of the permanent farmhouses was begun, the soil was prepared for planting and they sowed wheat, oats and rye. Work progressed rapidly, and Kit told his wife, when he went home to Taos to spend a Sunday late in May, that he hoped the family could move in another eight weeks.

In June a bombshell was exploded in the form of a letter from Captain Fremont, which an express rider brought to the ranch on the Cimarron. Fremont informed his friend that he had embarked on his third expedition and requested that Kit join him at Bent's Fort as soon as possible, bringing with him anyone whom he considered a valuable addition to the party.

The letter gave Kit one of the worst shocks of his life. He had invested all of his capital, a sum in excess of four thousand five hundred dollars in the farm. His wife and daughter could think and talk of nothing but the new life the family would lead. But—and it was a very large "but"—Kit had promised Fremont when they had parted the previous year that he would always be available if needed again.

Perhaps he had merely said what he considered polite, though it is doubtful, for he always weighed his words. Regardless of his intentions at the time, he felt he had no choice now. He had lived too long under the code of the Mountain Men, to whom a spoken promise was sacred. Kit realized he could not live with himself if he broke his word.

In four whirlwind days he disposed of his property, obtaining only two thousand dollars for it and taking a large loss. He broke the unpleasant news to his wife, gave her the money and said goodbye to her and his daughter.

Owens, who had no desire to remain if Kit was leaving, sold his farm, too, and rode with his friend to Bent's Fort on the Arkansas River, where Fremont and his company were waiting for the guide. Both men were enrolled, and Fremont, who learned something of Kit's personal situation from St. Vrain, voluntarily doubled his wages.

Before setting out, Kit asked Bent and St. Vrain to put his family under their protection, and they agreed. But he was never to see Bent again, and almost lost his wife, daughter and the new baby too. In the summer of 1846, soon after American troops captured the town of Las Vegas, the United States formally took possession of the New Mexico Territory and Bent became its governor. In January 1847, the Mexicans of Taos rebelled, Governor Bent was killed and Mrs. Carson, who was regarded as a traitor to Mexico by many of her former compatriots, was marked for death too. A servant warned her of the impending uprising only a few minutes before the actual rioting began, and she fled with the children to the home of American friends, who hid her and barricaded their doors.

Her own house was burned to the ground, destroying all of the worldly goods she and Kit possessed, but the loss of her property was the least of her worries. An armed mob ruled the town for forty-eight hours, and toward the end of that period Mrs. Carson and the children were smuggled out of Taos. Swift horses were provided, a volunteer escort formed and the refugees started on the long trail toward Bent's Fort.

A few hours after setting out they encountered a battalion of American militiamen marching toward Taos to restore order, but Mrs. Carson had no desire to return to a house that had been reduced to a charred hulk. She continued on her journey, and when she reached Bent's Fort, she and the children were given a warm welcome. Ironically, the only dwelling available there was the cabin in which Kit and his Indian bride had lived years earlier.

Many months passed before Kit learned what had happened to his family. Mrs. Carson and the children lived at the post until the latter part of the war, when Kit was finally in a position to give them his personal protection and take them off to a new home.

In the summer of 1845, Fremont may have known that a violent storm was brewing, but Kit certainly did not. He had made his difficult decision and, putting the past behind him, threw himself into work he knew so well. He and Fremont studied the maps the captain loved, and plotted the course they would take. Fremont had conceived an audacious scheme, but its execution depended on Kit's willingness to take a great risk.

Directly west of Great Salt Lake was a desert of unknown proportions. The Indians, Kit knew, were afraid of it and it was commonly believed by trappers that no one could survive on the wastelands where there was no water, grass or game. Fremont wanted to make his way across the desert, if a method of making the expedition relatively secure could be found. Then, he said, the Sierra Nevadas would be crossed, and the company would march straight into the Sacramento Valley.

The idea appealed strongly to Kit. Like Fremont, he wanted to explore places never before seen. But he shared the commander's caution, and had no desire to lose his life on a foolish venture. He promised to think about the matter on the march.

The company comprised a total of sixty-two men, seven of them western mountaineers. Fremont, who had come to understand and respect the Mountain Men, put the band under Kit's command, with orders to use them as he saw fit. On the trail to Great Salt Lake, Kit led the main column, and sent the others ahead as hunters.

Fremont was still fascinated by the huge inland body of salt water, and spent several days studying it in detail. Then the expedition moved around the south side of the lake, halting at a mountain-fed pond that stood on the eastern side of the desert. Again Kit went into conference with Fremont, and together they worked out a plan of action.

Kit, accompanied by Maxwell, the hunter on Fremont's first expedition, and two other mountaineers, would ride ahead into the desert, traveling for two to three days, if necessary. Fremont would climb to the peak of a mountain that dominated the area, and would keep watch through his telescope for a sign from the scouts. If Kit burned a large bale of pine cones that produced a particularly heavy black smoke, Fremont would know he had found water and grass. If he was also fortunate enough to find game, he would burn a second fire at a distance of about a quarter-mile from the first.

Kit and the men he had chosen to accompany him made careful preparations for their venture into the desert. They cleaned, dried and gummed several large deerskins, which they planned to use as water bags, made enough pemmican to last them for more than a week and gathered generous quantities of fodder for their horses. They oiled their guns with special care because firearms sometimes dried out in deserts, and they optimistically filled two muslin sacks with pine cones.

The entire company assembled to see them off, and as soon as they had started, Fremont and a few of his men began their ascent of the bleak mountain.

The desert was the most barren wasteland Kit had ever seen. Coarse sand and bald rocks stretched out toward the horizon, and there was no sign of a tree, shrub or even a tiny tuft of grass anywhere. When the little party had ridden less than a mile, a rattlesnake that had been sunning itself on a rock uncoiled slowly and began to glide toward the horses. Maxwell, who was on that flank, blew off its head with his pistol. No other sign of life was seen anywhere through the rest of the long day.

The heat was intense, but soon after the men made their camp at sundown, the weather turned bitterly cold. Kit had anticipated the chill, and a fire was made with kindling and logs that had been carried for the purpose. Shortly before daybreak the fire was extinguished with sand so the smoke would not mislead Fremont, and after eating a hasty breakfast started out again, as Kit wanted to cover as much ground as he could before the heat became too intense. He could see some mountains ahead now, which encouraged him to believe that he would soon reach the end of the desert, and before noon the men rode into the foothills of what later became known as the Toano Range. There they found both water and grass, and jubilantly prepared to send their signal to Fremont.

Kit made no immediate effort to search for game, however, for a difficult problem confronted him. He estimated that he and his companions had traveled a distance of anywhere from seventy-five to one hundred miles, and he needed all of his pine cones to make a fire large enough for

Fremont to see. Several dead trees were cut down, a fire was made and, when it was blazing, the pine cones were heaped onto it. A faint breeze was blowing down from the mountains, but was not strong enough to disturb the smoke, which rose high into the clear air.

There was no way of knowing whether the signal had been seen, so the scouts had nothing to do but wait. They pitched their camp and, after eating and watering their horses, set out to explore the immediate area. Kit discovered a pass that promised to lead them through the mountains, but no game was seen.

Captain Fremont set his expedition in motion as soon as he saw the signal, and for three days the company toiled across the desert. The men and horses suffered no permanent ill effects, but several of the pack mules collapsed and had to be shot.

The reunited party rested for a day or two in the grasslands, then started out toward the west through the vast expanses of what later became the state of Nevada. There were several Mexican settlements and missions in the southern portion of the territory, a Canadian trapper had discovered the Humboldt River in the western portion of the region and—although the members of the expedition did not know it—a small American party had blazed a trail across the center of the area on a journey to the west. But no civilized man had ever seen the portion of the territory through which the expedition traveled.

Kit rode twice as far as any other man in the company, for each morning he went out in advance of the party to find an appropriate route, then doubled back late in the day to report his findings to Fremont, who followed the path that Kit had laid out the previous day.

In the main, Kit led the company west by moving from one small river to another. Unfortunately, most of these streams ran in a north-south line, so progress was very slow. Occasionally deer and elk were found, but Fremont had to feed his men on the huge supply of provisions he carried. Bands of Shoshone Indians roamed through the region, but Kit was able to speak to them in a mixture of dialects they understood, and assured them of the company's peaceful intentions. The savages were curious, and remained friendly.

At last the explorers came to the Humboldt, and Kit followed it toward the southwest. Here was virgin territory completely unknown, and Fremont's topographers worked feverishly. The daily marches became still slower, but game was relatively plentiful in the foothills of the Humboldt Range, and the journey through what came to be known as the Humboldt Valley was pleasant.

Kit was forced to rely completely on his instincts and experience, and often roamed far on both sides of the route he selected. The extent of his travels is reflected in the places that bear his name. He found Lower Carson Lake, Carson Lake, the Carson River and the huge Carson Sink, an area rich in salt deposits. Shortly before the Civil War, Carson City was founded and named in his honor.

Winter had come by the time the explorers, moving toward the west now along the banks of the Carson River, reached the Sierra Nevada Mountains. Memories of the previous winter crossing were vivid in the minds of Kit, Fremont and the other veterans of the second expedition, but the commander preferred not to wait until spring before crossing into California. Kit, as always, was willing to leave at once.

The company was divided, as Fremont was anxious to explore and map as great an area as possible. Kit acted as the guide for the leader's group, and the other was instructed to cross elsewhere and rejoin the main body at Sutter's Fort.

The snow was not as deep as it had been in the winter of 1843–44, and Kit found several low-lying passes, so Fremont's party suffered no severe hardships and after reaching California, went on to Sutter's Fort without incident.

There they waited in vain for the other group, and finally went out to search for the lost platoon. Fremont spent the better part of the spring looking for his subordinates, but did not confine his activities to the hunt. He made careful maps of every area he saw, and it was not accidental that he visited every American settler. The Mexican authorities may be forgiven for becoming apprehensive.

Kit finally located the missing group, and the company was again reunited. Fremont needed supplies of all kinds, and when a young Mexican officer visited him for the purpose of finding out why he was wandering all over the province, declared he was going to the town of Monterey for his purchases. Sutter, he said, didn't carry all of the items he needed. A large Mexican garrison was stationed at Monterey, and when the commandant learned that a company of Americans, led by an officer in the United States Army, was marching toward him, he lost all patience.

A messenger met Kit on the trail, and was taken to Fremont, who handed him a letter ordering him to leave Mexican soil at once or face the consequences. Fremont and Kit decided the commandant was bluffing, and ignored the warning. But they realized the Mexicans meant business when a regiment of approximately six hundred infantrymen and cavalrymen, supported by artillery, marched out to meet them.

Fremont had been ordered by the War Department not to start a fight, so he was forced to bow to the ultimatum. With Kit in the lead, the explorers started for Oregon, crossed the northern spur of the Sierra Nevadas and reached Klamath Lake in midsummer. It was Fremont's intention to move on to the Columbia River, but the men and horses badly needed a rest, so he pitched his camp on the shore of the lake and prepared to stay for several weeks, as game was plentiful.

While the men were taking their ease at the bivouac, an express rider arrived with a dispatch for Fremont from the

War Department. He was informed that a Mexican army had crossed into American territory on May 1, and that the United States had officially declared war on May 13.

That night a band of Indians attacked the camp unexpectedly, killing three men before Kit, aided by Owens and Maxwell, succeeded in rallying the company, killing several of the savages and driving off the others. Kit scoured the area the following day, as Fremont believed the attack had been inspired by the Mexicans, but the guide found no evidence to substantiate the theory.

Fremont decided to return to California at once, and all of the company enrolled as militiamen under him. The men were soldiers now, not explorers, and military discipline was instituted. Fremont had no authority to grant commissions, but appointed Kit to the rank of acting lieutenant and placed him in command of a ten-man vanguard. It was possible that the Mexicans would send a column of troops north, knowing that the company had gone into Oregon, so the march was made by way of a different route than that used previously.

Kit and his squad unexpectedly found the main village of the Klamath Indians in the forest, where the savages were drying salmon for winter use. A Mountain Man could not allow himself to miss the opportunity to obtain vengeance for the attack on the camp at Klamath Lake, so the vanguard immediately opened a furious assault. The warriors tried to make a stand, but their most potent weapons were bows and arrows, which were no match for rifles, and they fled into the forest.

All food was removed for the expedition's use, and the village was burned to the ground. By the time that Fremont, who had seen the smoke in the distance, hurried forward with the main body, the cedar lodges of the savages were an inferno.

The company had not seen the last of the Klamath Indians. The following day, when Fremont was riding with the vanguard, a band of warriors ambushed the party. Kit's rifle jammed, and Fremont saved his life by riding down a brave who, at short range, was about to shoot an arrow at the guide. The savages continued to harass the company on its march to the Sacramento Valley; several skirmishes were fought, and in each the warriors were dispersed. Kit killed two braves, further enhancing his reputation as an Indian fighter. He was now thirty-six years old, and by the standards of the frontier was well advanced into middle age, but he was still in the best of physical condition and his energy remained inexhaustible.

He needed his strength in the weeks that followed, for Fremont and the Mexicans marched and countermarched incessantly without coming to blows. A squadron of United States Navy ships occupied Monterey, and Fremont made his headquarters there for a short time. Then, his growing battalion augmented by marines and volunteer militiamen, he marched south with one hundred and fifty men and captured the towns of Los Angeles and San Diego.

Fremont wanted to send dispatches to the War Department, and Kit was the obvious choice as the express rider to carry them, so in mid-September he and several other Mountain Men started out in the direction of New Mexico. They intended to play the role of trappers if they were intercepted by Mexican troops. Several patrols halted them, but allowed them to go on their way again, and Kit had good reason to hope they would reach American territory.

On October 6, 1846, the travelers met an augmented regiment of Americans under the command of Colonel S. W. Kearny, who had captured Santa Fe in mid-August and was now marching to California under orders from the War Department to take charge of operations there. None of Kearny's men knew the country through which the regiment was marching, so the colonel requested Kit to act as his guide and send the others east to Washington. As

Kearny was Fremont's superior, Kit obeyed without question, and retraced his steps.

The march was uneventful, but Kearny learned, when he arrived at the California ranch of an American named Warner on December 3, that a strong Mexican force stood between him and San Diego. Kearny immediately decided to push forward, and on December 5 and 6 the decisive Battle of San Pascual was fought.

Kit, still acting as the column's guide, rode at the head of the cavalry vanguard, and played an important part in the skirmish with Mexican cavalry that opened the battle. Several men on each side were killed, and Kit, according to the report of the vanguard commander to Colonel Kearny, was responsible for the death of two Mexicans.

Kearny regrouped his forces and, in the general attack that followed, sent all of his cavalry, sixty soldiers aided by twenty-five American residents of California, in a wild charge that was to be followed by an infantry assault.

Kit's services certainly were not required as a guide at this point, but he took his place in the front rank, along with two captains and three lieutenants. His horse was shot out from under him when the Mexicans opened fire on the advancing Americans, and he narrowly escaped being trampled to death as the entire squadron swept over and past him.

For a few moments it appeared as though he would not be able to rejoin the cavalrymen, but he saw the riderless horse of a dragoon who had been killed. First snatching the animal's bridle, he took the dead man's rifle and ammunition, and galloped forward again. The Mexicans held firm behind their hastily erected breastworks, and the majority of the American horsemen were either killed or wounded. Kit's luck held good, and he escaped without a scratch.

Kearny brought up his cannon, but the Mexicans captured one of his howitzers, and Kit was ordered to regain possession of the gun. He and fifteen horsemen who accompanied him rode toward the enemy breastworks, but the Mexicans who had taken the cannon reached their own lines in safety, and the Americans were forced to retire. Colonel Kearny brought his infantry forward in an attempt to dislodge the foe, but at nightfall the Mexicans still held firm, and operations were suspended until morning.

At daybreak on December 6 it was discovered that the Mexicans had retired during the night to take up new positions in the hills. Kearny, realizing that the opposing forces were evenly matched, wanted reinforcements from the garrison at San Diego held by the Navy and Fremont. Kit immediately volunteered to go through the enemy lines for help.

He set out at once, accompanied by Lieutenant Edward F. Beale, and few of his exploits won him greater renown than his successful dash past Mexican sentries. He and Beale crawled two miles over rocky terrain, removing their boots when they heard Mexican sentinels nearby. They were forced to halt and hide repeatedly, but managed to reach the rear of the Mexican camp without having been detected.

Then they started toward San Diego on foot, and after walking two nights and a day reached the garrison. A relief column was sent out at once; anticlimactically, Kearny had won his battle by the time the reinforcements arrived on the scene. The Mexicans had scattered, the most important military engagement to take place in California was now history and Kearny was unopposed on the remainder of his march to San Diego.

Kit was the hero of the American Army, and Kearny enthusiastically commended him in the official dispatches he wrote. The members of the command shared their colonel's rapture. A young sergeant from Hartford, Connecticut, wrote to his parents, "Never has there been a man like Kit Carson. All that has been said about him, and more, is true. He is as fearless as the lion, as stealthy as the panther, as strong as the oxen that pull our baggage carts. If the Colinel [sic] should grant his permission, I believe that Carson would attack a fort filled with Mexicans single-handed, and if he should perform such a deed, would drive them off."

Virtually every American in California volunteered for a place in Kearny's growing command, and in January the little town of Los Angeles was taken without a shot fired by either side. Kit, at his own request, was transferred to the command of Fremont, now a temporary major.

There is no evidence to indicate that he took part in the dispute that arose between Kearny and Fremont. The explorer-engineer believed that his instructions from the War Department gave him the right to act independently, and he refused to place himself under Kearny's command, although Kearny's orders, which had been issued at a later date, clearly gave him the over-all command of all forces operating in California. The unfortunate affair was to result in the court-martial of Fremont; President Polk would uphold the findings of the board that Fremont should be rebuked, and the angry, disgusted officer would resign from the service.

Perhaps Kit might have become embroiled in the dispute had he remained in California, for he was always loyal to his friends. Fortunately for his own future, Kearny sent him to Washington with dispatches in March 1847. He was accompanied by Beale and fifteen enlisted men, and crossed the continent in slightly less than three months, arriving in the nation's capital in June. The official account of the journey that he and Beale submitted to the War Department was laconic, and there is no mention in it of the Indian attack on the party that, according to Dr. Peters, took place. The long ride from the west coast to the east in so short a time was in itself an accomplishment that needs no cake frosting. Perhaps, as Dr. Peters wrote, such an attack did take place, and Kit saved his little company by commanding the men to conceal themselves behind their pack saddles in order to avoid being struck by bows and arrows. Or it may be that a nineteenth-century biographer could not resist the temptation to add an extra laurel to the already crowded brow of his hero.

The facts of the long journey speak for themselves. While traveling through the mountains and prairies, Kit acted as the party's hunter, and supplied his companions with meat. Only when he arrived in St. Louis did he put away his rifle.

Senator Benton happened to be in St. Louis, and himself made the arrangements for the final stages of the journey. For the first time in Kit's life he traveled by railroad, and if he was impressed by steam engines and rolling stock, he confided in no one. Trains, it seems, did not fascinate him, but to the end of his days he was always partial to steamboats.

Mrs. Fremont met his train when he arrived in Washington late in the evening of June 7, 1847, and insisted that her husband's friend accept her hospitality. Kit went with her, and was her house guest during the three weeks that he remained in Washington.

On the morning of June 8 he went to the War Department with his dispatches, and created a sensation. Officers and civilian employees lined the corridors to stare at the short, compactly built man in faded, stained buckskins and worn moccasins who nonchalantly carried his long rifle slung over his shoulder. "Mr. Carson," Mrs. Fremont wrote to her husband, "was embarrassed by the attention drawn to him, so great was his modesty. I ventured to suggest to him that he might appear less conspicuous if he wore the more conventional attire favored by others, but he was reluctant to change his manner of dress."

Had Kit known what lay in store for him, he probably would have fled from Washington at once. Then, as in later days, the capital was not reluctant to greet a celebrity, and for the first time in Kit's life he was made to realize that he had become famous.

9. THE DRAGOON

Kit Carson was living proof that the West, vast portions of which the United States hoped to own if the Mexican War ended in victory, was as ruggedly picturesque as newspaper writers and romantic authors claimed. Every hostess in Washington wanted to exhibit the Mountain Man as a prize, and even the wives of foreign ambassadors showered him with invitations. Members of Congress were proud to be seen with him, and both senators and representatives jockeyed for the privilege of escorting him to Capitol Hill. Ordinary citizens stopped him in the muddy streets of Washington to shake his hand, and children followed him wherever he went.

He was completely bewildered by the attention and acclaim he received, and the prospect of playing a social lion's role was so alarming that he told Mrs. Fremont he preferred to see no one during his short stay. He bitterly resented the idea of paying for transportation, and thought it outrageous that public carriage drivers should charge a fee for their services. Senator Benton's office solved the problem for him by providing him with a horse for the duration of his visit.

Kit probably would have left the capital without delay had the War Department not asked him to remain. He was given no explanation, but on his third day in the city he received a brief note written in the hand of Secretary of War William L. Marcy, asking him to call at his earliest convenience. Amused gossips said he presented himself at the War Department a quarter of an hour later.

Marcy told him that President Polk wanted to see him, and would receive him on June 14 to discuss a matter of official government business. Marcy, shedding no light on what that business might be, merely asked if Kit was an American citizen. Satisfied with the reply, the Secretary wrote a brief note which he sealed and sent to the White House, then asked Kit to dine at the Marcy home the following evening.

The terrified hero could not refuse, and found himself the guest of honor at a large party. French cuisine had become popular in Washington, and although Kit was too polite to refuse anything offered to him, merely picked at the fish, fowl and meat drenched in rich sauces. Guests later reported in letters to friends that he ate all of the vegetables placed before him and appeared to enjoy his ice cream and cake. He did not touch any of the wines, but was pleased to accept a second cup of coffee. When the ladies retired to the drawing room at the end of dinner, Marcy pressed a *cigarro* on him, and he puffed on it without comment.

He came into his own only when the men asked him his opinion of the progress of the war in California. Among those present were several high-ranking War Department civilians and at least two generals, all of whom listened intently as he told them he felt certain that American forces had made most of California secure.

On June 14 Marcy accompanied Kit to the White House, where he was taken without delay to the private office of President James K. Polk. Shyness overcame Kit at first, according to what Polk subsequently told his wife, but eventually he responded to questions and described the current state of affairs in California to the best of his ability.

The President concluded the meeting by offering Kit a temporary commission as a first lieutenant in the Army. Kit was so stunned that he stammered his thanks. The President explained that both the infantry and the cavalry wanted him, and that Secretary Marcy had worked out a compromise. He would be commissioned as a lieutenant of rifles, which was fitting for a man whose marksmanship had made him famous, but he would serve with the dragoons, a suitable place for one whose horsemanship was renowned.

Kit was sworn in at the War Department that same day, and was presented with a set of uniforms already made to his measure. A manservant in the Fremont home had obtained his measurements, and Senator Benton, who had followed Kit to Washington, insisted that he accept the uniforms as a personal gift.

The day's excitement had scarcely begun, for a messenger from the White House arrived with a dinner invitation from Mrs. Polk. Mrs. Fremont wrote to her husband that Kit turned pale when he read the message.

The dinner was highly successful, however, for the Polks had learned from the Marcys' errors. The men drank whiskey and water before the meal, and Kit accepted a glass. No wines were served, and the main course was a rare roast of beef, which the President himself carved. The frontier was not unknown to the Polks, for the President had grown to manhood in the little town of Columbia, Tennessee, south of Nashville, at a time when Cherokee Indian raids had still been common in the district. Mrs. Polk was a Tennessean, too, and both the President and First Lady made efforts to put their guest at his ease.

They succeeded admirably, according to a letter that Mrs. Polk wrote the following day to her mother in Nashville. "Lieutenant Carson reminded me of many men we have known in the old Mero District," she said. "He is courteous to a fault, slow-spoken, and with becoming modesty turns aside suggestions that his deeds have been more valiant than those of lesser men. He seemed to be at his ease when talking with J., Mr. Buchanan [Secretary of State James Buchanan], Mr. Marcy, and the other gentlemen. But he remained the soul of diffidence with the ladies, and replied to those remarks addressed to him by us in so few words as to indicate that our interest disturbed his peace of mind.

"His manners at table I found to be faultless. I must confess I watched him to see how he handled his fork, which he used with dexterity. That he thinks highly of Major Fremont was made known to all of us, much to the satisfaction of Mrs. Fremont and Senator Benton, but when J. asked him to describe for our edification how he eluded the Mexicans when carrying dispatches to San Diego, he grew red in the face and would not speak."

Kit's self-effacing unwillingness—or inability—to discuss his exploits and his embarrassment in the presence of women were traits that the press, in later years, extolled as virtues. Thus, unwittingly, he became the founder of a tradition that other men of the West later imitated. Probably some of these later heroes felt as he did; others, certainly, did not. But Kit was the founder of a breed, and those who followed in his bootprints abided by the patterns he established. Although he didn't know it, his personality formed the mold from which hundreds of minor folk heroes were cut. He was probably the inspiration for the protagonist of Owen Wister's enormously popular novel, *The Virginian,* published in 1902, which solidified the concept of the westerner as a taciturn lover of justice for its own sake, a hard-riding, fast-shooting foe of evildoers who became tongue-tied in the presence of ladies.

The President and First Lady liked the reticent hero, and he received a second invitation to dine at the White House. No record of what transpired at this family meal has survived, but James K. Polk and Kit Carson certainly were kindred spirits. Polk was a practical dreamer who had envisioned his nation as a mighty land that stretched from the Atlantic to the Pacific. His dream had already come true, for a full year had now passed since the United States and Great Britain had signed the Oregon Treaty, bringing the future states of Washington and Oregon and parts of

Wyoming and Montana under the American flag. The war with Mexico was progressing satisfactorily, for late in February General Zachary Taylor had administered a crushing defeat to the Mexican dictator, Santa Anna, at the Battle of Buena Vista, and General Winfield Scott was now marching on Mexico City with a powerful army of ten thousand men. It was common knowledge in Washington that the President would not be satisfied with less than the formal acquisition of all Mexican territory north of the Rio Grande, the vast province of New Mexico and that of Upper California.

All of these lands were part of the great range that Kit Carson knew and loved. He had probably traveled through them more extensively than anyone alive, and he was in a position to describe these territories to a President whose belief that it was the Manifest Destiny of the United States to spread from sea to shining sea had been translated into fact. Polk, Kit was to say in later years, made the United States a great nation.

The sojourn in Washington was not an uninterrupted triumph for Kit, however. He heard for the first time that his good friend, Governor Bent, had been assassinated in Taos, and he learned from War Department records that rioting in the town had been severe. But he could discover nothing about the fate of his own family, and according to what Mrs. Fremont wrote her husband, became highly agitated. His concern for his wife, daughter and the baby he had never seen may have been responsible for the unusual orders he received from the War Department late in June. He was directed to carry dispatches across the continent to Kearny, now promoted to the rank of brigadier general. And he was directed to take the long route, traveling by way of Santa Fe to deliver other official communications to the civilian administrators of New Mexico. Obviously he would go by way of Taos and find out for himself what had happened to his family.

Kit left Washington at the end of June, going by train

as far as St. Louis, then riding alone to Fort Leavenworth, Kansas. There he learned that the Comanche Indians, taking advantage of American preoccupation with Mexico, were on the warpath against the United States. The colonel in charge of the garrison assigned a detail of fifty men to act as Lieutenant Carson's escort. Kit protested that he could travel faster alone, but he was under military orders now, and the escort went with him.

On the trail he overtook a somewhat smaller cavalry patrol that was guarding a wagon train en route to Santa Fe, and took over-all command. Soon after leaving the prairies the unit was attacked one morning at dawn by Comanche warriors attempting to steal horses, and an inconclusive battle was fought. Three soldiers were wounded in the fray. Comanche losses were much higher, but the savages managed to take a number of horses and cattle with them. Had Kit been free to follow his old habits, he would have pursued the savages, retrieved the animals and obtained vengeance. It must have pained him to continue on his journey, proceeding with due haste, as ordered, without making a counter-raid.

The party traveled by way of Bent's Fort, and on its arrival there, Kit unexpectedly found his wife and children. Nothing is known of the reunion other than the fact that Kit remained at the trading post for forty-eight hours. Remaining true to his principle of not discussing his personal life, he neither wrote anyone about the meeting nor discussed it in detail with friends whom he subsequently encountered in New Mexico. Apparently he thought that Mrs. Carson and the children would be safer at Bent's Fort than in New Mexico, for they did not accompany him on the last, long stage of his journey to Santa Fe.

The officer in command of the garrison at Santa Fe relieved Kit of his escort, and authorized him to hire fifteen men familiar with the wilderness to accompany him on the journey, by way of the Old Spanish Trail, to California. He obtained recruits quickly, and departed.

Soon afterward there occurred an incident reported only by Kit's nineteenth-century biographers. If it actually took place, he himself considered it too trivial to mention in his own official report to his superiors after he reached California. Three hundred Indian warriors, members of an unspecified tribe, approached the camp of Kit and his men one evening and, professing friendship, wanted to approach the fire. Kit refused, the braves became ugly and he told them to leave immediately. When they were slow in obeying, he and his companions opened fire on them, an inhospitable act that sent the survivors fleeing in all directions.

Had such a band of warriors really appeared, and had their behavior aroused Kit's suspicions, he certainly would have speeded their departure for other parts. But braves traveled without their families only when hunting or at war. The group was too large to be a hunting party, and if three hundred savages were on the warpath, it seems likely there would be some mention of the fact in documents other than the biographies of Kit Carson. The story may be eyebrow-raising, but cannot be disproved, and in any event, is a good tale.

Incident or no incident, Kit reached Los Angeles in late September. Game had been scarce on the trail, so he and his men rested for a few days, then went north to Monterey with the dispatches. Thereafter he was assigned to a company of dragoons that made its headquarters at Los Angeles, and was sent out into the field with twenty-five cavalrymen to patrol the passes of the San Jacinto Mountains.

His first duty was to report the possible approach of a Mexican army, which neither Kearny nor his immediate subordinates considered likely. Secondly, he was ordered to apprehend any Indians who stole the sheep and cattle of American ranchers living in the fertile valley south and

west of Los Angeles. Kit followed orders, and the winter
of 1847–48 passed uneventfully. Word was received to the
effect that General Scott had captured Mexico City in September, and it was the unanimous opinion of officers stationed in California that the war would end soon.

In March 1848, Kit was given dispatches to carry to Washington and was provided with an escort. Spring rains slowed
the progress of the party across the swollen Colorado, Gila
and lesser rivers, and several of the men lost rifles and
equipment in turbulent waters. A party of Apache Indians
was encountered, and Kit ordered the savages to keep
their distance, threatening to open fire on them if they
came too near. They took him at his word, and a clash was
averted.

The dispatch riders reached Taos late in the spring, and
Kit discovered that his family had just arrived there from
Bent's Fort. The war with Mexico was over, a peace
treaty having been signed early in February. Kit decided
that, under the circumstances, no one would blame him if
he took a few days to look after his own affairs. Workmen
were hired to build a new home on the site of the house
that had been burned to the ground in the riots that had
cost Bent his life, and Kit waited until the actual labor had
begun before going on to Santa Fe to report to the officer
in charge, a colonel of Illinois Volunteers.

There a shock awaited him. The colonel informed him
that his appointment as a first lieutenant of rifles had not
been confirmed by the United States Senate.

This news created a sensation in Santa Fe and Taos. Kit's
friends felt certain he had been rejected on personal
grounds because of his friendship with John Fremont, who
had by this time resigned from the Army following his
court-martial. Kit flatly refused to express an opinion, and
neither then nor later said anything about the court-martial
or its aftereffects.

His friends urged him not to submit to further indignities,

and told him that, as he was not an army officer, he should not carry the California dispatches to Washington.

Kit's reply to this advice is quoted in meticulous detail by Dr. Peters: "I was intrusted [sic] with these dispatches, having been chosen in California, from whence I come, as the most competent person to take them through safely. I would try to fulfill this duty, even if I knew it would cost me my life. It matters not to me, while I am performing this service for my country, whether I hold the rank of a Lieutenant in the United States Army, or am known merely as an experienced mountaineer. I have gained some little honor and credit for the manner in which I have always conducted myself when detailed on any special and important business, and I would on no account now wish to forfeit the good opinion formed of me by a majority of my countrymen because the United States Senate did not deem it proper to confer on me an appointment which I never solicited, and one which, had I been confirmed, I would have resigned at the termination of the war."

Having expressed himself in these terms, or perhaps in others somewhat less verbose, he also collected some dispatches from the commandant at Santa Fe. Again pausing for a few days at Taos, he resumed his journey, cutting his own path through the wilderness and avoiding the trails in order not to meet the Comanche, who were still on the warpath.

He arrived safely at Fort Leavenworth, where his escort remained, and he went on alone, making the last stages of the trip by rail. It is impossible to determine whether he himself believed that his friendship with Fremont was responsible for the failure of the Senate to confirm his appointment. But, after having been entertained by both President Polk and Secretary of War Marcy, he certainly must have been bewildered.

The simplest of explanations awaited him in Washington. He himself accepted it without question, although in later

years Fremont's political supporters tried to gain sympathy
for their stalwart by claiming that Kit had been deliberately
persecuted because of his intimacy with Fremont.

The pressures of other business had prevented the Senate
from acting promptly to confirm the appointments of many
temporary officers, and Kit's name happened to be included on one of the long lists still awaiting action when
the war ended. Numerous civilians had received commissions in both the Army and Navy, but the Senate literally
forgot routine matters to concentrate on determining which
of the new territories would be slaveowning, and on similar
vital questions. The energetic Polk kept both houses of Congress so busy that confirmation of military appointments
lagged far behind schedule.

By the time the oversight was called to the attention of
the lawmakers, a peace treaty had been signed with Mexico,
and there was no longer a need for the civilian officers in
the armed forces. The situation was embarrassing to everyone concerned, particularly in view of the fact that Chief
Justice Roger B. Taney of the Supreme Court had declared,
informally, that the Constitution's prohibition of the passing of ex post facto laws made it legally impossible to create
new officers for the purpose of serving in a war that was no
longer being waged.

The War Department made the best it could of the
dilemma by declaring that all men who had held such un-
confirmed commissions were entitled to call themselves by
their wartime ranks. And Congress rather sheepishly passed
a bill authorizing the full payment of wages to these non-
officer officers.

Kit Carson's situation was no different from that of many
hundreds of others who had served the country, and neither
his friendship with Fremont nor a personal bias against him
on the part of Senate members had blocked his confirmation.
If he wished, he could call himself First Lieutenant Carson.
And during his brief sojourn in Washington, he received the

better part of the pay due him for services rendered during his brief tour of duty in the Army. He also received an order on the Treasury for wages authorized by Fremont on his third expedition.

Kit was now wealthier by several thousand dollars, and must have realized he had no political enemies. Perhaps a sour taste lingered in his mouth, however, for he stayed in Washington for no more than a few days.

Virtually no details of that visit are known. If he was invited to the White House, no record of that meeting still exists. John and Jessie Fremont still owned their Washington home, but the explorer was currently traveling to California with a private expedition which he and his father-in-law had financed. He hoped to find a route for a railroad that would span the continent, and as he had not been able to get in touch with Kit, had hired the unreliable Bill Williams as his guide.

Apparently Kit did not stay as a guest at the Fremont home, but Mrs. Fremont may have been in St. Louis, preparing to join her husband on the estate he intended to purchase in California. In any case, Kit's visit to the capital created no stir. The United States, now a coast-to-coast power, had swallowed vast amounts of territory and was trying to digest its meal. There were many visitors from the western lands in the city, some clamoring for public office, and all with axes to grind. Buckskins were a common sight on the muddy stretches of Pennsylvania Avenue, and Kit, still wearing his uniform, went unnoticed.

He neither craved nor sought attention, and when Secretary Marcy extended him a dinner invitation, he declined on the grounds that he intended to leave for his own home at the first possible moment. Incidentally, it is unlikely that Marcy would have shown hospitality to someone in the bad graces of the Administration. Tact was one of the talented Marcy's greatest assets.

A few newspapers noted Kit's presence in Washington,

and a representative of the New York *Post* asked his opinion of Fremont's court-martial. He refused to comment, saying he knew too few of the facts to express an opinion.

Kit's last official act was to accept money given him by the War Department for his return journey to New Mexico. He traveled to St. Louis by train, and after spending a few days with his brother, bought himself a horse and two pack mules. His purse bulging with money, he set out for Taos to renew his acquaintance with the family he scarcely knew. His thirty-ninth birthday was only a few weeks ahead, and he looked forward to a quiet, uneventful life with his wife and children.

No man trying to assess his future could have been more mistaken about the life he was destined to lead.

10. HOME ON THE RANGE

Energetic American administrators injected a new note into the sleepy life of New Mexico. Territorial courts in Santa Fe, Taos, Pueblo and other towns dispensed justice with a brisk severity that astonished Mexican residents and bewildered the local Indians. Landowners filed deeds which described the boundaries of their property in detail, and were assured that the government would protect them against marauders and poachers. American businessmen were no longer harassed by regulations that limited their activities. Constabulary forces kept drunks and troublemakers from the streets of the major towns, prostitutes were told to take themselves elsewhere and respectable women could go where they pleased without fear of being molested, but were wise if they did not venture out of doors alone after dark, for paradise was not established overnight.

Schools, always a hallmark of American progress, sprang up everywhere. And a half-regiment of United States Army regulars arrived in the territory to keep the peace. The commander of the unit liked Taos and established his headquarters there, much to the disappointment of Santa Fe, which had grown accustomed to being the hub of the area.

In some respects the atmosphere was unchanged. Americans and Mexicans had lived side by side in peace for many years, and had learned to respect and like each other. The leaders of both communities agreed that it would be best to forget some of the excesses committed during the war, particularly the rebellion in Taos and the severe reprisals inflicted thereafter on the Mexicans.

The reconciliation of wartime foes was made easier by the fact that they had an enemy in common, the Indians of the Apache nation. These savages often attacked wagon trains, raided farms and ranches and, in general, were the terror of the region. Their leader, whom the Mexicans called Chico Velasques, may have been a half-breed; whatever his origin, he was an able organizer, a crafty thief and a man of courage.

The principal duty of the First Regiment of United States Dragoons at Taos was that of clipping the feathered head-dresses of the high-riding Apaches, and several expeditions were sent out in the winter of 1848–49 to tame the savages. The officers were hampered by their unfamiliarity with the mentality and habits of the Indian, and little was accomplished. When troops were in the vicinity, bands of warriors disappeared, only to return when the cavalry had gone elsewhere.

Kit Carson paid little or no attention to these maneuvers. He was preoccupied with his own future and, supplied now with enough money to invest in a venture that would give his family permanent security, he thought once again of becoming a farmer. He made several trips to the valley where he had been building a house when recalled to duty as a guide by John Fremont, and his companion on these journeys was another Mountain Man. Maxwell, who had been the hunter on Fremont's first expedition and one of Kit's subordinates on the third, had recently married a Mexican girl of family and wealth, and was anxious to settle down too.

After scouring the entire Rayado, as the Mexicans called the valley, the two men found land to their liking only five miles from the site of Kit's first farm. They purchased two large, adjoining sites, and again a small army of workmen poured into the valley. Wagons rumbled out of Taos, fifty miles to the east, laden with lumber, tools and equipment, and soon the ranch houses, barns and smaller buildings began to take shape. Kit and Maxwell shared a hut during this period of construction and, in addition to supervising the building of their homes, were busy breaking ground and planting crops of grain.

Both houses were built along similar lines, Maxwell's being somewhat larger than Kit's. Both were one-story buildings of simple Mexican ranch design, with inner courtyards and verandas that ran around the outside perimeters. Ceilings were high, windows were large and all rooms had cross-ventilation, for men who lived in New Mexico knew that the summers were hot. Each establishment had its own fowl yard, stocked with chickens, ducks and pigeons. There were kennels for the dogs, and the stables for the horses of men who had spent most of their adult lives in the saddle were enormous.

Mrs. Carson planted a vegetable garden behind her house, and Kit invested all of his remaining capital in cattle and sheep. On the far sides of his property were several scattered houses, which were occupied by Mexican tenant farmers with whom he made the customary arrangements: in return for their labor, they would keep fifty per cent of the crops they grew.

Late in the spring or early in the summer of 1849, Kit and his family moved into their new home. Taos was a booming community, so the house in town was sold at a good price, and there was enough money on hand to meet emergencies. The future was bright, and Kit worked hard, riding out into the fields at daybreak and not returning to the house until sundown. His first crop promised to be successful, and he had no pressing problems. It may be assumed that Mrs. Carson breathed frequent sighs of well-earned relief.

Her peace of mind was short-lived, for a bombshell exploded in the territory late in the summer. A Santa Fe trader named White had been traveling from the east with a wagon train of supplies, accompanied by his wife and child. Apache warriors had attacked the party, kidnaping the child and murdering Mrs. White. Settlers were alarmed, the Army was outraged and the blood of Mountain Men curdled. The tragedy, it was said, had taken place on the banks of the Red River, a tributary of the Arkansas, in the mountains.

A company of cavalry was ordered to proceed to the spot at once, find the killers and, if possible, rescue White's child. Every mountaineer in the area volunteered his services, and the dragoons, aware of their own inadequacies, accepted all of the offers. Kit and Maxwell were among the first to ride into Taos in buckskins, rifles under their arms.

A hard ride of several days brought the troops and their volunteer guides to the scene of the murder, and the trail of the Apache was found. The party followed it, but the next twelve days were among the most difficult Kit had ever known, for the retreating Apache had split into two, sometimes three and occasionally even more groups, each of which took a separate trail higher into the mountains. On the morning of the twelfth day the pursuers were reunited, however, and it was believed that the savages were not far ahead.

Kit led the advance, and when he saw through the evergreens that he was approaching the Apache camp, he called to the others, urging an immediate attack. The men behind him did not move, and various reasons have been advanced for their torpor. According to one, a mountaineer named Leroux was allegedly jealous of Kit and advised the captain commanding the expedition to confer with the savages in order to save the life of White's child.

Accounts of the incident become somewhat garbled at this point. According to some, Mrs. White had not yet been killed, but had merely been taken captive, and was murdered during this brief delay.

Whatever the cause, the pursuers hesitated, and Kit checked his own advance, knowing it would be foolhardy to ride alone into the Apache camp. The warriors were alerted by his shout, and one of their sentries, who was armed with a rifle, wounded the captain, thereby causing another brief delay.

These few moments made the difference between a decisive engagement and a half-victory. By the time the mountaineers and cavalrymen finally charged, the braves were in flight, leaving most of their possessions behind. The chase continued for several miles across rough terrain. Two warriors, members of the rear guard, were killed and several others were wounded. Several children in the Indian party, unable to maintain the rapid pace set by their elders, fell behind and were captured.

White's child may be assumed to have been one of them, for the chase was abandoned. Kit's biographers, maddeningly, do not mention the child specifically, and there are no other records of the incident. The modern reader is free to make his own guess, for the story ends on as inconclusive a note as the chase itself. It would appear that the moral, an integral part of nineteenth-century storytelling, was that the expedition would have enjoyed complete success had Kit's advice been taken.

There is an ironic footnote. In Mrs. White's personal belongings, which were recovered, was a novel portraying Kit as a great Indian fighter, a hero who had never lost a battle and did not know the meaning of defeat. It was the first such book Kit had ever seen, but Dr. Peters indicates that he displayed only a mild interest in it. He was far more concerned about the party's inability to come to grips with the Apache warriors.

A snowstorm in the mountains, which slowed the return of the party, heralded the approach of winter. Several men had followed the example set by Kit and Maxwell, and had built ranch houses in the Rayado. The cattle in the valley were a sure magnet for Indian raiders, so a squad of ten dragoons under the command of a sergeant was sent to the valley to protect the lives and property of the settlers.

The winter of 1849–50 passed quietly, the ranch owners augmenting the troops with a rotating detail of two guards from their own ranks. In the spring an expected Apache attack materialized shortly before sundown one day, and a large number of horses and mules grazing in a pasture were stolen. Both of the sentinels on duty were wounded, but one managed to give the alarm, and the other ranchers immediately gathered at Kit's house with the dragoons.

Night having fallen, it was too late to set out in pursuit of the bandits, so the men waited impatiently until daybreak, when they departed. The trail was easy to find and easier to follow, as so many animals had been stolen, and Kit led the company on such a hard ride that, soon after the raiders were sighted in the foothills ahead, four horses gave out and their riders were compelled to fall behind.

Kit and the others, eleven men in all, continued the chase, and gaining ground on the raiders, soon were able to count their numbers. There were twenty warriors in the escaping party, thus making the odds against the settlers and dragoons almost two to one. By the standards of Mountain Men, such a ratio was trifling. Kit and his companions eventually overcame the braves' lead, and a running battle took place, a fight of the kind familiar to anyone who has ever seen a Western movie or television play.

Kit and his comrades won, killing or wounding a number of the braves and recovering all but a few of the stolen horses and mules.

Several logical questions arise as a result of this encounter. Why, in battles with the Indians, was Kit Carson seldom—if ever—defeated? His courage and that of his colleagues was not superior to that of warriors who had learned from earliest childhood to endure pain. Nor were Mountain Men, settlers and cavalrymen better horsemen than braves who were taught to ride before they could walk. The answer, obvious on reflection, is that mountaineers, soldiers and even settlers were familiar with firearms, which few Indians could handle.

In the years prior to the Civil War, the majority of Indian braves carried bows and arrows, which certainly could wound but rarely inflicted mortal injury. Even the most belligerent of the western tribes—among them the Apache, Cheyenne and Comanche—had gained possession of few rifles. Those which they had acquired were usually stolen, and they suffered from a shortage of ammunition and gunpowder. Consequently they lacked practice, so when they did manage to go into a battle armed with firearms, their aim was poor.

Another factor in their frequent defeats was their inability to fathom the complicated mental processes of civilized men. The tribesmen were barbarians who, when making war on each other, followed basic, dog-eat-dog rules. Men who had enjoyed a better education were able to devise strategies and tactics that bewildered the savages. Not until the Indians acquired a greater degree of sophistication, which they learned from their conquerors, were they able to fight successful pitched battles. By then, in the late 1860s and 1870s, it was too late to stem the swelling tide of immigration into their territory.

Whatever the causes of Kit Carson's success in his Indian fights, he had learned the knack of how to overcome the tribesmen of plains and mountains, and it is self-evident that he must have enjoyed these battles for their own sake. A man of forty who had already lived a full life need not have gone off in pursuit of the Apache horse thieves himself. The dragoons had been stationed in the Rayado to do such work for him, but he unhesitatingly placed himself in command of the avenging expedition. If Maxwell accompanied the party, his name was inadvertently omitted from all accounts of the incident. Therefore it may be assumed that Maxwell, having reached his middle years, was willing to let others do his fighting for him.

Kit, on the other hand, was unable to resist a challenge. It may be that this quality of character, more than any other, made him a folk hero.

Neither advancing age nor increased responsibilities cured him of his wanderlust either. He was a husband, the father of a growing family and the owner of a large ranch whose affairs needed supervision. But, soon after his return from the Apache-chasing expedition, he smelled spring in the air, and the mountains beckoned. Unable to resist the lure of the wilderness, he and a mountaineer named Thomas Goodel set out from Taos on May 5, 1850 for Fort Laramie, more than five hundred miles away.

To be sure, the reason Kit gave for making the journey was sound. Gold had been discovered in California, men by the thousands were making their way across the continent to the Pacific, and supplies of all kinds were bringing unprecedentedly high prices. Every man traveling to California wanted horses and mules almost as much as he wanted a pick, a shovel and a sieve. Kit owned a large herd, and decided he could reap enormous profits from the immigrants who stopped at Fort Laramie.

He took a herd of fifty animals north with him and, arriving at Laramie in June, stayed there for about one month. As he had anticipated, he sold the entire herd for sky-high prices and made the best profit he had ever enjoyed. Certainly he had justified heeding the call of the wild.

It was during Kit's stay at Fort Laramie on this occasion that his renown paid dividends for the first time. Men who arrived at the post on their way to California were eager to shake his hand, women and children stared at him in silent awe, and those who bought his horses and mules boasted that their newly acquired animals had come from him. His prices were higher than those of his competitors, but travelers willingly paid them.

Few of the almost countless anecdotes told about Kit Carson indicate that he was endowed with a particularly keen sense of humor, but one, relished by both Burdett and Peters, indicates that he was not as solemn as might otherwise be supposed. During Kit's stay at Fort Laramie, he was approached one day by an Arkansas farmer seeking a fortune in the gold fields. The man had heard that the famous Kit Carson was at the post, had the hero pointed out and, approaching without ceremony, wanted to know if he was addressing the celebrated Kit.

No longer embarrassed by such confrontations, Kit admitted his identity.

The stranger could not hide his disbelief. Standing before him was a short, slender man with graying hair, who was dressed in shabby buckskin trousers and a faded woolen shirt. Such an insignificant-looking person could not possibly be the trapper and hunter, Indian fighter and great guide whose name had become synonymous with that of the West.

Kit, aware of the disappointment in the stranger's eyes, glanced around at the company chatting in the central compound. Some feet away stood a tall, burly man dressed in a magnificent hunting shirt and leather leggings. From one side of his belt hung a pistol in a holster, and from the other dangled a long knife with an intricately fashioned bone handle. Any true Mountain Man could recognize at once that this splendid specimen had bought his clothes and weapons in one of the eastern cities.

But the immigrant from Arkansas knew no better, and Kit told him that the handsomely attired giant was the Kit Carson he was seeking. The farmer went off, stared for some time at the man and then departed, completely satisfied. Kit kept a straight face the whole time.

Although such incidents amused Kit, he was not pleased when total strangers claimed they were his close friends. But wherever he went now, he encountered such men, many of whom did not know his true identity. In years to come, he would meet them in Taos, too, and invariably became annoyed by these false claims. Apparently he was never able to understand that he was paying the price demanded of every celebrity.

Kit's friend, Goodel, earned such a handsome profit at Fort Laramie that he went off to California with the gold seekers, and Kit returned to Taos with a Mexican friend. No biographer of Kit Carson could resist the opportunity to embroil his hero with hostile Indians when making such a journey, so Kit allegedly was forced to make a longer than necessary trip in order to avoid a party of Apache warriors. Thanks to his vigilance, he escaped from danger.

In any event, he arrived at the Rayado to find that a party of Apache thieves had made off with a number of his cattle, as well as animals belonging to his neighbors. This time he sensibly allowed the dragoons to conduct the search for the missing animals. The mission was successful, the cattle were returned and Kit was able to devote all of his time to his family and the development of his property.

The acquisition of larger herds and the success of the farm made it necessary for Kit to hire more men, and this in turn complicated his existence. His laborers were Mexican Indians, and under the terms of their employment he was obliged to provide them with their food, a practice which had been followed for generations in feudal New Mexico.

Any foodstuff brought to the territory from the eastern parts of the United States was prohibitively expensive, so Kit found a happy solution. He spent part of each day hunting, accompanied by one or more of his dogs, and the table of his laborers was one of the best in New Mexico. He often shot deer and wild turkey, and occasionally brought down other game. Inevitably, Kit Carson enthusiasts exaggerated their hero's prowess, and claimed that he also shot elk and antelope. If he did, no one else in the vicinity of Taos enjoyed his luck. Elk did not live as far south as New Mexico, and the North American antelope,

an unusually shy creature, sought the privacy of uninhab-
ited mountain valleys.

Regardless of what Kit shot, he was still a skilled professional hunter. His marksmanship kept his food bills down,
and he enjoyed his outings. It may even be suspected that
he preferred these hunting trips to the more prosaic work
demanded of a farmer and rancher. He did not neglect
his duties, however, and the value of his holdings increased.

Only one adventure interrupted Kit's domestic peace
during the latter half of the year 1850, which was the least
active he had ever known. That incident created a great
deal of attention, however, and placed Kit permanently in
the ranks of those who were striving to maintain law and
order in a frontier territory.

Two men from an eastern city, named Weatherhead and
Brevoort, engaged a number of men to act as their guards
on their return from New Mexico. As they had no furs or
other baggage of consequence, it was assumed by some
of Taos' less reputable residents that they wanted guards
because they would carry large sums of cash on their persons. One of these men, whose name was Fox, conceived the
idea of persuading others of similar morals to join the company with him and murder Weatherhead and Brevoort.

A desperado whom Fox tried to recruit went to the commander of the dragoon regiment with his tale, unfortunately waiting, however, until Brevoort, Weatherhead and
their company of guards had started east. The colonel, conscious that speed was essential, hurried to Kit with the
news and sought his help. The assistance of an experienced
guide was needed, for the informer had said that Fox and
his companions were taking their intended victims east by
way of one of the many "plains trails" through the Pan-
handle of Texas and what later became the state of Oklahoma, a route that was longer but less rigorous than that
through the mountains. Not many people traveled that way,
and if men were murdered somewhere on the vast expanse

of the prairies, wolves could be relied on to dispose of the evidence.

Kit loaded his rifle, took his blanket roll and saddlebag from a shelf and declared he was ready to start at once. Military red tape, the plague of every army in history, delayed the departure. Troops had to be relieved of other duties, then assigned to accompany the volunteer guide, and not until the following day were a sergeant and a squad of eight men ready to start. Kit carried orders, signed by the colonel commanding the dragoons, granting him the power to deal with Fox and any others involved in the conspiracy as he saw fit.

The party cut through the mountains and foothills of New Mexico, then traveled east at a rapid pace across the prairies. Two days out of Taos they encountered a detachment of army recruits, marching in the opposite direction. The captain of the company placed the bulk of his command under one of his lieutenants, and joined the expedition with twenty of his men. Kit was pleased that his ranks had been increased, but the presence of the newcomers was a mixed blessing, for the recruits could not ride as rapidly as veterans.

Therefore it became necessary to resort to forced marches, the party spent several long days on the road and almost a week passed before the company of Weatherhead and Brevoort was overtaken. Kit immediately placed Fox under arrest and, as was to be expected, the man vehemently protested his innocence. Three soldiers were detailed to stand guard over him, with orders to shoot him if he tried to escape. Brevoort and Weatherhead found it difficult to believe they were the intended victims of a robbery and murder plot, but Kit, who knew virtually everyone in the Taos vicinity, carefully pointed out to them that the majority of their guards were men with unsavory reputations.

Thirty-five members of the company of fifty were dismissed and told to leave the camp at once. None of the suspects argued with Kit, who stood before them with a loaded rifle, the blue-uniformed troops ready for action. If some of those dismissed were innocent, it was too bad, for frontier justice was as rough as it was swift.

Weatherhead and Brevoort offered Kit a reward for saving their lives, but he declined, much to the disappointment of the troops, who would have shared the prize. The following day the two easterners resumed their journey, and Kit turned back toward Taos. Fox was paraded through the streets of the town to the jail, a one-story building of sun-dried clay, and there he languished for many weeks.

By the time his case was tried, the informer had conveniently disappeared. The colonel and Kit were the principal witnesses for the prosecution, but Fox was set free, for he had committed no overt criminal act and the evidence against him was slim. He immediately left Taos for parts unknown, and was not seen in the vicinity again.

The incident had two results. The people of the area now thought of Kit as a law-enforcement officer, and from that time on, citizens frequently called on him to quell breaches of the peace. He always responded to such appeals, even though he had no legal right to interfere. It was said that his mere appearance in Taos, riding down dusty roads with his rifle tucked under his arm, miraculously cooled tempers.

The second result was concrete. In 1851 Kit received a pair of engraved, silver-mounted pistols from Brevoort and Weatherhead. They were the most expensive weapons he had ever owned, and they remained in his possession for the rest of his life.

The winter of 1850–51 passed quietly, as did the following spring. The ranch-farms of the Rayado were now sufficiently productive to warrant a trip to the east to dispose of merchandise, and in the early summer Kit set out for St. Louis in command of a wagon train laden with wheat, oats and rye that he and Maxwell had grown. He left his horses and wagons in the boom town of Westport

Landing, Kansas—soon to become Kansas City—and, trans-
ferring his cargo to a steamboat, traveled the rest of the
way to St. Louis via the Missouri River.

In the city he purchased large quantities of supplies that
he and Maxwell needed, carried them by boat to Westport
Landing and started out for home by way of the familiar
mountain trail that would take him to Bent's Fort. When
the wagon train reached the mountains, there occurred an
incident that Kit himself later verified, and that was also
authenticated by several of the hired men who accompanied him.

Warriors of the Cheyenne nation were furiously angry
because they believed their whole tribe had been disgraced
a few days earlier, when a young brave had been caught
stealing a blanket from an army bivouac and had been
whipped. Kit and his company of fifteen rode up into the
mountains innocently, completely unaware of what had
taken place. But when pairs of warriors appeared fleetingly
in front of the caravan, behind it and on its flanks, Kit
knew that something obviously had gone amiss. He signaled
to one of the warriors, indicating that he wanted to confer
with the Indians, and a few hours later his request was
granted. A party of fifty braves appeared on the trail ahead,
all wearing war paint on their faces.

Kit quickly ordered his men to form the wagons in a
circle, barricade themselves and prepare for action. Then,
accompanied by two of his company, he walked unhesitatingly toward the warriors, his new pistols hanging from
his belt, his rifle slung under his arm. For many years the
Cheyenne had been his friends and blood brothers, his
first wife having been a member of the tribe, and he con-
fidently expected to iron out any difficulty quickly.

To his astonishment the warriors addressed him in the
tongue of the Sioux, the lingua franca of western savages.
It was no wonder that the Cheyenne did not recognize him,
for he had gained weight, his hair was gray and, instead

of the buckskins of his youth he wore the modest wool suit, half-boots and broad-brimmed hat of a successful farmer.

He and his two companions sat down with the warriors, a pipe was passed and the leaders of the band aired their grievances at length, still speaking in the language of the Sioux. Some of the younger warriors, impatient with the formalities, addressed each other in their own tongue, and agreeing that the ceremony should be cut short, proposed that the intruders be killed at once.

Kit had heard enough. He jumped to his feet and, cocking his rifle, made an impassioned speech in the language of the Cheyenne. He identified himself, reminded the braves of his past association with them and told them he still considered himself their friend. But he indicated that, if they felt otherwise, he was prepared to kill at least three members of the band with his rifle and pistols before they could touch him. He added the hope, however, that reason rather than violence would prevail.

The warriors were bewildered. Most were members of a generation that had come to manhood since Kit had lived in the mountains as a trapper and hunter, but they were familiar with his name and reputation. Their desire for vengeance disappeared, at least temporarily, and they promised they would not molest him.

Kit accepted their word with a grain of salt, knowing that Indian moods were mercurial. He sent the youngest member of his party, a teen-aged Mexican boy, ahead to Taos to ask for a military escort, and spent several days at Bent's Fort in order to give a relief column time to set out. Soon after he left the trading post, however, he found signs that the warriors were still hovering nearby, and alerted his men for trouble.

He spent a sleepless night standing guard over his wagon train, but in midmorning of the following day, when he had reached a point approximately twenty-five miles southwest of Bent's Fort, the cavalry escort arrived. The Cheyenne vanished into the mountains, and the incident ended.

The affair was far more significant than Kit or anyone else realized at the time. His conference with the warriors marked the first occasion of consequence that he had sat down to reason at length with Indians. His understanding of the savages' mentality, his ability to speak their language and his blunt courage had preserved the peace. His tongue rather than his marksmanship had saved lives and property, and in years to come his talents as a conciliator would bring him the greatest fame he had yet known.

For the present, however, he was still a farmer and rancher. He went out hunting every morning, then devoted the rest of his day to his crops and livestock. He arose at the same time every morning and went to sleep every night in a featherbed. He listened to the domestic problems of his wife and tried to help his children with their school work.

He spent many of his evenings during the winter of 1851–52 sitting before the huge fire in the living room hearth that warded off the chill of New Mexico nights, and an old, familiar sense of restlessness began to stir in him. Like other men of middle years he hated to admit, particularly to himself, that he was growing older. And as he dreamed, the vague outlines of a wild idea began to form in his mind.

11. THE LAST FLING

Kit's neighbor and friend, Maxwell, was a kindred spirit. They and their wives saw a great deal of each other during the winter of 1851–52, and the men, withdrawing to one end of the room, shut out the sound of talk about servant problems, how to marinate a venison steak and the character of the new schoolteacher in Taos. The Mountain Men reminisced about their glorious youth in the wilderness, and their nostalgia for those bygone days became so overwhelming that Kit made up his mind to take the direct action for which he was noted.

One evening, early in March, he proposed to his friend that they round up a band of veterans and go out together into the mountains on one last trapping expedition. Both employed competent foremen, he argued, and their ranches would not suffer during their absence. Maxwell agreed instantly, they shook hands and the compact was formed.

There were many former mountaineers living in Taos and its vicinity, and the friends selected their company with great care. Troublemakers and eccentrics were excluded from the ranks, and only men with whom they had worked in the past were invited to join the band. When it was learned that Kit Carson was planning to go trapping, he was swamped with applications. Men rode north from Santa Fe for the purpose of begging to be permitted to accompany him, and a number of applications were sent by express riders from Texas.

Only experienced trappers, all of them old friends, were admitted to the circle. Faded buckskins were taken from

old chests, traps were oiled and guns cleaned. Kit and Maxwell made an advance trip into the prairies to the east to
shoot buffalo for pemmican, and in their mounting excitement they could think of little other than their venture.

Early in April sixteen former trappers joined their two
hosts in the Rayado, and their reunion was boisterous. All
were graying and the majority had paunches, but they
tested themselves shooting at targets on a range behind
Maxwell's house, and none had lost their skills.

The band set out in high spirits for the South Platte,
where they began trapping, and in the summer that followed they traveled countless miles through country all
of them had known intimately. They shot game for food,
living exclusively on unsalted, roasted meat, and they sat
late around their campfire every night. But they worked
hard, too, for all had been professional trappers and the
catching of beaver was serious work.

Perhaps they moved from river to river somewhat less
rapidly than in their youth, but they more than made up
in experience what they lacked in speed and agility. By the
time they reached the end of their planned route, on the
Arkansas River, they had accumulated enough furs to give
each man a purse of nearly one thousand dollars, an im-
pressively large sum in view of the fact that the beaver
market had become less active.

The whole band returned to the Rayado, where Kit and
Maxwell each gave a farewell party, and at last the group
disbanded. Kit and his neighbor were satisfied, at least for
the present, and devoted their full time and attention to
their families, their crops and their livestock. They were
model husbands, fathers and ranchers during the autumn of
1852 and the winter of 1852–53.

With the coming of spring, Kit's blood began to race at
a faster pace, and when he heard in Taos that sheep were
bringing exceptionally high prices in California, a new
idea began to form in his mind. His previous summer's out-

ing had been a mildly profitable holiday, but he was a mature man with responsibilities, and could not go out again in search of his lost youth. Perhaps, however, he could combine business with pleasure.

He questioned travelers who came to Taos from California, and they confirmed the story he had heard. Sheep were selling in the land of gold for as much as five dollars per head. The news settled the last doubts in Kit's mind, so he went to a valley south of Santa Fe and invested most of his floating capital in sheep, buying close to seven thousand animals at one dollar and fifty cents per head.

Two friends who were ranchers followed his example, and all three set out for California with their herds, accompanied by a number of their hired men. They left Taos in the spring and traveled north slowly by way of Fort Laramie and Salt Lake, then going west on the trail that Kit had blazed when he had been Fremont's guide.

There were large Indian tribes encountered on the journey, among them the Apache, Sioux and Cheyenne, but Kit was confident he would have no trouble with them. Realizing he could not pass unnoticed through their territory when driving thousands of sheep, he made a point of greeting the tribesmen ceremoniously, making gifts of sheep to their chiefs, elders and principal warriors. Thanks to his diplomacy and bribery, no sheep were stolen, and he reached California safely, his reputation among the Indians greatly enhanced.

His ability to handle the Indians peacefully by dealing with them in terms they understood and appreciated had grown and matured through the years. His first marriage is proof that he never shared the prejudices of many Mountain Men, and his conduct over the period of more than a quarter of a century had gained him the grudging respect of every tribe acquainted with him. He was known as a man who had never fought without cause, who had never been the first to attack and who always kept his word.

Now, in a period when immigrants by the thousands were moving into the western territories and changing the region beyond recognition, the frightened and defiant Indians saw their whole world crumbling. Badgered and cheated, hounded and persecuted, they realized that Kit, who knew their way of life and respected their traditions, was their friend.

In his last years, shortly after the Civil War, when a visitor complimented him for the cleverness he had shown by making gifts of sheep to prominent Indians in order to assure himself a peaceful journey to California, he is alleged to have replied, "I believe I would have been allowed to pass freely even if I hadn't given them sheep. I didn't know it at the time, but most of the Indians already thought of me as their friend."

His efforts on that journey were rewarded, for a pot of pure gold awaited him at the end of the rainbow trail in the Eldorado that had fired the imaginations of men everywhere. Kit found that the reports on sheep prices were not exaggerated, and he sold his flocks, sixty-five hundred sheep in all, at five dollars and fifty cents a head. He pocketed $35,750, of which almost $25,000 was clear profit. It was the largest sum he had ever earned in his life, and although the deal did not make him wealthy, he was relieved of pressing financial concerns.

Kit paid another visit to his brother Moses, who had become a man of substance selling supplies to prospectors drawn to California by gold. While Kit was resting at Moses' ranch, a messenger arrived with a letter from Maxwell, who had originally disapproved of the speculation in sheep. Kit's friend had changed his mind, and at the time of writing was traveling west on the Carson River. He asked Kit to wait for him so they could return to New Mexico together.

Kit had time to burn, so Moses took him to San Francisco, the fastest-growing boom town in the United States, to see the sights. When Kit had first visited the place in his youth, he had seen a small Mexican garrison at the Presidio and a colorless mud village of domesticated Indians. The lusty metropolis that had sprung up out of nowhere startled him.

At the time of his visit, San Francisco boasted between thirty-five and forty thousand permanent residents, and was growing so rapidly that the harried city officials could not keep an accurate count of the population. New homes, streets—even entire districts—came into being overnight. There were more restaurants, taverns and inns than any one person could identify, most of them catering to the male gold seekers. Bordellos were everywhere, as were gaming houses and other palaces of "entertainment," where those who had struck it rich were painlessly relieved of their gold dust.

By the standards of civilized men, San Francisco was a lawless community. It was estimated that two or three men were murdered every day, and no one thought of going out of doors unarmed. By its own standards the city had become positively decorous. "Old residents," men who had been there for three or even four years, recalled that in 1851 there had been at least fifteen murders every day. There were those who claimed that someone had died a violent death every hour, right around the clock, and no one could prove them wrong or disputed their word. Then respectable citizens, alarmed by the chaos, had formed their famous Vigilance Committee. They had taken the law into their own hands, hanged every murderer and suspected murderer they could catch and, by use of stern counter-violence, had restored at least partial order.

Kit received a thunderous welcome from the inhabitants. He was the living embodiment of the spirit of adventure that had drawn San Francisco's thousands to California, and the ferocious warmth of the city's greeting stunned him. Owners of restaurants and taverns refused to let him pay for his meals. Saloon keepers urged him to accept the

courtesies of the house. And he was embarrassed when
the owner of the circumspect hotel at which Moses habitually stayed on his visits to the city insisted that the brothers
were his personal guests.

A night of sightseeing was exhausting. The proprietors
of several gambling houses begged Kit to honor them by
cutting cards, shooting dice or playing poker in their es-
tablishments. When he replied that he had never liked games
of chance, they promised him they would make an exception for him and use neither marked cards nor loaded dice.
The owners of bawdy houses opened their doors to the
famous Mountain Man and asked him to sample their
wares free of charge. Kit fled to the sanctuary of the hotel
room he shared with Moses.

It was impossible for him to appear on the streets without attracting a crowd, and people followed him everywhere.
According to a story he himself later told, he left his hotel
very early one morning in the hope that he could stroll
down to look at the fabulously beautiful bay he remembered
so vividly from his previous visits. But a throng of five
hundred accompanied him, and he was forced to turn back.

Many of the livelier and more imaginative Kit Carson legends date from this visit to San Francisco. Several of the
tales appear in retrospect to have been inevitable.

According to one, a gang of bullies accosted Kit, but he
sent them flying by drawing his pistols and wounding two
men before anyone else could draw. According to another,
he deliberately took the place of a sickly young man who
had been challenged to a duel by a hulking brute and,
of course, killed his opponent with a single shot. A third,
milder than the majority on the long list, states that he
engaged in a target-shooting contest with San Francisco's
best marksmen and beat all of them with ease.

There is no real evidence indicating that he drew either
of his pistols at any time during his visit to the city. And it
is unlikely that he took his rifle out of the baggage he left

in his room, for the more prominent citizens treated him as a man of substance, an honored guest. They hailed him as an explorer who had opened many parts of the Far West for the first time, a pioneer who had known the land when it had been a wilderness and an army officer whose historic march to San Diego had been one of the great personal triumphs of the recent war.

Kit appreciated the homage paid to him. But praise made him so uncomfortable that he quietly refused to allow a banquet to be given in his honor. He asked only one favor, that he be allowed to rent a small steamboat for a ride around the bay. A vessel of one hundred and twenty tons was provided for him the following day, and when he went on board he was greeted by a roaring crowd of the great, near-great and other well-wishers. His hosts refused to let him pay for either the boat or the sumptuous meal they served on board. He responded with as much grace as he could muster, and even went so far as to drink a small glass of the mildest wine that was served. The San Franciscans, of course, drank liquor so hard that they took care to prevent it from spilling onto the deck for fear it would blister the varnish.

During his visit Kit received a number of flattering business offers from shrewd men anxious to exploit his name. He might have made considerable amounts of money but, unlike celebrities of later eras, thought it would be immoral to lend his name and reputation to the enterprises of others.

In all, the San Francisco interlude placed Kit in a new perspective. He realized at last that many of his fellow Americans regarded him as a great hero and were inclined to look at him through a magnifying glass. He reacted by cutting short his visit and returning to Moses' ranch, where he waited for Maxwell.

At last Maxwell arrived, having disposed of his own sheep at an enormous profit. The two friends decided to return home by the way of the southern route, for the season was already far advanced and they had no desire to cross the Sierra Nevadas in winter. First, however, Maxwell wanted to see San Francisco. And he proposed they make the first stage of their journey in one of the coastal steamers that now made regular runs between the great new city and the towns of Los Angeles and San Diego in the south.

Kit countered with the suggestion that Maxwell enjoy the sights and steamer voyage. He himself would make the necessary preparations for the return to New Mexico, would travel overland and meet his companion in Los Angeles. Explaining his reasons, he told Maxwell and Moses one of his closest-held secrets, which did not become public knowledge until his biographers revealed it many years later. On one occasion during the Mexican War, he said, he had been a passenger on a navy steamer between Los Angeles and Monterey, and had become violently seasick. He had promised himself that never again would he go out into open salt water, and he intended to keep his vow.

Maxwell accepted the new plan, and arrived in Los Angeles two weeks before Kit reached the town with his horses and pack mules. The pair started out a few days later, accompanied by the hired men who had gone to California with them. They soon found that the autumn weather had been unusually dry, and consequently grass was scarce. But everyone was anxious to reach home by Christmas, and Kit believed he could lead the party on a short-cut through river basins that, regardless of the weather, were certain to be grassy enough for fodder.

So, a short time before his forty-fourth birthday, he blazed a new trail through the southern portions of what later became Arizona and New Mexico. The whole company was in high spirits on the journey, and Kit's biographers, notably Burdett and Peters, relate that his companions teased him unmercifully, a new experience for him. The rousing welcome San Francisco had given him was directly responsible. Whenever he hesitated, halted or groped for bearings on the new trail, Maxwell led the chorus: "Are you really the famous guide, Kit Carson? Do you know where you're going, or are you lost?"

Basic American humor, it seems, has not changed appreciably in the past one hundred and eleven years.

Kit enjoyed the last laugh, for he led the party into Taos early in December after spending only eight weeks on the trail. The sheep traders had come home for Christmas with time to spare.

An official letter from the United States Government awaited Kit at his house. He was informed that President Franklin Pierce had appointed him Indian agent for the territory. If he accepted, he would be sworn in by the governor of New Mexico, and would be required to post a bond of one thousand dollars.

He wrote a letter of acceptance at once, and rode back to Taos to arrange for his bond. That day, he said, was the happiest he had ever known.

12. THE INDIAN AGENT

The vastly expanded United States of America was living up to its potential by the end of 1853. The Industrial Revolution was gaining momentum, and new manufacturing plants were springing up from old New England to the recently incorporated Kansas City. Land in the West, the promise of opportunity and the chance to live as one pleased were magnets drawing ever increasing numbers of immigrants to the New World from the Old, and the melting pot bubbled furiously as more than one third of a million newcomers came to the country from Europe in 1853.

The controversy between the industrialized North and rural South was sharpening in intensity. The rights of the states as opposed to those of the federal government comprised the main issue, but the fundamental difference, that of slavery and human rights, had risen to the surface. Thoughtful men were afraid that if tempers continued to soar, a civil war might break out, but most people were confident that President Pierce, who favored compromise, could find a patchwork solution with the help of Congress.

Mass media publications had come into their own. Every city and town of consequence boasted a large number of newspapers, book companies were printing novels by the thousands and tens of thousands, and each month saw the appearance of new magazines. New universities and colleges were opening their doors, too, many of them in the Midwest.

The Indians, who had been pushed farther and farther west since the early seventeenth century, were now caught in a vise, for rapidly growing California had become a state in 1850, and the savages were hemmed in by civilized men on both east and west. Nowhere was the problem more acute than in the enormous territory of New Mexico, whose precise boundaries had not yet been defined by map makers. Roughly, it included the present states of New Mexico, Arizona and Colorado, and within this area lived a number of nations, among them the Comanche, Cheyenne, Navajo, Arapaho and several large branches of the Apache.

The federal government had become acutely conscious of Indian problems, most of them caused by friction between settlers and savages, and was aware of its responsibilities to the Indian. The attitude that had prevailed for more than two hundred years had not been discarded, but the social consciences of men in high places was beginning to stir. And the necessity of avoiding bloodshed was urgent.

The dispatch of army troops to a troubled area was not enough to insure the keeping of the peace, Washington had discovered. Therefore greater reliance was being placed on Indian Agents, men who represented the federal government in an area. Such positions had existed since the earliest days of the Republic, and the ideal agent was someone who knew and understood the Indians, and whom they, in turn, trusted. It was his duty not only to act as Washington's spokesman, but to bring the grievances of the tribes to government attention. A good agent was a mediator in disputes, a man who used diplomacy and fair dealing as well as troops to prevent uprisings.

Nowhere was the post of Indian agent more important in the 1850s than in the huge New Mexico Territory, for the simple reason that nowhere in the United States were there more undomesticated Indians. Therefore Kit Carson overnight became one of the most important and powerful federal officials in the West. He had made no personal move to get the place for himself, but his appointment could not have come as a surprise to him. An informal group of lobbyists was looking after New Mexican interests in Washington, and among them were men Kit numbered among his closest friends. St. Vrain and Ewing Young, two of the territory's most potent spokesmen, had publicly declared that they considered him perfectly qualified for the position. Several prominent newspapers, among them the Baltimore *American* and New York *Herald,* had predicted his appointment as early as July of 1853.

It is as unlikely, too, that a man as timidly conservative as Franklin Pierce would have sent Kit's name to the Senate had he expected the prospective agent to reject the post. Kit must have told someone he would accept, and that news must have been passed along to the President. His confirmation was passed quickly by the Senate, which acted on a voice vote and without debate. Those who were still annoyed because Kit's first lieutenancy in the Army had never been approved by the Senate must have felt that their hero had been vindicated.

Kit wrote two identical notes in which he expressed his great pride and pleasure, sending one to Secretary of War Jefferson Davis and the other to Secretary of the Interior Robert McClelland. And Young sent an enthusiastic letter to Senator Stephen A. Douglas of Illinois, who was preparing a bill reorganizing the western territories, in which he declared that all of New Mexico rejoiced. No man, he said, was better equipped to serve the United States as an Indian agent than Kit Carson.

Kit made his headquarters at his own ranch in the Rayado, but had less time now for his own affairs. He could still supervise the ranch operations, but was forced to leave most of the day-to-day details in the hands of a foreman. It was his duty to visit each of the Indian nations in the region, a task that could not be accomplished on a single journey, and he was on call at all times. Obviously he would spend many weeks of each year on the trail again, and the knowledge could not have been displeasing to him. Mrs.

Carson's reaction to the appointment is not known, but it must be presumed that by this time she had resigned herself to her husband's wanderlust and thirst for excitement.

Kit performed his first duty as agent before he was actually sworn in. He intended to go to Santa Fe for the ceremony immediately after Christmas, but shortly before he departed he learned that a war party of several hundred Apache, members of the so-called Jicarilla branch of the nation, had camped in the hills about twenty-five miles north of Taos.

Armed only with his authority and his personal weapons, he rode alone into the camp of the savages, an act that required great personal courage and that may have bordered on the reckless. The Apache were bitterly hostile to the settlers and, ever since the United States had gained formal possession of the area in the Mexican War, had stubbornly refused to sign a treaty with Washington. Therefore Kit was risking his life by going alone to meet the tribesmen.

He demonstrated that he knew what he was doing, however. Had he asked for a cavalry escort, the garrison commander at Taos would have given him troops, but the Apache would have considered him a coward. Realizing they respected courage, he went alone.

The chiefs of the tribe knew him, and admitted him to their camp. The scene that followed was one that was repeated many times in the next few years. Kit sat down with the chiefs, elders and senior warriors, and a pipe was passed from hand to hand. The Indians made long speeches, airing their many legitimate grievances. Then it was Kit's turn, and for a man who disliked rhetoric, he did exceptionally well. He told the Apache they had to accept the facts of life, and that foremost among these was that the United States had become the master of the area.

But the government he represented had no quarrel with the Apache, and wanted to live side by side with the tribesmen in peace. His people, Kit said, were fair and believed in justice. He did not elaborate on this point, and in view of the harsh, shortsighted policies that had been pursued in Washington for decades, it is difficult to understand how he could have persuaded even the most ignorant barbarians that they had been treated fairly.

He was in a position to paint the future in brighter colors. If the Apache felt they had been robbed or cheated, he directed them to come to him. Army troops would capture and punish wrongdoers and avenge the tribe. But the Apache must not take the law into their own hands. If they robbed travelers, if they stole the horses and cattle of ranch owners, if they attacked wagon trains or isolated homes, the soldiers would punish them.

It was difficult for Kit to impress on the Apache that he represented a nation whose manpower was, for all practical purposes, unlimited. If the Apache killed tens of soldiers, he said, hundreds would come to take their places. If they killed hundreds, thousands would come. But their own resources, he emphasized, were limited. When a warrior died in battle, there was no one to step forward; the Apache would have to wait until their boys grew to manhood and became warriors.

As proof of his own good will and that of the government he represented, Kit said, he would soon receive from Washington a bag filled with gold. He would give that gold to the Apache as a gift. Then they would have no need to steal, for they would be able to buy their horses and all else that they required. Each year, he continued, he would give them another, similar bag of gold.

The Apache may or may not have been impressed by what they heard. This was not the first time they had been told they would receive money, but payments had been infrequent, and when they had been given a bag, considerable quantities of gold had disappeared from it. There was a difference, however. The man who had made them the new promise was Kit Carson, who always kept his word.

So the chiefs made another series of long speeches. Carson, they said, was their friend. Therefore the government of Carson was their friend. They would live in peace with the settlers, and never again would raid, murder, pillage or burn.

Kit accepted their pledge, but was privately relieved to see that the band had only a few horses. Dismounted braves were relatively harmless. He realized, however, that a dangerous situation existed: there were hundreds of horses on the ranches in the Taos district, and the savages might not be able to resist temptation.

Taking no chances, he paused in Taos on his way to Santa Fe and warned the commandant of the garrison that it would be prudent to keep an eye on the band. Kit then went on to Santa Fe, and in his absence a bloody battle was fought, with both the Apache and a company of dragoons suffering heavy losses.

At this late date it is impossible to determine which side was at fault. The officers in charge of the cavalry were young, hot-blooded and, with good reason, nervous when a large body of Indians was loitering in the vicinity. The Indians, on the other hand, did not regard a promise as sacred, particularly when required to give their word under duress.

While the fight was raging, Kit—accompanied by Mrs. Carson, who was making one of her rare public appearances—was taking his oath of office as Indian agent for the territory of New Mexico. He returned to Taos to learn that the dragoons had suffered the worst defeat ever inflicted on them in a battle with Indians. Twenty soldiers had been killed, forty had been wounded and the survivors had been forced to retreat. A relief force, arriving at the scene of the action the following day, found the mutilated and scalped bodies of the dead, all of them stripped naked.

Kit's new career was off to an inauspicious start. The officers and men of the Taos garrison were outraged, the ranchers were alarmed and rumors were flying. It was said that the Utah Indians of the mountains to the north, who were allies of the Jicarilla Apache, were gathering in force to join their friends in all-out war on the settlers. It was also claimed that other tribes of the Apache nation were on the warpath.

Colonel J. L. Cook, commander of the Second Regiment of United States Dragoons, was making feverish plans to lead an expedition against the savages in person. A volunteer force of American and Mexican ranchers under the command of one of Kit's neighbors, James H. Quinn, was mobilizing to join the cavalry, and the air of crisis was so intense that a number of the sleepy, peace-loving Pueblo Indians of the neighborhood had offered their services and had been accepted.

Unfortunately, no one knew where the Apache had gone, as they had taken advantage of the time at their disposal after their victory and had covered their tracks.

Kit faced an uncomfortable dilemma. Colonel Cook asked him to act as the expedition's guide, believing him to be the only man capable of flushing out the enemy. In view of his lifelong experiences, he could not refuse such a request. On the other hand, he had just sworn on a Bible to uphold the peace, to hear the grievances of the savages and act as a mediator in their disputes with settlers. He solved the problem by agreeing to accompany the expedition in the dual capacity of guide and Indian agent.

Kit found the trail of the Apache, and led the column of cavalry and troops north into the mountains. Unseasonably warm January weather had caused flash floods, and great difficulty was encountered in crossing swollen rivers, but no lives were lost. For several days the trail remained faint, but suddenly it became fresh and strong, and the colonel gave the command to prepare for action. By this time Kit had apparently abandoned any desire he might have entertained to become a mediator. He was engaging in an enterprise that was as natural to him as roasting a buffalo steak over an open fire.

The column overtook the Apache after a ten-day march, and the savages were surprised by a hasty assault on their rear. But they enjoyed several advantages, and made good use of every one. They and their animals were fresh, while their pursuers were tired after the long, forced march. Of even greater benefit to the Indians was the site of the assault, a narrow, boulder-strewn canyon. The Apache fled, and only a few members of their rear guard were killed or wounded. The troops continued the chase, but neither the soldiers nor the civilian volunteers were a match for the agile warriors. Before nightfall the Apache made good their escape, and the regiment was forced to halt.

The pursuit began again the next morning, but the alerted tribesmen were no longer dallying, and Cook's men made long, forced marches on trails that crisscrossed the mountains. Even the veterans were exhausted, and their miseries were compounded when they ran short of food and had to be put on half-rations.

In this campaign Kit lived up to his public image. He had no intention of abandoning the chase. But men of half his years lacked his stamina, and after spending two more fruitless weeks in the mountains, Cook reluctantly decided to retire to the fort of Tierra Amarilla in northern New Mexico, almost due south of the San Juan Mountains that form a part of the Continental Divide and, ironically, only a short distance from the present-day Jicarilla Apache Reservation.

There the troops rested, and Cook, wanting relief for his weary men, sent a messenger to Santa Fe, where a major general was now in command, asking for help and instructions. A number of scouting parties remained in the field during this period and one of them brought in a captive Indian warrior.

Kit was summoned to interrogate the brave, and discovered to his horror that the Indian was a member of the Utah nation. Tribes had been known to go to war for lesser indignities inflicted on them. He immediately had the warrior's status changed to that of an honored guest, and sent several Mountain Men north into Utah country to ask the chiefs of the nation to join him for a conference. He had the foresight to send each of the chiefs a gift of food, so they responded to his summons.

Kit was in his best form at the day-long meeting that was held when the Utah chiefs gathered. He explained the error at length, and offered the Utah reparations, which they accepted. He distributed gifts with a lavish hand, giving them axes, cooking pots and bolts of cloth. Then he paraded the troops for their benefit so they could see he was motivated by a sense of justice rather than fear, as they would be certain to go to war if they thought the Army was afraid of them.

The tactics were successful, and Kit scored an impressive victory, winning not only a pledge from the Utah that they would remain at peace with the United States, but obtaining their promise to sign a treaty.

Two battalions arrived at the fort from Santa Fe, consisting of three hundred cavalrymen from the First Regiment of United States Dragoons and more than two hundred soldiers from the Third Regiment of United States Infantry. Cook was needed at Taos to keep the peace in the district, and the attack force was placed under the command of Major R. W. Carlton of the dragoons. Kit shed the coat of Indian agent and again donned that of chief guide.

The troops moved toward the north, and as a number of guides were being employed, Kit ordered them to fan out and search for signs of the Apache. Several were found, and Kit studied each of them; at last he came across one that he believed to be new, and took charge himself. He felt certain he was on the right trail now, and the whole command pushed forward.

The men marched steadily for five days, and on the morning of the sixth Kit told Carlton he was convinced the Apache had gone into their spring hunting camp. The column, he declared, would arrive there at two o'clock that afternoon.

The major found it impossible to accept such a flat statement. No man, he said, could accurately predict the precise time that more than five hundred troops would arrive at an unknown mountain destination on the basis of the examination of a few broken twigs and an occasional footprint. He offered the bet of a new hat that Kit was wrong, the wager was accepted and one of the most famous incidents in the saga of Kit Carson was in the making.

At two o'clock—according to letters written by some members of the expedition, the precise time was 2:02 P.M.—the cavalry vanguard approached the Apache camp.

Carlton immediately surrounded the bivouac, maintaining complete secrecy, and then asked Kit to order the Apache to surrender. Kit called out to them in their own tongue, telling them they were trapped. The warriors, about three hundred in number and equipped with inferior arms, made two futile attempts to break out of the circle, suffering heavy casualties.

Again Kit demanded that they surrender, and they realized they had no choice. Never had a band of warriors been subjected to such complete humiliation, and the success Kit and Carlton enjoyed that day became the talk of the whole country. Kit informed the defeated tribesmen that, as a punishment, they would receive no gold from the United States until the following year. Then the warriors were forced to scatter, and troops under Kit's supervision sent them off in many different directions.

Late in the year Kit received an expensive hat purchased in St. Louis. It bore the inscription, *"At Two O'Clock. Kit Carson, from R. W. Carlton, U. S. Army."*

The hat became a prized memento, and the additional

renown that Kit acquired as a result of the incident was enormous. It is possible that as many as a dozen officers and men heard the bet being made. But by the time the two battalions reached Taos on their way to Santa Fe, every member of the expedition was willing to swear that he had been an eyewitness. Soldiers wrote to their families in every part of the United States, the story crept into print and within the next two years reappeared at the climax of at least three novels.

Kit was now hailed everywhere as the successor to the mantle of Daniel Boone, and his place as a folk hero was secure for all time. His personal reaction was one of embarrassed silence.

The tracking of the Jicarilla Apache and their surrender had concrete, immediate results. Kit returned to the Rayado after spending four months on the trail, and did not find it necessary to leave his own ranch for the remainder of 1854. News of the Apache defeat spread through the mountains, and one by one the other tribes sent their leaders to confer with the Indian agent of the region.

Kit received each delegation on his own property. They pitched their tents on his land, he roasted venison and sides of beef for them, and then conferred at length with the chiefs and elders. The Indians knew they would suffer the fate of the once proud Apache if they broke the peace, and each nation swore it was now the friend of the United States. For the first time in the history of the area, there were no recorded Indian raids on wagon trains, travelers or the homes of individuals that year.

Washington recognized this unique situation by sending an assistant superintendent of Indian affairs to New Mexico early in 1855. A grand council was summoned, and the chiefs, elders and senior warriors of every nation gathered. The Indians made speeches, the assistant superintendent made speeches, Kit made speeches. The Indians enjoyed the rhetoric, but were more appreciative of the many hundreds of blankets, the axes, mirrors and cooking utensils that were freely distributed.

All was not sweetness and light at the council, however. The Indians were intelligent men who realized their rewards were paltry compensation for the steady encroachment of settlers on their shrinking domain. They wanted the right to lead the nomadic existence they had always known, and were not satisfied with token bags of gold or wagonloads of blankets and mirrors.

Men who had ears could hear the rumbles of discontent, but the assistant superintendent wasn't listening, and happily returned to Washington. The thunder became louder. Kit, who was increasingly alarmed, sympathized with the Indians and wrote a number of letters to officials in high places. But Jefferson Davis had more on his mind than the plight of the Indian, and others were also preoccupied.

Kit's pleas for a new, more enlightened Indian policy went unheeded. The country had not been prepared for a major change, and only those who actually lived on the frontier realized that the Indian was finding it next to impossible to survive. To everyone else he was a romantic, dream-world figure, a sly villain who robbed and murdered for sheer sport. Not until the great Indian massacres of the period from 1854 to 1867 had become history would the people of the United States feel a great sense of revulsion for what had been done and make a serious attempt to cope with a problem that had become a national catastrophe.

Men who had acquired fame as "Indian fighters"—and Kit stood foremost in their ranks—felt no hatred for the savages. When they fought, they did so because it was necessary to restore order. The principle Kit had observed since he had first arrived in the West almost three decades earlier, and which his father and brothers had followed in his childhood, was one of never starting an argument with Indians. Virtually all other frontiersmen believed as Kit did, and acted accordingly.

Certainly those who hailed Kit as an Indian slayer conveniently overlooked the fact that his first wife had been a full-blooded Indian and that his eldest child, whom he loved dearly, was a half-breed. He was impatient with the arrogant new type of settler arriving in the territory, and felt sufficiently aroused that he made a tour of the region around Taos early in 1855 to warn newcomers that they were asking for trouble when they deliberately insulted the warriors who, in ever increasing numbers, visited Santa Fe and Taos.

These settlers were as deaf as Washington officialdom. Braves who had been cursed in the streets visited the ranch in the Rayado to air their complaints, then vanished into the mountains again. New rumors began to spread. It was said that the Utah Indians were suffering from a plague of smallpox and were blaming settlers for the disease. It was said that two young Apache women had been violated by members of a covered wagon caravan traveling to California. An Apache elder who was ill went to Santa Fe to be treated by a physician; while on the road he was robbed and murdered by a desperado. The killer was captured some days later in one of the small towns between Santa Fe and Taos, but was carelessly guarded and escaped.

Kit braced for trouble, and it was not long in coming.

Late in the winter of 1855, probably in March, before the spring thaws came, representatives of every branch of the far-flung Apache family of tribes and of their cousins, the Utahs, held a secret meeting in the valley of the little Blue River, deep in the mountains of north central Colorado. There they pledged themselves to wage all-out war to the death against the interlopers who were depriving them of their pastures and hunting grounds.

No hint of the preparations was heard by civilized men in the towns and villages of the West. The attacks were launched simultaneously by a score of war parties soon after the spring thaws came, and the settlers were stunned.

Bands swooped down on wagon trains and waylaid small groups of travelers. Ranches were looted, then burned and whole families were killed. Raids were made on dozens of villages and small towns. Overnight the whole of the mountain country seemed to be on fire, and everywhere there were reports of fresh murders, kidnapings and robberies. Men were killed outright, women were tortured before being put to death and children vanished, some to be adopted by the tribes, others to become slaves.

New Mexico was too dazed to react quickly. Santa Fe and Taos were almost completely cut off from the outside world, for every road leading out of the two principal communities of the territory was blocked. At first no one realized that the uprising was so widespread, but several men managed to get through the passes from the forts and trading posts in the north, and at last it dawned on the leaders of the area that an undeclared war of unprecedented proportions was being waged.

Settlers from isolated districts left most of their belongings behind as they fled to Taos and Santa Fe. Those who stayed behind to guard their homes and herds tried to band together for mutual protection, but many were not strong enough to repel the marauders who attacked without warning. A state of near-anarchy prevailed, and the governor placed the entire territory under martial law.

As soon as it was learned which of the Indian nations were taking part in the war, common sense dictated that, even as defense preparations were being made, other tribes should be persuaded not to join in the conspiracy. This was a task for Kit, in his capacity as agent, and certainly no one was better equipped to perform it. It was impossible to spare a large body of troops to accompany him, and twenty dragoons were assigned as his escort. Maxwell and several other old friends decided to go into the mountains with him, too, and when he rode north from Taos early in April 1855, there were thirty-four in the party.

The number of skirmishes the group fought will never be known. Legend makers have had Kit fighting several battles each day, performing countless feats of valor and repeatedly escaping with his life after outwitting cunning foes. No man could have done all that was claimed on his behalf during the next three or four months.

The results of his journey speak for themselves, however. He first went into the land of the Cheyenne, and was successful in persuading that nation not to take part in the war. The Comanche also agreed to remain at peace, and he then went far north, where he met the Arapaho, who tentatively offered to take the side of the settlers, but later thought better of the idea.

Oddly, he did not travel into the land of the largest and most powerful Indian nation of the region, the Navajo. This tribe, which numbered more than ten thousand persons, owned vast flocks of sheep, large herds of cattle and cultivated many thousands of fertile acres. Had their chiefs decided to take part in the war, the odds against the settlers would have been considerably higher. No one has ever learned why the Navajo decided to remain neutral in the struggle. They believed themselves superior to the other nations, and it had long been their policy to stand aloof in the quarrels of their neighbors, but they shared the grievances of other tribes, so it is logical to assume that they must have been tempted.

The fact of the matter is that they stood aside. Perhaps their decision was made known to the New Mexico authorities, for Kit made no attempt to ride into western New Mexico and Arizona, their domain. It is one of history's ironies that the Navajo War of 1863–64 should have been an even bloodier conflagration.

Kit later referred to the return journey from the land of the Arapaho in northern Wyoming as "difficult." He had expected to reach Taos again in early July, but did not appear there until late in August, by which time many of his friends assumed that he had been killed.

The strain of the journey had been exhausting, but he spent only one night at his own home before setting out for Santa Fe to report that his mission had been successful As he rode south, he saw that order of a sort had been restored. Patrols of soldiers were constantly on the move up and down the roads, and every farm, every ranch was guarded by armed civilians. Yet, in spite of the precautions, war parties of Apache and Utah braves were still attacking settlements.

Many despairing citizens were ready to abandon their properties, but had nowhere to go and could not, under any circumstances, flee either to the eastern states or to California. There was a rumor, unsubstantiated but persistent, that Mexico intended to take advantage of the American difficulties by sending troops north in an attempt to regain possession of the vast area it had surrendered.

Washington was concerned, but no troops could be spared for duty in New Mexico, as a minor civil war was raging in Kansas, where the issue of slavery had erupted. Bands of pro-slavery and anti-slavery "ruffians" were terrorizing the countryside, and regiments were being ordered to proceed into the disputed area with all haste.

New Mexico was on her own.

13. THE APACHE WAR

When Kit Carson arrived at Santa Fe in mid-April 1855, he found the leaders of the territory frantically preparing for a war that everyone believed would last for a long time. Regular army troops numbered eight hundred and forty-three officers and men, and there was virtually no hope that the War Department could send out any reinforcements. Log forts were being built at strategic points throughout the area by the docile Pueblo Indians, and the owners of large ranches were contributing grain, meat and other supplies which were being stored in warehouses built for the purpose.

A militia had been authorized by decree, and recruits were flocking to the banner. Each man was promised wages of thirty dollars per month, the same rations that regular army troops were issued, a rifle and "those portions of uniforms which are available in the Quartermaster stores."

A total of four hundred and eighty men responded to the call, and were formed in six companies of eighty men each. The response would have been even greater had not each volunteer been required to furnish his own horse. The overwhelming majority of the militiamen were Mexicans. This fact, among others, may have deterred the Mexican Government from giving either direct or indirect aid to the Indians. The fears that a column was being organized in Mexico to take part in the war had been dispelled, for several scouts had been sent south of the border and had returned with the word that all was quiet there.

The over-all commander of the field forces was Colonel T. T. Fauntleroy of the First Dragoons, who decided he could safely use only half of the regulars in the territory as the nucleus for his assault force. The others would be needed for garrison duty at the many posts scattered throughout the region, and several companies would have to be kept in reserve for use as a counterforce in the event that the Indians unexpectedly launched a major attack in a weak salient.

The volunteer militiamen therefore made up the core of the New Mexican field units. Cerin St. Vrain, who now made his home in Taos, was given the command of the regiment, with the rank of lieutenant colonel, and officers of the regular establishment were assigned to train the recruits. Several cannon, including three howitzers, had been made available to the militia, and St. Vrain ambitiously decided to employ one of his companies as a field artillery battery. But he soon discovered that citizen soldiers could not be trained to handle large guns in a short period of time, so the cannon were returned to the regulars and the unit was converted into a rifle company.

When Kit arrived at headquarters, he was offered a variety of posts. Fauntleroy and St. Vrain wanted him to become second in command of the militia with the rank of major, but were willing to give him the company of scouts if he preferred. He refused to take a commission, believing he would compromise his permanent status as Indian agent. It was still his duty to settle the dispute by peaceful means, if possible, and to persuade the warring tribesmen to lay down their arms.

The immediate problem confronting Fauntleroy and St. Vrain was that of finding the Apache and Utah in the mountains, and as no one was better able to find and follow a trail, Kit was approached again. He consented to act as the principal guide for the expedition provided he remained a civilian. In order to emphasize his independence, he refused to accept wages.

Headquarters were moved to Taos, and when the hasty

training program was completed late in the spring, the field forces marched one hundred miles north to a log garrison in the mountains, Fort Massachusetts. Kit and the scouts immediately went out into the wilderness to search for signs of the enemy, but conducted a fruitless hunt for more than one month.

Fauntleroy's regulars were content to wait at the fort, where they ate three hot meals each day and slept indoors, but the ardor of the militiamen began to ebb. The volunteers had enlisted for a period of one hundred and twenty days, and St. Vrain had good reason to fear that many would return to their homes if the Indians were not located and defeated within that time.

Therefore the volunteers were moved out of Fort Massachusetts, and the guides redoubled their efforts. Early in July a trail was found, word was sent to Fauntleroy and the dragoons rode out into the field to join the militia. Kit took charge of the scout company, which was under the command of a lieutenant of regulars, and the guides moved at such a rapid pace that the main body found it difficult to keep up with them.

Eventually the Indians were found in the main valley of the South Platte, a few miles south of the present-day city of Denver. The guides unexpectedly came upon a force of two hundred and fifty to three hundred mounted Apache and Utah warriors. One of the leaders of the conspiracy, a half-breed Utah chief who was known to the settlers as Blanco, allegedly was a member of the war party.

The sudden confrontation startled both sides, and for a few moments neither budged. Then, while one of the scouts rode to the rear to notify Colonel Fauntleroy that the enemy had been found, Kit advanced several paces. Speaking in the tongue of the Apache, he requested a peace conference.

The warriors were in no mood for talk, for they apparently assumed that the scouts were alone. Unable to regard the small company of scouts as a serious threat, they replied with scornful shouts, and Kit was forced to retire.

Had the regiment used employed the tactics generally applied in Indian warfare, a sweeping victory might have been won, for the troops outnumbered the savages by a ratio of approximately eight to three. But the soldiers displayed a lack of common sense. Bugles blew loudly and repeatedly, alerting the Indians, who promptly turned and fled.

The dragoons advanced in some semblance of order, but the militia could not resist the temptation to charge at a full gallop. Volunteers enthusiastically waved swords over their heads, and many forgot to fire their rifles. Ranks were broken, and soon every man was on his own.

The ragged chase continued over broken ground for a distance of six to eight miles, and officers tried in vain to form their units. As a result of this amateur bungling by men who had forgotten their military training, the Apache and Utah escaped. The pursuit was halted at sundown, and the volunteers made unsuccessful efforts to persuade each other that they had won an important victory.

The warriors had retired into the mountains to the west, and that night a number of campfires could be seen on the heights. Kit and the other veterans paid no attention to these signs, however, knowing that the Indians were trying to mislead them.

The following morning the column started out again, with each man carrying several days' supply of food. The quartermaster wagons were left behind in order to attain greater mobility, and traveled at a slower pace. The regiments rode up into the mountains, and pushed forward for three days, sometimes following misleading trail signs that the braves had left in order to confuse them. Supplies began to run short, the men were placed on half-rations and the militia grumbled.

Had it been necessary to continue the hunt indefinitely,

the amateur soldiers might have rebelled, but Kit came across a trail that, he believed, was the right one. The scouts followed it, and on the fourth day of the chase the Indians were located high in a narrow pass near Gray's Peak, east of the Continental Divide.

Blanco and his warriors elected to make a stand, which was a mistake, for the Apache and Utah were badly outnumbered and their firepower was far inferior to that of their opponents. The battle site they had chosen gave them an advantage, however, and Fauntleroy was forced to direct repeated attacks on the position before the savages were finally dislodged. Both sides suffered heavily, the Indians losing approximately one hundred killed or seriously wounded. The survivors scattered, making further pursuit impossible.

Colonel Fauntleroy had won a battle that heartened his tired, hungry men. And the dispatches would make pleasant reading in the major towns of New Mexico. But the Indians were still strong enough to renew hostilities when and where they pleased, so the victory was inconclusive. A council of war was held—in which Kit may or may not have taken part—and it was decided to return to Fort Massachusetts. The men needed fresh provisions, and many of the volunteers spoke openly of going home. New shoes were needed for the horses, too, and many of the animals had to be replaced.

It was hoped that, while the expeditionary force took a deep breath, the enemy might consolidate. Perhaps civilized troops might have reacted to the challenge by banding together, but the warriors preferred to continue operating in four or five separate groups. Raids on frontier outposts continued while the soldiers were recuperating.

St. Vrain had more than his share of troubles, for almost half of his men decided to go home when their periods of enlistment ended. This made it necessary to recruit and train new companies of militia, and barracks were erected at

Taos while the active command remained at Fort Massachusetts. Winter came, and garrison life at the post in the mountains was uncomfortably cold, but reports of fresh raids on isolated ranches made it necessary to prepare for a campaign that could not be allowed to fail.

Kit may have spent a few weeks during the winter of 1855–56 at his own home in the Rayado, as he was not needed either at Fort Massachusetts or at the training camp at Taos. There is sketchy evidence indicating that he did go home, for he accompanied St. Vrain's new companies to the garrison late in February or early in March 1856. Obviously the situation was urgent, for St. Vrain did not wait for spring weather to move his men.

A study of maps pin-pointing the spots where raids had been made during the autumn and winter convinced Fauntleroy that the enemy war parties were operating out of two principal bases. One, used jointly by the Apache and Utah, seemed to be in the high mountains to the north, where the previous summer's fighting had taken place. The other, a stronghold utilized only by the Apache, appeared to be somewhere in southwestern Colorado. So he divided the regiments, sending St. Vrain's militia toward the west and assigning his own regulars the more difficult task of moving high into the Rockies, finding and conclusively defeating the combined forces of the two nations.

Kit accompanied the dragoons as chief guide, and the regulars started out from Fort Massachusetts in mid-March, one month before the spring thaws were expected. It was extremely difficult to march a body of four hundred cavalrymen north through snow-crusted mountain passes, but the strategy was sound. The Indians knew that civilized men always waited for warm weather before moving through the mountains in force, so there was a good chance they would be caught off guard. It might be possible, too, to attack them at their winter camp before they broke up into smaller war parties in the spring.

The admirers of Kit Carson claim that he was responsible for this plan of operations. It may well be that the idea was his, but others knew the habits of the savages, too, so he cannot be given complete credit. The ultimate responsibility was Fauntleroy's, and the Colonel undoubtedly realized that he was taking a grave risk by exposing his men and horses to the elements.

To Kit, however, belongs the full glory for leading the regiment to the winter camp of the Apache and Utah. The achievement, officially recorded in Colonel Fauntleroy's report to the War Department, was one of Kit's more spectacular feats and won him praise throughout the United States. He himself subsequently belittled the part he had played in the campaign, however, saying that any experienced mountaineer could find trail marks in snow. He declared, too, that he was aided by Comanche friends whom he met in the mountains, and insisted that he deserved no credit.

The extent of his accomplishment indicates that he was being unduly modest. He led the column up the Arkansas River, then made his way north through some of the most rugged terrain to be found anywhere in the United States. Eventually he came to a little valley, only a short distance east of the Continental Divide, where towering mountains cut off sharp winds and permitted the grass to remain green during the winter months. There, at the place where the city of Boulder, Colorado would be founded two years later, was the main winter camp of the Apache and Utah.

As many as three thousand members of both nations were living there in lodges that had been constructed the preceding autumn, this number including women and children, of course. Colonel Fauntleroy later estimated that seven hundred to eight hundred warriors took the field against him.

The dragoons swept down on the village out of the mountains, taking the Indians completely by surprise. The savages fled, but the braves rallied in time to counterattack twice, and the battle that ensued lasted the better part of three hours. The ground underfoot was dry, for a hot, early spring sun had melted the snow at the approaches to the valley, and the water had run off. Therefore the terrain was perfect for cavalry maneuvers, and the dragoons gave a good account of themselves.

The troops were outnumbered by a ratio of approximately two to one, but enjoyed many advantages. They were disciplined regular army men who could trot, canter or gallop in formation. Their firepower was infinitely superior to that of their foes, and they had relatively unlimited quantities of ammunition and powder. The warriors fought valiantly, but were no match for their attackers, and at last the survivors were compelled to surrender.

Fauntleroy obtained vast quantities of the Indians' stores, including dried meat, parched corn and other food supplies. All of the personal belongings of the Indians, which had been left in the lodges, also fell into his hands. Many of the vanquished warriors fled in all directions, and the victory was the most complete ever won against Indians in the West.

The deeds of valor supposedly performed by Kit on the field of battle that day are legion. His marksmanship was even better than usual, he rode tirelessly up and down the field, and whenever he saw a platoon or company of dragoons faltering, he rallied the men, then led them in a fresh assault.

Whether he actually took part in the fighting is questionable. He was a civilian, not a soldier, and was supremely conscious of his position as Indian agent. Perhaps he performed many dazzling deeds, as his enthusiastic friends later claimed, but no mention of his activities during the fight were mentioned in the official dispatch to the War Department.

He did do his country a great service, however, learning from several prisoners that another winter camp of Utah was located about forty miles to the south and that Blanco was living there.

Kit questioned the prisoners closely, then told the colonel what he had found out.

Fauntleroy saw an opportunity to deal the savages a blow that would make it impossible for them to continue the war. Although the day was already far advanced, he ordered the tired troops to remount, and two hours before sundown the column was making its way south again. A halt was called in the early evening, then was resumed when the stars and moon appeared and, with Kit guiding them, the dragoons made their way along the rim of the Continental Divide.

The unit halted at midnight for a few hours of rest; the march started again at daybreak. It was the colonel's hope that he could surprise Blanco before the Utah chief learned what had happened to his own people and their allies in the previous day's battle.

Only Kit knew where he was going, and he was taking the word of the captured warriors, so the commander and his staff realized they might be engaged on the wildest of goose chases. The area was one that Kit knew well, so he encountered no real difficulty on the trail, and the dragoons were willing to follow him anywhere. He maintained a rapid pace, and by late afternoon had gone the better part of forty miles. The regiment showed remarkable stamina in covering so much ground in such a short space of time.

Some of the defeated veterans had already carried the news to Blanco, for the Utah chief appeared suddenly on the trail. He called out, in Spanish, that he wanted to confer. Kit replied in the Utah dialect, demanding that Blanco come forward accompanied by no more than three of his warriors. The Indian obeyed, and Kit rode forward with the colonel.

Blanco then declared that he and his people were tired of the war and wanted peace. Fauntleroy told him he could have permanent peace if his braves would surrender their arms at once and return to their own land.

The chief protested, saying that if his warriors were deprived of their arms, they would be attacked by the Cheyenne and Arapaho, his people's traditional enemies.

The logic of his argument made sense to Kit, who entered the negotiations in his capacity as Indian agent. He proposed that the Utah be allowed to keep their weapons but surrender the better part of their ammunition and powder. They would have to promise to sign a treaty with the United States and, effective immediately, terminate their alliance with the Apache.

Blanco, who had no real choice, accepted the terms. Two of his sons and a nephew of a lesser chief agreed to accompany the regiment to New Mexico as hostages. Three hundred and fifty Utah warriors gave up large quantities of bullets and gunpowder, and the dragoons remained nearby to make certain they kept their word and dispersed. Fauntleroy's subsequent report to the War Department indicates there were no other incidents of note, and that Blanco repeated his vow of peace and friendship before the braves started north.

The victorious regiment traveled south to Fort Massachusetts, and soon after reaching the garrison learned that St. Vrain's volunteers had fought several successful skirmishes with the Apache. Only one of these engagements had been sufficiently large to be worth calling a battle, for the roaming bands of warriors had lost much of their strength and had fled whenever they had encountered the superior force of the militia. In the one battle that had taken place, the braves had set fire to a field choked with the previous year's high dry grass, but St. Vrain had set the example by galloping forward, and his men, close on his heels, had killed a large number of the marauders.

For all practical purposes, the Apache War was at an end. The militia companies were dismissed and marched off to their homes, and the regulars returned to their permanent bases. But Colonel Fauntleroy intended to take no chances and, after conferring with Kit, sent a number of platoons into the mountains on permanent patrol duty. If they should discover that the Indians were gathering again, the war would be resumed.

Kit's work was not yet finished, for he was afraid that the Cheyenne and Arapaho would take advantage of the weakened state of the Utah to attack them. Therefore he returned to the mountains, sought the chiefs of both nations and persuaded them that it was in their best interests not to go on the warpath. The leaders of both tribes listened to him, and finally agreed not to raid the Utah. No doubt the knowledge that troops would be sent to their own villages if they failed to keep the peace was a strong influence in convincing them that Kit was right.

Finally, late in the summer of 1856, Kit returned to his ranch in the Rayado. With the exception of a brief visit the preceding winter, he had spent more than a year in the mountains, and he was very tired. His forty-seventh birthday was approaching, and when he paused for an overnight rest at the home of Ewing Young en route to his own house, he told his old friend that he was cured of his wanderlust.

His homecoming was quiet, and he neither wanted nor expected praise for what he had done. But the news of the victory over the Utah and Apache fascinated the rest of the country. Sectional strife was growing more intense throughout the United States, and with the chances of a civil war becoming more alarmingly real every day, people were glad to turn for relief to the affairs of the remote never-never land of the frontier. Citizens of New York and Richmond, Boston and Atlanta, Chicago and Cincinnati and Nashville, most of whom had never seen an Indian, eagerly sought every detail.

Few facts were forthcoming, so the inventive editors of the more popular newspapers and magazines cheerfully filled in the gaps. It was enough that there had been an Indian war, that Kit Carson had played a leading role in it and that the Apache and Utah had been defeated. Exaggerated accounts of Kit's accomplishments appeared in numerous publications, and it was irrelevant that most were written by men who had never ridden a horse, climbed a mountain or caught a glimpse of an Indian. The imaginary exploits of Kit were the fairy tales that helped people forget the ominous war clouds gathering overhead.

It is significant that Kit took no active part in the Presidential election of 1856, for his old friend, John C. Fremont, was running against James Buchanan for the nation's highest office. New Mexico was far from the political arena, it is true, but a statement from the popular folk hero might have won Fremont some votes. No such statement was issued, nor does Fremont appear to have solicited Kit's help. Had Kit voted, he undoubtedly would have cast his ballot for his friend, but there were no polls in Taos.

In the years immediately following the Civil War, Kit's supporters, who were sensitive to a possible charge that he had shown a lack of loyalty to one who had been his mentor and had done more than anyone else to bring him to the attention of the whole country, claimed that he had written a long, warm letter to Fremont after Buchanan's election on November 4. It may be that Kit did write such a letter, but it does not appear in Fremont's correspondence. Other friends of Kit declared that he could not have written to Fremont or anyone else because, they said, he was illiterate.

This statement was responsible for a widespread belief that Kit could not write. A number of documents that he wrote in his own hand during the Civil War still exist, however, so the confusion was compounded by Carsonites who glibly announced that he learned the fine art of writing during the war.

The contradictory claims aside, the simple facts of the

matter are that Kit, who showed no interest in politics, did not actively support the candidacy of Fremont, who expected no such support.

Kit's commission as Indian agent expired at the end of Franklin Pierce's term of office in the White House, but he was reappointed to his post by President Buchanan, and his service was uninterrupted. He remained in the position throughout Buchanan's presidency, but he had told Ewing Young the truth when he had confided that his traveling days were ended.

The Indians came to him now, and several new buildings were erected on his ranch in the Rayado to accommodate visiting chiefs and elders. The Apache, Comanche, Utah, Cheyenne and Kiowa were under his jurisdiction, and peace on the frontier having been firmly established, brought their disputes to him for settlement. He dealt with them fairly, and it was a tribute to him that the chiefs came to his house, for they were reluctant to visit the homes of settlers.

The hunting grounds of the Indian nations were gradually being reduced, and the problem of their survival was becoming increasingly acute. Kit, like other Indian agents, believed that the dilemma could be solved by giving the tribes large tracts of farmland, teaching them to cultivate it and helping them to become self-sufficient. It may be that Kit was actually the author of the famous statement attributed to him: "Only hungry Indians go on the warpath." But there is no record of that declaration anywhere, so it must be assigned to the realm of myth.

In any event, Kit discharged his duties efficiently during the years of the Buchanan administration. He had won the trust of the Indian nations of New Mexico, and there were no major disputes or battles that marred the peace. It is ironic that these four years, when both the North and the South were preparing for armed conflict, were the most serene that Kit had ever known.

He tended to the affairs of his ranch, which continued to prosper.

Scores of friends attended the wedding of his eldest daughter, who married a young man she had met in St. Louis and went with him to live in California. This social event was probably the largest ever held at the house in the Rayado, and sides of beef were roasted in an open pit for the guests. The chiefs of every tribe in the district attended the affair, but it is not known whether they, like the other guests, were served hard liquor. Kit had long been opposed to the selling or giving of intoxicating alcoholic beverages to the Indians.

A few close friends celebrated Kit's fiftieth birthday at the ranch in 1859, among them Maxwell, St. Vrain and Young. The Cheyenne learned of the party, and appeared on the appointed day with a gift, the freshly killed carcass of a large fat deer. Kit was delighted, of course, and the venison was roasted in the open pit near the house, even though the weather was cold. No one noted for posterity what became of the meal that Mrs. Carson had planned.

Certainly Kit was content to spend the rest of his days living quietly on his property, tending to his own affairs and serving as the Indian agent for the territory. But neither he nor any other American was allowed to rest on his laurels. On December 20, 1860, South Carolina seceded from the Union, six weeks after the election of Abraham Lincoln as President. In January 1861, an unarmed federal ship was fired on in Charleston Harbor, and in the days that followed, one southern state after another followed the example of South Carolina. In February the Confederate States of America were formed, in March Lincoln was inaugurated and the die was cast.

The Civil War began in April, and men on both sides rushed to the colors. In far-off Taos, Kit Carson stirred, breaking the only prolonged period of peace he had ever known—or would know—in his life.

14. THE SOLDIER

The problems New Mexico faced at the outbreak of the War Between the States were unique, and neither the Union nor the Confederacy was able to count on her support. In recent years the territory had been greatly reduced in size for the sake of administrative and other conveniences, but was still huge, consisting of areas that later became the states of New Mexico and Arizona. This sprawling region of deserts, mountains and river valleys stood as a buffer between Confederate Texas and Unionist California.

Slavery, as such, was virtually non-existent in New Mexico, in part because the territory was still in an early stage of both agricultural and industrial development. The demand for labor on farms and ranches, in factories and mines was light. And there were large numbers of Mexican Indians already there, eager to work for small wages. Therefore only a handful of the wealthiest families owned slaves.

The overwhelming issue of states' rights versus those of the federal government did not arise, because New Mexico was not a state. The territory was slow in maturing politically, and her citizens were pragmatists who worried about their real, day-to-day affairs. No one was concerned about what approach to take on some far-distant day when New Mexico became one or more states.

Emotionally, however, the people were being pulled in both directions at the beginning of the war, and in some respects their situation was similar to that of citizens of border states. Like many Marylanders, Kentuckians and Tennesseans, New Mexicans literally were unable to decide which way to turn. But the confusion of the western ranchers and townsmen was caused by ignorance. Elsewhore in the country men had been debating living, vital issues for years. Those issues were virtually meaningless in New Mexico.

The choice was simple. Many favored the cause of the Confederacy because they sympathized with their neighbors in nearby Texas. Others, in the main immigrants from northern states, chose the Union.

Kit Carson remained loyal to the Union because, as he explained in later years to General William T. Sherman, he could not imagine himself becoming a citizen of any nation other than the United States of America. He was one of the first New Mexicans to offer his services to the Union, volunteering to perform any useful task.

His attitude and that of several others in Taos and Santa Fe swung New Mexico into the northern column, and newspapers in New York, Washington and Chicago boasted—prematurely—that the territory was safely in the Union camp. Confederate sympathizers found it prudent to keep quiet, and several wealthy Santa Fe residents who had migrated to New Mexico from southern states sent an urgent plea to Texas for help.

It was obvious to the military leaders of both sides that the territory would fall into the hands of the side that first established military control. No one was better aware of the situation than the regular army commandant, Colonel E. R. S. Canby, who issued a call for militiamen soon after he received official word that hostilities had started. Hundreds responded, among them Kit Carson.

A territorial commission as lieutenant colonel of the First New Mexican Volunteer Infantry was granted to Kit in May 1861, and he received his federal commission on July 25. The regiment had already gone into training at a camp south of Taos, and Kit was slated to become the unit's executive officer, with a regular to take over as commander.

Pending the appointment of a superior, however, he was the acting head of the regiment.

Many of his men were the sons of friends and neighbors, and he had known scores of them since they had been children. Certainly every soldier in the regiment knew him, at least by reputation, and men from every part of the territory eagerly joined the unit. Members of a rifle company, acting without Kit's knowledge, began to circulate a petition requesting the War Department to make him the permanent commander of the First Volunteer Infantry.

Every enlisted man signed, then the officers added their names. Someone told Kit about the petition, and he made an attempt to recall it, but was too late, for it had already been forwarded to Canby. Kit was embarrassed, and calling all of the officers to a meeting, gave them what one later described as "a nasty tongue lashing."

Colonel Canby heartily approved of the suggestion, and forwarded it to Washington with his endorsement. Secretary of War Simon Cameron of Pennsylvania had long enjoyed reading about the exploits of Mountain Men, and had been a Kit Carson admirer for years. He initialed the final authorization himself, and on September 20, 1861, Kit was promoted to the rank of full colonel.

New Mexico seemed to be in no danger from the Confederates. Meanwhile various Indian tribes in the new Colorado Territory were taking advantage of Washington's preoccupation with more important matters; roaming bands of Apache and Comanche, Cheyenne and Utah soon reverted to their old violent habits. It was obvious that the best of all possible cures for the situation was to send Kit into the area, so the First New Mexican Volunteer Infantry marched north into the mountains that Kit had known for thirty-five years.

His presence in a blue uniform at the head of a column of seven hundred men gave the Indians good cause to reconsider. The Utah remembered their sacred treaty with the United States, and went home. The Apache and Comanche scattered, and the Cheyenne hurriedly sent delegations to their old friend with protestations of their friendship. The brief campaign became a peaceful, triumphal training march for the regiment.

During its absence, however, the tide of civil war swept over New Mexico. A strong Confederate force of two brigades, augmented by two battalions of cavalry and three artillery batteries, marched north from Texas through the Rio Grande Valley. The Confederate commander, Brigadier General H. H. Sibley, relied on speed and surprise, and his tactics were so successful that he occupied Santa Fe without firing a shot.

The First Volunteer Infantry returned to Taos to find the better part of the territory in enemy hands. Colonel Canby, who was soon to be promoted to the rank of brigadier general, had retired in good order and his forces were intact. He summoned Kit to a conference of regimental commanders, and it was decided that the Confederates had to be driven out of New Mexico regardless of the cost.

The two armies spent the better part of the winter of 1861–62 skirmishing, for the troops on both sides were untried, and no colonel wanted his men to take part in battle before they were ready. Actions during this period were confined to the company and platoon level, and Kit rotated his units in order to give as many men as possible the experience of undergoing enemy fire.

Only the Indians benefited during these months. The Apache began raiding ranches and villages again. And farther to the west, the mighty Navajo nation began to stir. The residents of present-day Arizona and western New Mexico fled from their homes when Navajo marauders went on the warpath, and people throughout the western lands became alarmed. The Navajo, with a population of more than ten thousand, were the wealthiest, strongest and most stable of all the Indian tribes of the mountains. They lived in their own towns, had many thousands of acres under cultivation and owned large herds of cattle and sheep.

Settlers had encroached on their domain, but they had seen punitive expeditions sent out against other tribes, and had quietly accepted injustice. Now, however, with soldiers in blue and soldiers in gray pitted against each other, they believed their time had come. They struck expertly and repeatedly. Virtually every ranch, every farm, every general store that had been established in what is now northwestern New Mexico and northeastern Arizona was systematically looted and burned.

Frontiersmen protested in vain, and could do nothing to protect their wives, children and homes. The sons of settlers were in uniform, and as few wagon trains of armaments had yet arrived from the munitions factories in the great cities of the East, even weapons were scarce. Families that escaped with their lives were fortunate.

The Navajo, emboldened by their success, sent out still more raiding parties. Soon southern Nevada and large portions of Colorado were threatened. It was rumored that Navajo warriors would occupy Las Vegas, and householders in Taos shuddered.

But the Union defenders of the area had no troops to spare, and were in a desperate situation. The Confederates had been reinforced by an augmented regiment, and Canby sent a plea to Colorado for help. A volunteer regiment was already in the process of formation there, but before it could be sent south to join him, New Mexico's first major engagement took place on February 21, 1862. Both sides claimed a victory, but the Battle of Valverde was inconclusive, for the Union forces held strongly fortified positions and could not be dislodged in spite of repeated Confederate attacks. The commanders of both armies knew it would be necessary to meet again.

The Confederates tried to strike another blow as soon as

possible, but Canby evaded them, desperately stalling for time until the Colorado regiment joined him and he received additional arms from the East. For approximately one month his army played a game of grim hide-and-seek with its enemies, and both doubled back and forth through mountain passes.

Valverde marked Kit Carson's baptism of fire as the commanding officer of a major military unit. Although no one doubted his personal valor, of course, there were many—including friends in Taos and critics in the major cities of the North—who considered him unsuited for a post of such responsibility. In his younger days he had led loosely organized bodies of Mountain Men in Indian fights, but neither in the Mexican War nor in his later service with the Army had he performed duties other than those of a guide and courier. So there was good reason to question whether he was capable of co-ordinating the efforts of a body of seven hundred men.

Kit demonstrated at Valverde that he was a natural-born soldier who had learned a great deal through the years and had forgotten nothing. His understanding of battle tactics was instinctive, and although he seemed less certain of strategic concepts at this time, he had few opportunities to plan or operate on a large scale.

Canby relied on a simple battle order. A regiment of regulars held the center of his line, Kit's First Volunteer Infantry was stationed on the right flank and the left, the weakest part of his line, was held by several unaffiliated battalions and companies of volunteers, supported by all of the artillery Canby had been able to muster. The Union forces, although outnumbered, had selected the ground, and the terrain favored them. The units entrenched themselves behind boulders at the upper edge of a rising plateau, and breastworks of earth and stones formed connecting links between boulders to make a solid defense line. Equally important, the field that stretched out before them was very rough and therefore unsuited for the superior Rebel cavalry.

Sibley nevertheless opened the battle with a cavalry charge against the enemy right flank, led by two squadrons of elite Texas Rangers. Kit rode up and down the line, exposing himself to Confederate fire as he exhorted his men to hold firm. The First Volunteer Infantry held, and the attack was repulsed.

A probe then was directed against the Union left flank, but the artillery, consisting in the main of light howitzers, forced the horsemen to retreat. Had Canby been stronger, this would have been the appropriate moment to launch a counterattack. He sent for his senior commanders, and in the council of war that followed, Kit was one of the officers who recommended caution. It was better, in Kit's opinion, to hold a prepared line than venture into the open.

Canby continued to stand, and the Confederates were forced to try another, even more vigorous assault. Sibley tried to soften the enemy with artillery fire, but his gunners were inexperienced and the bombardment did little or no damage. Then his entire army advanced, cavalry in the van, followed by infantry. The Union forces did not budge.

Kit's regiment was opposed by a full brigade, so he was outnumbered almost two to one, odds familiar to him since his days as an Indian fighter. But the Rebels, most of them Texans, were superb soldiers, not undisciplined savage warriors. The First Volunteer Infantry held the line grimly, pouring a steady stream of fire at the enemy. The second in command of the regiment, a Lieutenant Colonel Pfeiffer, had a horse shot from beneath him, but Kit, although exposed throughout virtually all of the charge, escaped unscathed.

He calmly directed the return fire, and even though the Rebels threatened to overrun his position at one point, he remained cool. Judging the situation less critical than it appeared, he deliberately refrained from committing two companies he was holding in reserve. After about one hour of bitter fighting, the attack was repulsed.

The center also held firm, but the left wing buckled, and the entire Union line was threatened. Canby restored order there by sending his cavalry into the sector and redoubling his artillery fire. His gunners were no better than the Confederates, but their fire frightened the Rebel horses, and when Sibley's cavalry withdrew, his infantry pulled back, too.

Both sides took a breathing spell, and there was an unofficial truce while the dead and wounded were taken to the rear. Then Sibley launched his third and most determined assault, knowing that if he failed his day's efforts would have been in vain. He advanced in strength along the entire front, and a squadron of Rangers almost succeeded in penetrating the First Volunteer Infantry's line.

Kit immediately galloped to the scene, accompanied by the members of his small personal staff, several other officers and his scouts, the regiment's only mounted unit. Hand-to-hand combat was a type of fighting he knew and understood, and he threw himself into the battle with the reckless courage for which he was renowned. His marksmanship was still unerring, and two pistol shots brought down two Rebel horsemen. Then he flailed at the foe with his saber, the others rallied to his side and the Confederates were compelled to withdraw.

Kit realized that this was the right moment to send his reserves into action, and he personally led his two uncommitted companies into the open. He knew he still faced a larger force, so he contented himself with a quick, powerful thrust that punched holes in the enemy's line, then pulled both units back to safety behind the breastworks.

Sibley's offensive power was broken, and the Confederates broke off the engagement at sundown.

After Valverde, no criticism of Kit's appointment to the rank of colonel was heard anywhere. He had earned his spurs as a regimental commander, and the War Department rightly regarded his unit as one of the most efficient and reliable in the entire Southwest.

In the other, more important theaters of operations, the Confederates held several distinct advantages. The majority of West Point graduates were southerners, so the Confederate officer corps was made up of professionals who were, in the main, superior to their opposite numbers in the Union ranks. And, man for man, the Rebels, who were fighting for a cause in which they believed passionately, were better soldiers.

The situation in the Southwest was different. There a hard core of West Pointers directed the Union army. Other officers were neither politicians nor businessmen without military experience, but war-hardened frontiersmen. Many of the senior commanders were, like Kit, former Mountain Men, and others were Mexican War veterans who had subsequently settled in New Mexico. The soldiers were hardbitten young men from lonely ranches and farms. Almost without exception they knew how to handle firearms, march for day after day through the mountains without tiring and live under field conditions that softer, city-bred troops found intolerable. Certainly the New Mexican Union troops were as strong, able and dedicated as their fiery opponents from Texas. The two forces were evenly matched.

In mid-March Canby was reinforced by the strong regiment of Colorado volunteers, and several companies of regulars who had been on Indian duty also joined him. There were complaints from settlers, who now had literally no one to defend them from marauding tribesmen, but Canby correctly reasoned that with his limited strength he could fight only one enemy at a time. It was his strategy to defeat the Confederates, drive them out of New Mexico and then turn his full attention to the Indians.

Everything depended on his ability to smash General Sibley's army. Sibley, as the defender, could not sit quietly in Santa Fe while a strong Union force threatened him, so another major encounter was inevitable.

The so-called Battle of Apache Canyon was fought on March 28 and 29, but unlike Valverde, was not a classic military engagement in which two opposing armies faced each other on a single field. Canby, strengthened by the arrival of small arms and ammunition as well as by reinforcements, elected to fight in the Indian style with which the men of the territory were familiar.

Senior commanders, Kit among them, planned the operation with great care. Units of company size were assigned specific Confederate units as targets, and were ordered to strike swiftly, withdraw and then attack again. This process was to be repeated until the Rebels either withdrew or fled. If they retreated from New Mexico, they were to be harassed, if possible, until they crossed the Texas border. If they advanced, the Union soldiers were to disengage, regroup and attack again. Pitched battles were to be avoided, as were clashes with overwhelmingly superior enemy forces. If a company encountered a large Confederate unit, the vanguard and rear guard were legitimate targets, and hit-and-run raids on flanks were permissible.

Company commanders were given great freedom of movement, and were told to use common sense at all times. They were also directed to keep in touch with battalion headquarters, and the majors commanding battalions were ordered to maintain close liaison with regimental leaders. Thus, if one or another unit found itself in great trouble, others could be summoned to its help.

Kit was in his element in planning of this sort, and for all practical purposes became Canby's deputy. The two men realized that the success of the venture depended on their ability to contain the fighting within a limited arena. If the Union companies scattered over too broad a region, their strength would be dissipated. Therefore it was essential to maintain inter-unit communications, and the most competent horsemen were chosen to perform this vital task.

Sibley's troops, marching north through the mountains, literally did not know what hit them. Confederate companies were subjected to rifle fire, and when platoons were sent in pursuit of the foe, snipers isolated these small units. By the time that Sibley himself realized what was happening, it was too late for him to pull his regiments together and make a determined, united stand.

He tried desperately to rally his disorganized forces, but the Union commanders maintained their pressure thoughout the night of March 28–29 after attacking all of the previous day, and the Rebel units were shattered. They withdrew from New Mexico as they had come, through the Rio Grande Valley. They had suffered heavy losses and could have been destroyed had it been possible for the Union troops to adhere to the original battle plan. But soldiers who had fought for more than twenty-four hours without pause were too tired to pursue their vanquished foes, and Sibley was able to retire into Texas.

Throughout the battle Kit performed executive duties befitting his rank, and at no time took part in personal combat. Messengers brought him reports of progress in various sectors, and he spent virtually all of his time studying maps, conferring with subordinates and shuffling units, relieving a company in one place, sending platoons of victors into battle in another.

He maintained constant liaison with Canby throughout the battle, and was cited in the commander in chief's report to the War Department. He proved, both to his own satisfaction and that of his superior, that he was capable of functioning on the level expected of a full colonel. He was close-mouthed, as always, about his personal reactions, and if he was disappointed because he had not fired a pistol or lunged with a saber, he kept his thoughts to himself.

Kit's growth in stature during the eight months he had been commander of the First New Mexican Volunteer In-

fantry was remarkable. He was no longer just a picturesque
Mountain Man with unique personal qualities, but a proven
military leader whose ability could not be questioned. New
Mexicans knew him and were not surprised, for they had
long recognized his talent. Elsewhere his feats long went
unrecognized, for by the time the full story of what was
considered a minor campaign was made known in both the
Union and the Confederacy, the Battle of Shiloh—fought
only ten days after Apache Canyon—crowded all other
news out of the headlines.

It is ironic that Kit never received the credit due him for
his activities during the New Mexico–Texas campaign.
Other, more justly renowned military men were making
news, and when Kit's fellow citizens east of the Rocky
Mountains thought of him, they inevitably coupled his
name with Indians.

The Battle of Apache Canyon was the last major engagement he fought against the Confederates during the Civil
War, and his work thereafter continued to contribute to the
legends of the super-guide and foe of the Red Man. Few
people stopped to think that, from the early spring of
1862 until the conclusion of the Civil War in 1865 he repeatedly proved himself an officer worthy of high command.

New Mexico became a Union possession again after General Sibley's retreat, and was destined to remain in northern
hands. Had the Confederacy been able to spare troops for a
major campaign there, the story might well have been different, but the South was plagued by an ever worsening
manpower shortage, and regiments of Texans were urgently
needed elsewhere to oppose the huge armies being raised
in the industrial North.

Canby could not afford to take chances, however, and
remained prepared to face a new column raised by General
Sibley. From time to time rumors crossed the border to the
effect that brigades were being mustered for a new invasion, and these reports kept one third to one half of the

Union troops in New Mexico in a constant state of alert.

Nevertheless it was possible, after the Rebel retreat, to devote attention to the Indian problem, and the task of paci-
fication was assigned to Kit and his regiment. It was hoped
that a campaign against the powerful Navajo could be
avoided, and Kit decided to quiet the other tribes first.
It was his theory that, if he succeeded, the intelligent Navajo would retire to their own citadel of mountains and
fertile valleys. Being a realist, he preferred not to become
embroiled with such a large and powerful nation.

His first step was to halt raids in northern New Mexico
and Colorado, and the mere appearance of his regiment in
the mountains convinced the Apache, Cheyenne and Arapaho that he meant business. The savages knew Kit could be
the most dangerous of their foes, for he understood them
thoroughly and had seven hundred men to do his bidding.
He marched as far north as the new town of Denver, a
rapidly growing, four-year-old community on the South
Platte River.

The atmosphere was reminiscent of San Francisco when
Kit had paid his last visit to California, for gold had been
discovered in Cherry Creek, where the first Denver settlers
had built their huts in 1858. Most of the inhabitants were
adventurers, but a few merchants and other men of business provided a stable element.

When Kit arrived there at the head of his regiment, the
Rocky Mountain News was a flourishing, three-year-old
newspaper, telegraph lines to the East had been opened,
there were two theaters in the town and several self-styled
"hotels." Most of the community's females reminded Kit
of the women he had seen in his youth in Santa Fe and,
later, in San Francisco. He made a vain attempt to declare
the bordellos out of bounds for his troops.

Denver, with a population of two to three thousand,
greeted Kit enthusiastically and tried, on a small scale, to
match the welcome San Francisco had given him. Here was

a man who epitomized the West, and his presence in the
town aroused the excitable citizens. Men lined the streets
and fired pistols in the air to celebrate his arrival, the El
Dorado Hotel offered free drinks to the officers of the regiment and the local bank declared a holiday.

Kit received more dinner invitations than any one in-
dividual could accept, and protested in vain that he was a
colonel on active military duty in time of war. His hosts
cheerfully replied that even colonels had to eat.

He established his camp on the outskirts of the town, and
bands of Arapaho warriors loitering in the vicinity soon disappeared. This "victory" made Kit even more popular,
but his relations with some of the citizens took a turn for
the worse when his quartermaster tried to buy supplies.
Denver was suffering from boom-town inflation, and when
Kit learned the prices being charged for beef and flour, he
announced he would prefer to go off into the mountains and
shoot game for his troops. Eventually the quartermaster was
able to purchase provisions at reasonable prices.

A new regiment of volunteer infantry was in the process
of formation, and relations between Kit and its commander,
Colonel J. M. Chivington, a former clergyman, were cool
from the outset. Kit took an instant dislike to Chivington
and, being a blunt man, made no secret of his feelings.
Chivington, a newcomer to Colorado, belonged to the school
that advocated extermination as the solution of the Indian
problem, and Kit openly expressed his contempt for anyone
so shortsighted and lacking in humanity.

The two men were not to meet again for several years.
When they did, Kit—by that time a brigadier general—took
pains to snub Chivington, who was responsible for the
Sandy Creek Massacre of Cheyenne and Arapaho men,
women and children in the spring of 1864. That attack,
made without cause, took the lives of more than three hundred Indians and set off a bitter war that lasted for more
than three years.

Kit, condemning Chivington and his men for the raid, used one of the strongest phrases ever attributed to them when he called them "dogs and cowards."

The infamous incident was still a year and a half in the future, however. Aside from Chivington, Kit was friendly with everyone he met. The authorities of the Colorado Territory heartily agreed with his suggestion that he call a meeting of the tribal chiefs of the area, and he summoned the leaders of both the Arapaho and Cheyenne to a conference.

His government, he told them, wanted and needed peace with the Indian nations in order to fight a much bigger war with brothers who had gone astray. He asked them, in the name of his own friendship with them, to give him their word they would return to their lodges and stay there. The chiefs and elders had ample opportunity to see the men of the First New Mexico Volunteer Infantry parade with their new, powerful rifles, and readily smoked a pipe of peace with the man who had been their Indian agent.

Another celebration was held before the regiment departed, and both officers and enlisted men discovered that the cold mountain air helped to clear their heads as they moved south.

Snow was deep in the passes by the time the men marched into New Mexico late in October. Various branches of the Apache nation were on the warpath, but were being held in check, and it was rumored that General Sibley was planning another invasion, this time from the northeast. Kit was sent to block a Confederate approach from that direction, and the regiment spent the better part of the winter on patrol duty. The threat did not materialize, and early in the spring Kit was summoned to a conference in Santa Fe. He left at once, leaving Colonel Pfeiffer in temporary command.

The territorial authorities asked Kit to accept what, on the surface at least, appeared to be an impossible assignment. The Navajo were still raiding ranches, farms and villages, and had murdered a three-man delegation sent to negotiate with them. It was obvious that they would have to be defeated in open war, and Colonel Christopher Carson was ordered to wage a campaign against them.

Kit had only his own regiment for the purpose, and no other troops could be spared. Seven hundred men were being sent against a strong nation of ten thousand persons who lived in a natural "fortress"—an area comprising many thousands of square miles protected by mountains and cliffs.

Kit accepted without question.

His Navajo campaign was undoubtedly his most brilliant undertaking. The actual campaign lasted for the better part of a year, and even though the war in the major theaters of operation was being waged with unprecedented fury during that period, Kit captured his share of newspaper space. People in both the Union and the Confederacy were able to forget, for a little while, the terrible blood-letting at Gettysburg and Chickamauga as they read of the incredible Indian war being waged in the Southwest.

Kit made careful preparations for his campaign, obtaining vast quantities of ammunition, food supplies and medicines from Canby's quartermaster general. Unable to get help from other troops, he appealed to the Indians for assistance, and the normally peaceful Pueblo, who were the ancient enemies of the Navajo, responded to his call with unprecedented enthusiasm.

Approximately three hundred warriors joined him, but he confided to Canby that he considered them unreliable, for their own tribal organization lacked discipline. He placed the older braves with the baggage train as guards, and split the younger warriors into small, easily controlled groups, which he stationed on his flanks.

The troops were granted leaves of absence before the campaign began, and Kit himself spent ten days at a house in Taos that he had purchased for his family early in the war. The ranch in the Rayado had suspended operations for the duration of the hostilities, in part because of the master's prolonged absence, in part because it was difficult in a time of war to hire dependable workers. The ten days that Kit spent with his wife in Taos was the longest holiday he took during the entire Civil War, and as his personal aides, Colonel Pfeiffer and several other staff officers were also in the town during that period, he took advantage of their proximity to hold a number of conferences with them.

He had been granted the right to wage the war in any way he saw fit, and gradually formed a strategic plan that was bold, farsighted and relatively humane. It was plain to him from the outset that it would be courting disaster to fight a series of pitched battles. The Navajo were too strong. Similarly, he had no desire to expose himself to running guerrilla attacks that would decimate his regiment. He knew only too well that he would be pursuing phantoms if he tried to chase small bands of warriors into their mountain retreats.

His first act was to request as many cannon as Canby could spare, and he was given four light howitzers. These guns, he said, were all he needed, and he told his subordinates he would use them for the sole purpose of impressing the enemy with his power. The Navajo, who owned their own rifles and pistols, could not be frightened by small arms, but he felt reasonably sure that cannon—even light howitzers—would terrify them.

He intended to use the howitzers to keep the Navajo at a safe distance from the regiment. When the officers looked bewildered, he explained his strategy. Indian warfare of the conventional sort would be ineffective, partly because the regiment was not strong enough to defeat the Navajo in battle, partly because these natives were not nomads. Other tribes, which were smaller, had roamed the mountains and plains for centuries. Buffalo meat had provided their food, buffalo skins their tents and clothing.

But the Navajo nation was so large that it had been forced to abandon its wanderings in order to obtain meat and grain in quantity. They cultivated corn in their valleys, their fruit trees produced bumper crops, they owned thousands of cattle and the sheep grazing on their hillsides were numbered in the tens of thousands.

Kit hoped to hold the Navajo warriors at arm's length while the troops systematically destroyed the corn growing in fields and captured the Indians' livestock. If he could deprive the enemy of its basic food supplies, he believed, the chiefs of the tribe would surrender.

His theory was remarkably similar to the scorched earth policy adopted by General William T. Sherman following his capture of Atlanta in September 1864.

Kit's proposal was so unusual that his officers didn't know what to make of it, but they agreed that it might be effective. There seemed to be no alternative, so they were willing to try the scheme.

The regiment was ready to march on June 1, 1863, but the cannon did not arrive from Santa Fe until seven days later. Another week was lost while fifty picked men learned the rudiments of firing and handling the guns. A number of Apache came to Taos to watch the howitzers being fired, and Kit freely admitted them to his camp, hoping they would carry advance word of the guns' power to the Navajo.

Finally, on June 19, the expedition set out. A small fife and drum corps led a parade through the dusty streets of Taos, and Mrs. Carson sat in a carriage on the road at the western edge of the town, waiting to say a last goodbye to her husband. Kit joined her and, after watching his troops march past them on the road, mounted his own horse and moved to the head of the column. The campaign was under way.

The men marched almost two hundred miles due west through the river valleys and mountains of northern New Mexico. No troubles were encountered when they passed through the land of the Jicarilla Apache. But the Pueblo warriors had to be restrained when they wanted to raid some of the Apache villages. Kit preferred to fight one war at a time.

Navajo scouts maintained contact with the vanguard, but did not attack, and Kit refused to take the advice of subordinates who urged him to drive off the warriors. He saw no reason to keep his movements secret.

Early in July he arrived at a small settlement on the Chaco River, northwest of the Chaco Canyon, and a few days later established his headquarters on the river. He was now on the edge of the Navajo domain, and his first act was to send a battalion fifty miles south to drive and burn some grain warehouses on the Rio Puerco, not far from the present-day town of Gallup. This unorthodox act caught the Navajo completely by surprise.

The entire regiment then marched north to the San Juan River. Settlers in the valley there had been suffering heavily from raids, and the howitzers went into action for the first time when a large war party of undetermined strength moved to meet the troops. A few cannon shots dispersed the braves, and he met no opposition at a substantial native village. Women and children fled, and several hundred head of cattle were captured. After some hesitation, Kit decided to destroy the clay huts, and the entire village was demolished. Preferring to live off the land in order to conserve his own provisions, he ordered the cattle butchered.

Then the regiment turned south again, and in September made its way through the passes that separate the Unicha and Chuska mountain ranges, moving into the heart of Navajo country.

In the months that followed, the howitzers roared constantly as the regiment systematically looted, burned and destroyed in an area approximately one hundred and fifty miles wide and one hundred and seventy-five miles deep. The Navajo lived in a region bounded by the San Juan River on the north, the Colorado on the northwest, the Little Colorado on the southwest and the mesa wastelands above the present-day city of Winslow, Arizona on the south.

Scores of Navajo towns and villages on the main rivers and their tributaries were leveled. The regiment marched into seventeen river valleys, and when soldiers who had been farmers declared that plants that were merely trampled would spring up again, Kit ordered them pulled out of the soil by the roots. In one particularly fertile field, three hundred men worked for a full day and transformed a field of rich corn into a barren desert.

So many cattle and sheep were captured that the regiment could not use that much meat for its own use. Thousands of animals were slaughtered and their carcasses were left on hillsides to rot. The peach trees of the Navajo were the nation's great pride, and at least three thousand were cut down; the number may have been much higher, but Kit and his staff lost count. Grapevine roots were torn out of the ground, and hundreds of melon patches were laid bare. Granaries were smashed and their contents put to the torch.

From time to time the desperate Navajo attacked, but each sub-tribe remained in its own immediate neighborhood, and the chiefs were unable to unite their warriors. So the regiment, aided by its fear-inspiring howitzers, was able to drive off the war parties, and the troops sustained few casualties.

The more Kit's plan succeeded, the gloomier he became. "I can take no pride in this fearful destruction," he wrote to his wife. "My sleep is haunted by dreams of starving Navajo squaws and children. If the elders of the tribe would listen to reason, we could make peace. But they're stubborn men, so I must finish what I have started."

On at least five occasions in the winter of 1863–64 and
the early part of the following spring, Kit sent emissaries to
the Navajo in an attempt to arrange an armistice. The Indian leaders refused, even though they saw their entire
civilization being destroyed.

Kit's strategy completely crushed the Navajo. His Pueblo
allies wanted to take scalps, and were so eager for revenge
that, in February 1864, Kit had to send them home. He
continued to want no more fighting than was absolutely
necessary.

In April 1864, the broken, starving Navajo surrendered un-
conditionally.

Their herds, cornfields, vineyards and orchards had been
demolished. Their towns and villages had been reduced to
rubble. Their granaries and warehouses no longer existed.
And, unless they received immediate help from the United
States Government, the entire nation was in danger of starving to death.

Kit received orders to move the whole tribe to a reservation that had been set aside for the purpose in eastern
New Mexico, near Fort Sumner. He disagreed with the policy, believing it better to let the nation remain in its own
territory, but he was a soldier who did what he was told,
and his views were not solicited.

Two thousand or more of the Navajo fled into the mountains and canyons, but more than seven thousand marched
east in the greatest mass migration of its kind in American
history. The troops of the First New Mexico Volunteer Infantry guarded their captives on the trail, and the soldiers
felt great pity for the foes they had vanquished. Kit ordered
the Navajo fed from his own quartermaster stores, and by
the time he reached the reservation, his supplies had been
exhausted.

Kit was convinced that the government's policy was mistaken, and expressed his views in letters to the War Department and Department of the Interior. Unfortunately, he

did not live to see his beliefs vindicated. In 1868, several months after his death, the government reversed its Navajo policy. Setting aside a vast area in Arizona and New Mexico that had comprised the nation's domain, it allowed the Navajo to move back to their homeland.

The renown Kit acquired as a result of his Navajo campaign was greater than any fame he had accumulated earlier in his life. In both the Union and the Confederacy people had learned the meaning of war, but still thought of Indian fights as romantic. No one was surprised that the greatest of Mountain Men should have defeated a nation of ten thousand with a paltry seven hundred men. Kit had surpassed his own records, and his place in legends was secure for all time. Once again his exploits had provided people with escape from reality, and in this instance the reality of civil war was relentlessly grim, the achievement of the folk hero so fantastic that it was almost beyond belief.

Kit himself felt no sense of pride in his victory. Raids on the ranches and farms of settlers had been halted, the western portion of the New Mexico Territory was at peace and troops were freed for duty elsewhere. But the cost in human suffering had been high.

Mrs. Carson, in one of her few statements recorded for posterity, told General Sherman in 1867, when they met at dinner, that the misery of the Navajo was ever present in her husband's mind.

The campaign had not been the sort that Kit enjoyed waging. Circumstances and his shortage of manpower had forced him to use techniques never before attempted by Mountain Men. At best, the colonel commanding the First New Mexico Volunteer Infantry could console himself with the thought that he had done his duty and completed his mission successfully.

15. TWILIGHT

New Mexico and the other territories enjoyed few of the benefits that were helping the Union win the Civil War. Northern arms plants and factories were turning out huge quantities of guns, ammunition and uniforms, but the army commanders in the West received only a small trickle of munitions and supplies. Recruits by the thousands were joining the corps of fighting men who were destroying the last hopes of the Confederacy, but none could be spared for duty in the mountain lands, where the enemies were Indians rather than Rebels.

The territories were still relying on their own resources, in the main, and too many regiments and battalions of volunteers were commanded by men like Chivington of Colorado, who knew little about their foes and cared less. The use of diplomacy rather than force might have persuaded the Indian nations to lay down their arms after Kit Carson won his stunning campaign against the Navajo. Instead, the troops of the West, many of them newcomers to the region, went on rampages of their own, frequently attacking the tribes without cause.

The warriors, certain they faced extermination unless they defended themselves, reacted violently. Cheyenne and Arapaho, Comanche and Utah daubed on war paint and went out to raid farms and villages. The Blackfoot, quiet for several years, became restless. And the Kiowa, the largest and strongest of the plains tribes, tore up their peace treaty with the United States. Ranches were raided, homesteaders and their families were murdered, wagon trains were attacked and looted.

Members of the First New Mexico Volunteer Infantry who had hoped to go home on furlough after smashing the Navajo were bitterly disappointed when they learned they would be granted no rest. After marching the men, women and children of the Navajo nation to the dusty reservation in eastern New Mexico, the regiment was ordered to return to the field immediately. Kit's men were veterans now, as efficient as regulars, and were treated accordingly. In the latter half of 1864 the regiment saw service in Colorado, Nebraska and Kansas, then was dispatched to northwest Texas by way of Oklahoma. A large force of Kiowa and Comanche was gathering, and Kit's orders from the War Department directed him to smash the insurrection.

His scouts brought him word that three thousand braves had banded together, and he realized that, even if the reports were exaggerated, a unit of seven hundred soldiers was probably too small to disperse the warriors. The days when a handful of marksmen could scatter a horde of Indians had come to an end, for the braves carried firearms of their own now, and no brave was foolish enough to go into battle with bow and arrow.

Kit requested reinforcements. Santa Fe regretted that no troops could be spared, and a similar message was sent to him from Denver. A company was dispatched from Fort Kearney, Nebraska, and the captain commanding the unit carried a letter explaining why it was impossible to release more men for service with Colonel Carson. Fort Leavenworth, Kansas, promised to send two batteries of artillery as soon as they could be organized, but thought it unlikely that the cannoneers would march before January or February.

Tightening his belt, Kit marched his own regiment and the company from Fort Kearney into northwest Texas. There, in barren hill country, he fought an engagement on

November 25, 1864, the Battle of Adobe Walls. The reports on the strength of the enemy had been somewhat inflated, as he had guessed, but he still faced an overwhelmingly superior force. According to the best estimate he could obtain, the Kiowa and Comanche were sending approximately twenty-three hundred men against him, so he was outnumbered by more than three to one. More of the warriors were mounted, while his own men were on foot.

Knowing that his situation would become dangerous if he should be surrounded, he assigned his two companies of cavalry the task of keeping open his line of communications to the rear. He still had the howitzers he had used so effectively against the Navajo, and decided to employ them again, even though this would limit his ability to maneuver freely. He would lose little or nothing, he reasoned, because it would be difficult in any event for infantry to move at will when facing horsemen.

Picks and shovels were used on November 23 and 24, and breastworks four feet high had been thrown up by the time the Comanche, who opened the Indian attack, rode down from the higher hills on the morning of the twenty-fifth. The howitzers thundered, their shells whined as they arched high into the air, then exploded as they crashed to the ground, and the advance of the savages was slowed. But it was not halted, and Kit knew at once that he was in serious trouble.

The warriors realized it too, and the Kiowa galloped at full tilt at the soldiers in blue. Accurate rifle fire, the "secret weapon" of the Mountain Men, forced the warriors of both tribes to retire. But there was no rest for the regiment, as the braves launched a second attack, then a third. At midday Kit had to content himself with the knowledge that his troops were holding their own.

By three o'clock in the afternoon all of the howitzer ammunition had been spent, and company commanders reported that the supply of rifle ammunition would be exhausted soon after sundown. He promptly ordered them to hold their fire until the last possible moment. The warriors suffered such heavy casualties on their next charge that only one more attack was made before dark, when the savages finally withdrew into the hills.

It was obvious to Kit that he could neither resume the battle the following morning nor withstand the many small raids that the braves inevitably would make through the night. Consequently he utilized one of the oldest of military tricks: the troops built a number of campfires, then silently abandoned their positions and retreated. Kit rode with the rear guard, and the bone-weary men marched all night through the hills on the road to Fort Sumner. By the time the Indians discovered they had gone, it was too late, and contact was broken.

The battered regiment reached Fort Sumner safely, and Kit tried to cheer himself with his low losses. Only eleven men had been killed and seventy-three wounded. But he had lost a major battle, the first time in his life he had met such a resounding defeat, and felt himself disgraced. He wanted to resign his commission, but was dissuaded by his own officers and others who were on duty at Fort Sumner.

Actually, as he later learned, he had dealt the Kiowa and Comanche a blow from which neither tribe fully recovered. Both had suffered such heavy casualties at Adobe Walls that they were permanently weakened, and thereafter were unable to take the field in strength. They conducted many small raids, but never again could send an army into the field.

Kit spent Christmas at Taos in 1864, and celebrated his fifty-fifth birthday with his wife during a one-week leave of absence. Then he returned to duty, leading his regiment into Colorado. But there were too many brush fires for one regiment to extinguish, and Indian raids were so frequent that the War Department was flooded with complaints from the territories.

The Civil War was entering its final phase. On February
1, General Sherman began his march north from Georgia,
destroying railways, farm produce and machinery. Charleston, South Carolina, was taken by the Union fleet without
a shot being fired. And in a few weeks, on April 9, General
Robert E. Lee would surrender at Appomattox Court
House to General U. S. Grant. The War Department had an
opportunity now to devote thought to the plight of the territories.

Military forces in the territories were reorganized in a
single command, with all field units of both regulars and
militia reporting to one man. It was clear that the officer in
charge of operations should be someone intimately familiar
with the various tribes causing so much trouble, so on March
13, 1865, Colonel Christopher Carson was promoted to the
brevet, or temporary, rank of brigadier general. He was destined to hold that rank for the last three years of his life.

The struggle to subdue and control the Indian tribes took
an immediate turn for the better. Kit was responsible for a
vast domain, the territories of New Mexico, Colorado, Utah,
Idaho, the southern portion of Dakota and Arizona, which
had just been separated from New Mexico and given its own
status and government. Under his direct command were
three regiments of regulars and four of militia, together
with several smaller field artillery, quartermaster and cavalry units.

He established no permanent headquarters, but remained
in the field, traveling almost constantly through the mountains he had known all of his adult life. His foes, conducting
a desperate campaign for survival, remained elusive, and
he was further hampered because virtually all of the Indians
of the area were at war with the United States.

The most significant change in the development of the
Indian war after Kit's promotion was the Army's assumption
of the offensive. Warriors continued to make forays against
farms, ranches and villages, but these operations were con-

ducted by small bands of daring savages. The larger towns were no longer threatened, and the Indians, forced onto the defensive, expended most of their energies trying to elude the columns sent out against them.

It was impossible to achieve a lasting victory, however, for the warriors wisely refused to stand and fight unless cornered. Facing large, well-armed bodies of men, they preferred to vanish into the mountains. Most of the soldiers were men in their early twenties who had no previous experience in Indian fighting, and although they were courageous, neither they nor their young, company-grade officers understood the principles of such warfare.

"I have six thousand men under my command," Kit wrote to his wife in May 1865. "They are fine, true lads, but I would gladly replace them with five hundred mountaineers. Then I know I would spend the summer at home with you."

The end of the Civil War helped rather than hindered the Indian tribes, for the militia regiments of volunteers were demobilized, and the regulars were spread thinly over an enormous area. Kit asked the War Department for replacements, but not until January 1866 did his command total four thousand five hundred men. This was the largest body of regulars he commanded, and by spring of that year his force dwindled to approximately three thousand five hundred. At his repeated insistence, about half of this number were cavalry.

It was apparent to Kit that the Indian war would be a long one, so he returned to Taos late in the autumn of 1865 to sell his ranch in the Rayado. He believed it could not be operated profitably under absentee ownership. Mrs. Carson had let it be known that he wanted to dispose of the property, and soon after he reached Taos he concluded a deal with William A. Blair of Santa Fe, who bought the ranch, including all livestock, for $40,000, payable in four annual installments. Kit returned to the field, but managed to spend the last part of December and most of January 1866 at Taos with his wife.

He took part in only two operations after he became a general. In October 1865, he led a battalion of cavalry and infantry in person against the Comanche, and inflicted a defeat on a band of about three hundred without the loss of a man. In April 1866, he became impatient again and assumed personal charge of an augmented battalion that was searching the Colorado mountains for the Cheyenne. He found the savages, and in a brief battle killed about eighty, dispersing the rest.

Both of these engagements were minor, but the newspapers of the East, long accustomed to giving their readers a fare of war news, built them up in glowing words. People throughout the country were convinced that the invincible Kit Carson was once again performing super-feats.

But the folk hero was tired after four and one-half years of steady campaigning. Fortunately, his superiors understood his situation and sympathized with him. General Grant, who now held four-star rank, was the Chief of Staff of the Army, and Sherman, now a lieutenant general, was Kit's immediate superior. Both realized that a man in his late fifties found it difficult to live in the field, and in the late spring of 1866 the western command again was reorganized. The Kiowa, Cheyenne and Arapaho were the most troublesome of the Indian tribes, and the Army wanted to give Kit responsibility for dealing with them while, at the same time, reducing the physical burden he was being forced to carry.

At Sherman's instigation he was made commanding general of Fort Garland, Colorado, where he directed the efforts of eighteen hundred men, most of them infantry and cavalry. Mrs. Carson joined him there in the summer of 1866, bringing virtually all of their furniture and other personal belongings with her. They rented the house at Taos, and Kit never again visited the town that had been his home for so many years.

Newspaper reporters and magazine writers were attracted by the booming mountain country, now the last frontier in the continental United States, and Fort Garland was a natural magnet for them. Kit, following his lifelong custom, refused to discuss his exploits or any other phase of his personal life. But he became less taciturn on the subject of the Indians.

Military operations, he told newsmen in a number of interviews, were not the sole solution of the Indian problem. He made it plain that he sympathized with the savages, whom he considered his friends, and declared that those who advocated a policy of extermination were "unfeeling butchers." The only way to achieve permanent peace, he said, was to give the Indians large tracts of land where reservations would be established. Experts should teach the tribes to raise their own crops and livestock, and in time they would become self-sufficient.

"A man who owns his own house and fields won't go to war unless someone threatens him," he told a reporter from the New York *World* in November 1866. "Give the Indian his own land and he'll stop fighting."

Kit's views, widely publicized, were at least partly responsible for the change in government policy toward the Indians adopted during the administrations of Presidents Andrew Johnson and Grant. Federal lands were set aside as reservations and, as peace was made with one tribe after another, the Indians were moved to them.

In the 1870s, when the outrageous treatment the Indians had received finally aroused public sympathy, attempts were made to reconcile the image of Kit Carson, Indian fighter, with the more benign one of Kit Carson, humanitarian. Kit actually stood between these poles. He fought Indians when it was necessary, not because he enjoyed these clashes for their own sake. But his nineteenth-century biographers, who claimed he was one of the originators of the more enlightened policies adopted by the government, were gilding their hero. Kit, both as an Indian agent and as a soldier, executed policy, but at no time did he formulate it.

He approved of the plans made by others, for they were in accord with his own feelings. Certainly he used his great prestige to help create a favorable atmosphere for the administration of those policies. But there is no evidence available that suggests he was in any way responsible for their creation.

Kit worked hard to restore peace in the area under his command, and raids by the Kiowa, Cheyenne, Comanche and Arapaho gradually dwindled during the latter part of 1866 and the first months of 1867. Treaties had not yet been signed with the tribes, but attacks by war parties became infrequent. Owners of ranches and farms no longer found it necessary to carry firearms at all times, and travelers were rarely molested on the roads.

When a raid did take place, troops were dispatched promptly to find and punish the guilty braves. Tribal elders began coming to Fort Garland with their grievances rather than sending their sons on the warpath, and Kit did his best to obtain justice for warriors whom he regarded as his wards. He made few newspaper headlines, but contributed a great deal to the stability of the mountain country.

In the summer of 1867 General Sherman, who was making a tour of the district under his over-all command, paid a visit to Fort Garland and spent a week with the garrison commander. He accompanied Kit on several tours of inspection, and was the guest of honor at two dinner parties given by Mrs. Carson. On both of these occasions Kit was quiet, as always. Sherman was rarely garrulous, either, so others did most of the talking.

Newspapermen who were accompanying Sherman noted that when he and Kit were alone, both became animated.

Neither revealed what they discussed, either on official business or personal matters.

"I have great respect for the general," Kit said later.

"General Carson," Sherman told the press, "is a man of integrity. I have been privileged to meet few like him."

General Sherman departed, and General Carson resumed his attempt to pacify the Indians.

John C. Fremont, who had served as a major general in the Union Army during the first years of the Civil War and subsequently had been supported by the so-called radical wing of the Republican party in an unsuccessful attempt to beat President Lincoln for the party's nomination in 1864, now briefly re-entered Kit's life. Fremont was the head of a syndicate that was trying to raise funds for the building of a transcontinental railway through the Southwest, and late in the summer of 1867 he opened a correspondence with his old friend and one-time guide.

Fremont offered Kit the opportunity to invest in the enterprise, apparently feeling it would be good public relations to enlist the support of the Southwest's most romantic figure. Kit, who knew nothing of finance, wrote Fremont several short, cordial letters, but bought no stock in the company, and the correspondence ceased.

Kit's military career was terminated abruptly in October 1867, when he suffered an accident that ruined his health and, a few months later, took his life. He started out one morning on an inspection tour of the area in the immediate vicinity of Fort Garland, telling Mrs. Carson he expected to return in time for dinner that evening.

A single aide-de-camp accompanied him, and was riding behind him on the trail when Kit's horse suddenly bolted. There was no truth in the stories subsequently published in a number of newspapers to the effect that a band of Indians had been waiting to ambush Kit. The aide believed that a snake had appeared on the path, frightening the horse.

In any event, Kit was thrown from the saddle with such

force that he tumbled down a cliff at the edge of the trail, falling a distance of fifteen to twenty feet. He was unable to stand and was in such great pain that the aide hurriedly rode back toward the Fort. He encountered a platoon of cavalry, who accompanied him to the scene, and Kit was carried home on a stretcher.

He had lost consciousness by the time he was taken into his own house, and was immediately examined by the two physicians on duty. They agreed that he had ruptured a major blood vessel near the heart. Nothing could be done for him, Mrs. Carson took up a vigil beside his bed and he was not expected to live through the night.

He regained consciousness early the following morning, and began to rally. The doctors told him that complete rest was essential if he wanted even a partial recovery, and he spent the next month in bed.

In November 1867, he was retired from the Army with the rank of brigadier general. As his health was still delicate, the full courtesies of the post were extended to him, and he continued to occupy the same house in which he had been living.

In January 1868, President Johnson appointed him Indian agent for southeastern Colorado, with jurisdiction over the Kiowa, whom he had managed to tame. He and Mrs. Carson immediately moved to the old trading-post town of Boggsville, which later changed its name to La Junta. In March they bought a white, shingled house there and their furniture was moved in.

Kit made only one journey to visit the Kiowa, riding approximately thirty-five miles to one of their villages on Adobe Creek. He returned to his new house to find Mrs. Carson seriously ill, and thereafter remained constantly at her side.

On April 23, 1868, Maria Josefa Jaramillo Carson died after a marriage that had lasted for a quarter of a century.

Kit was deeply affected by her passing, and his own precarious health declined rapidly. A physician was sent from nearby Fort Lyon to examine him, and the colonel in command of the garrison sent two soldiers to act as the patient's orderlies. Kit said he needed no help, and was irritated when the orderlies insisted on staying with him.

He was stubborn to the end, refusing to take the medicines that had been prescribed for him. He showed no interest in food, and spent most of his days in the house. On a few occasions he went out to sit on his small front porch, but retreated when neighbors approached to offer him condolences.

On May 26 he suffered a heart attack, and was put to bed. The physician was summoned, and word was sent to one of his daughters, now married and living in Taos. On the night of May 27–28 the patient briefly regained consciousness, then fell asleep again.

Shortly before dawn on the morning of May 28, 1868, Brigadier General Christopher Carson, Mountain Man, died peacefully in his own bed at the age of fifty-eight.

He was buried the following day at Fort Lyon, following a military funeral. The *Rocky Mountain News* was the first to inform the world of his passing, printing a sedate obituary. Other newspapers were less accurate, mixing fact and fancy with a free hand. Stories that had been told through the years were embroidered by enthusiastic journalists, magazines vied with each other in an attempt to present colorful legends, and biographers went to work with a vengeance.

Within a few years the ever expanding myths hid the portrait of Kit Carson, the man.

PRINCIPAL BIBLIOGRAPHY

ABBOTT, J. S. C., *Kit Carson*, 1873.

ABBOTT, N. C., *Montana in the Making*, 1931.

American Heritage Book of Indians, Alvin M. Josephy, Jr., ed., 1961.

BANCROFT, H. H., *History of Arizona and New Mexico*, 1877, revised 1888.

——, *History of California, 1542–1890*, 7 vols., 1884–90.

——, *History of Utah*, 1890.

BREED, NOEL J., *The Early Development of the Wyoming Country, 1743–1853*, 1928.

BURDETT, CHARLES, *Life of Kit Carson*, 1859.

CARSON, A. C., *Colorado, the Top of the World*, 1912.

CAUGHEY, J. W., *California*, 1940.

CHITTENDEN, H. M., *History of Early Steamboat Navigation on the Missouri River*, 1903.

COAN, C. F., *A History of New Mexico*, 1925.

COTTERILL, ROBERT S., *History of Pioneer Kentucky*, 1917.

DEFENBACH, BYRON, *Idaho, the Place and Its People*, 1933.

ELLIS, E. S., *Life of Kit Carson*, 1899.

EVANS, J. H., *The Story of Utah*, 1933.

FLETCHER, FRED N., *Early Nevada*, 1929.

FREMONT, JOHN C., *Memories of My Life*, 1887.

——, *Report of the Exploring Expedition to the Rocky Mountains, 1842, and to Oregon and North California, 1843–44*, 1845.

GODDARD, P. E., *Indians of the South-west*, 1913.

GRANT, B. C., *Taos Indians*, 1925.

GREEN, C. R., *Early Days in Kansas*, 1912–13.

GREGG, J. J., *Commerce of the Prairies*, 1845.

GRINNELL, GEORGE B., *The Fighting Cheyennes*, 1915.

HEBARD, G. R., *History and Government of Wyoming*, 1919.

History of California, Z. S. Eldredge, ed., 5 vols., 1915.

History of Kentucky, Charles Kerr, ed., 1922.

HOUCK, LOUIS, *A History of Missouri*, 1908.

Journal of American Folk-Lore, 1880–1904.

KINGSBURY, G. W., *History of Dakota Territory*, 1915.

LINDQUIST, G. E. E., *The Red Man in the United States*, 1923.

LINDSAY, CHARLES, *The Big Horn Basin*, 1932.

LIPPS, O. S., *The Navajos*, 1909.

LYMAN, H. S., *History of Oregon*, 1903.

MACK, EFFIE M., *Nevada,* 1936.

MCCORMAC, EUGENE I., *James K. Polk,* 1922.

MEIGS, W. M., *Thomas Hart Benton,* 1914.

NEVINS, ALLAN, *Fremont, the West's Greatest Adventurer,* 1927.

PETERS, DEWITT C., *The Story of Kit Carson's Life and Adventures,* 1858, revised 1874.

POPE, W. F., *Early Days in Arkansas,* 1895.

REES, J. E., *Idaho Chronology,* 1918.

ROBINSON, W. H., *Story of Arizona,* 1919.

SABIN, EDWIN L., *Kit Carson Days,* 1914.

SCHARF, T. J., *History of St. Louis City and County,* 1883.

Southwestern Historical Quarterly, 1897 et. seq.

STOW, W. F., *History of Colorado,* 3 vols., 1918.

VESTAL, STANLEY, *Kit Carson, the Happy Warrior of the Old West,* 1928.

WALLACE, S., *The Land of the Pueblos,* 1895.

WISSLER, CLARK, *Indians of the United States,* 1956.

INDEX